LAROUSSE LIGHT FRENCH COOKING

**A gastronomic light eating program
to lose weight and stay slim
without ever being hungry
or losing your good disposition**

**by Dr. Alain Vanet
and Françoise Thiriet-Vuibout, Dietician
adapted in translation by Madeleine Kamman**

Recipes for the French Provincial Celebration Menus
and many other dishes by Madeleine Kamman

McGraw-Hill Book Company
New York   London   St. Louis   San Francisco
Toronto   Hamburg   Mexico

English translation and adaptation
copyright © 1981 by Librairie Larousse,
U.S.A., Inc.
LA CUISINE AMAIGRISSANTE
Copyright © 1976 by Librairie Larousse,
S.A., Paris

**Library of Congress Cataloging in
Publication Data**
Main entry under title:

Larousse Light French Cooking, with
provincial recipes.
    Rev. translation of La cuisine
amaigrissante par les basses calories by A.
Vanet.
    Includes index.
    1. Cookery, French.   I. Vanet,
Alain.   II. Vanet, Alain. La cuisine
amaigrissante par les basses calories.
TX719.V3413 1980   641.5944
80-14934
ISBN 0-07-067056-0

Editor-in Chief: Philip M. Rideout with
Inez M. Krech
Design: Bookgraphics
Map of France drawn by Corey Ann
Latham
Typography: Thomas D'Espinosa, DEKR
Corporation
Printer: R. R. Donnelley & Sons
8123-DON-1234

Dear Readers and Cooks,

As the translator and adapter of this book, may I introduce myself to those of you who do not know my name.

I am Madeleine Kamman, a cooking teacher, restaurateur, cookbook and food writer and as such, my life is full of ups and downs . . . on the bathroom scales that is! Since the days and nights of a food person are full of the dangers of overeating and overdrinking, if not in quantity at least in quality, daily meetings with the scale can be, to say the least, painful.

In June, after my cooking students were graduated, I met my yearly "Ides of June" and once more started on cottage cheese, plain yogurt, hard-boiled eggs, salads without dressings—in a word, all the foods that are thinning, healthy, good for every ill and so boring to look at, to eat, and to taste.

Unknowingly, my good friend, Philip Rideout at Larousse came to my rescue by sending me the present book, called in French *La Cuisine Amaigrissante*. As a proof that ideas go in currents, the book, it turned out, had been published in France the same year as Michel Guérard's *Cuisine Minceur*. Its great advantage for me was that it made use of my good old favorite French foods, down-to-earth vegetables and meats, which could take the indignity of being served butterless or creamless without giving me a guilt complex.

The introduction to the book proved most interesting and reflected the ideas of Dr. Vanet, a French "slimmer" by profession, and of Madame Thiriet-Vuibout, a dietician. I gave their method of cooking a faithful try for three months, from July through September, and the results were gratifying. I lost twenty pounds without ever being hungry, my very pressured businessman husband lost a good ten pounds, while our 13-year-old boy grew two inches, developed solid protein muscles and lost all his baby fat. Our 18-year-old, very proud of his thinness by birth, came along on the experiment without giving it a thought, until one day he was the one to venture, "Mother, how about a bit of relief from the diet; how about one of your little *gueuletons*? (the French vernacular for a dainty little meal, just rich enough to make one euphoric). So I decided to change the pattern a bit and introduce in the program a true feast in *cuisine nouvelle* after each five pounds of overweight lost. After all, one is human and needs special gratification once in a while. The family welcomed the milestone meals with such pleasure, that the idea was discussed among editors and a new section added to the book. It contains directions for delicious meals to rejoice with family and friends in celebration.

So thank you, dear reader and cook, for coming along on the most pleasant and gratifying trip down the scales and through the Provinces of France at the same time.

Happy light eating to all of you,
Madeleine Kamman

CONTENTS

PART I
LIGHT CUISINE

INTRODUCTION

DR. VANET'S ADVICE ON SLIMMING
as adapted by Madeleine Kamman

These guidelines are common sense, yet adherence to them in relation to eating specific foods, noted here, in portions properly sized for each individual's needs, should produce desired results while dining well.

▪ The first rule is to have only three meals a day: breakfast, lunch and dinner. Breakfast is your most important meal; make sure that it is substantial enough not to leave you the victim of hunger pains at midmorning. Coffee and a roll are your worst enemies, for at 10:30 A.M. you will already be feeling empty. Make sure on the contrary that half of your breakfast consists of at least 50% proteins. Here is a list of what you could have to reach 12 noon safely, without becoming hungry:

▪ Tea, coffee with skim milk if you want, but always without sugar. Sugar substitutes are acceptable if you allow them in your home (see later under Replacement for Sugar).

▪ One egg poached or panfried without fat, with 1 slice of high-protein bread and 6 ounces of tomato juice. Orange juice, if you prefer it, is most useful because of the potassium it provides for your system, but if you are slimming do not exceed 2 ounces if you are a woman and 4 ounces if you are a man.

▪ If you prefer, you can replace fruit or vegetable juices by ⅓ cup fresh berries, 1 peach, 1 nectarine or 1 apple.

▪ Should you, for other health reasons, have problems with eggs, switch to ½ cup cottage cheese or 1 cup plain unsweetened natural yogurt. A mixture of approximately 4 ounces of each is also excellent; this would amount to only 135 calories and represent barely any carbohydrate intake; at the same time, it is a rather filling concoction.

Now that we have made suggestions for breakfast, what exactly and how much can you have at lunch or dinner?

▪ First, learn to eat slowly. It takes approximately twenty minutes for the stomach to feel satisfied and lose completely the feeling of hunger. Whatever you choose to eat or however much you choose to eat, please eat as slowly as possible.

▪ Lunch of "soup and sandwich" is exactly what you should not have: too much bread, too much meat in our huge deli-style or white-bread sandwiches. Rather have 2 ounces of low-fat cheese with very little butterfat or 2 ounces of lean meat (chicken breast, turkey breast, shrimps, scallops, white fish) with mustard between 2 thin rye crackers, and a good solid bowl of crunchy salad with your own lean and slimming dressing. Top the whole thing with 1 piece of fruit and I doubt that you will feel hungry until dinnertime.

■ At dinner treat yourself to a first-course salad, 3 ounces of meat as a main course, 1 or 2 vegetables (please look at the lists on the following pages to choose), and a sugar-free dessert. I am very partial to a second piece of fresh fruit because I do not like the taste of artificial sweeteners, but if those are no bother for you, by all means indulge.

■ At lunch and dinner, one of the toughest propositions, as soon as I became used to light cuisine, was to eat out either at a restaurant or as a guest in a private home, where I seemed to run across all the spaghetti bolognese and the creamiest mashed potatoes ever. I took to scanning the menu well in a restaurant and to disciplining myself at a private home to locate those foods present on the menu or on the table which would allow me to stay on the light eating program. For example, when high-starch vegetables were offered I concentrated on the salad or took minute-size portions of starchy vegetables, or even none at all.

■ The second rule is not to succumb to anything between meals! Of course, you will be offered the usual tempting piece of candy or asked to taste your best friend's aunt's knishes or even be unmercifully submitted to the sight of the first apple pie of the season. Patience! You will find a very light pie recipe included, and you will be able to face it then, for by the time you can bake it, you will already have lost weight. At the beginning of the program, you still may feel hungry between meals, even if you have respected the rules of the game on breakfast. I am pleased to say that I never felt hungry between meals; but still, you may. In this case, try a glass of plain soda water or Perrier, it should fix that empty feeling and tide you over until the next meal.

■ Discipline yourself to drink a lot. A body that breaks down protein in larger quantities with relatively small quantities of fat and carbohydrate needs a lot of water per day. You will find that drinking this large amount of water has a fabulous effect on a women's complexion. Without exaggeration, mine regained the glow of my early thirties.

■ If you are a sweetened soda addict, it would be beneficial for you to switch to the sugar-free sodas, thus losing all the calories contributed by the sugar in regular soft drinks. I am personally not very partial to sugar-free sodas because they leave that layer of artificial sweetener on the palate which ruins my tasting capacities, but that is personal. My husband did well on sugar-free colas and lemon sodas. I chose to remain with diverse mineral waters: American, French or Italian.

■ Fruit juices, even orange and grapefruit juices, can be "sneaky" for they still contain quite a lot of natural sugars that one does not really need. Replace them by tomato or vegetable juices as already mentioned in connection with breakfast.

Tomato juice can be given a nice little lift in the summer by adding chopped fresh herbs or a tiny shallot, mashed and squeezed in the corner of a towel to discard the aggressive juices. With a juicer or a food processor you can prepare all kinds of excellent vegetable-juice cocktails; my favorite is cabbage juice, which I flavor with caraway seeds. This mixture is supposed to be a great healer of stomach ulcers and irritable stomachs. In a matter of minutes you can prepare a pitcherful that will represent your whole allotment of juice for the day; keep it refrigerated for freshness and vitamin preservation, and experiment with all kinds of spices and seasonings for a change of taste.

▪ Third rule: Consider all alcoholic beverages as your worst enemies since alcohol supplies your system with a large amount of fat-producing elements. For me that was no problem since I am only a wine drinker. It was a bit more difficult for my husband, who as a businessman had to face the cocktail of business luncheons. He simply switched to tomato juice with a lime slice for the sake of appearance; it resembles a Bloody Mary.

▪ At the lunch and dinner table on the days we felt like having a glass of wine, we opened only one half bottle and I always made certain that each of us had exactly half of it, which represents exactly 6½ ounces of wine per person, or approximately 65 calories.

PERMITTED FOODS

Although there is no denying that the surest way to lose weight is to be stringent about calorie counting, one can take a less gloomy approach to weight control by becoming aware of all those foods that will keep cuisine light and bring body weight steadily down. Familiarize yourself from the very start with those foods that you can have at any time. I have listed them here with useful comments when necessary and with their portion size and caloric content per portion. Please remember to control the size of the portion according to the needs of each individual as noted where appropriate.

MEATS
You can have all meats, provided that they are well trimmed of all fat and gristle. The list that follows is, as you can see, plentiful and many imaginative main courses can be built with these choices.

> lean well-trimmed beef
> lean well-trimmed lamb
> liver
> heart

veal

pork (the center of the loin only without fat at all)

chicken, both white and dark meats (without a trace of fat or skin)

turkey

FISH

Preferably choose those having as little fat as possible.

soles and their flounder cousins	sea and bay scallops
haddock	oysters
halibut	clams
red snapper	lobster
smelts	crab

The following fish are also excellent but much higher in fat content.

salmon

swordfish

fresh tuna

A good portion of meat or fish is 3 to 3½ ounces or 90 to 100 grams per meal. For those of you who have really a lot of weight to lose, limit your portion at lunch to 2 ounces until you have reached your goal, whether it is the loss of 5, 10, 20 pounds or more.

EGGS

These are also on your list. For other health reasons, you may want to limit your intake of eggs to no more than 5 per week.

1 egg (75 calories) is a good portion for breakfast or as a first course, boiled or scrambled without butter.

2 eggs (150 calories) are a good, high-protein main course for dinner or lunch.

VEGETABLES

A. Low low-calorie vegetables:

The vegetables in this list can be considered truly low-calorie vegetables. They produce approximately 18 calories per serving and yield 3 to 5 grams of carbohydrate per portion. Consider ½ cup of each vegetable a good portion for all solid vegetables or leafy vegetables that must be cooked, and 1 cup a good portion for all leafy salads.

asparagus

green beans

broccoli

green cabbage

red cabbage

celery

Swiss chard, leaf and rib

curly chicory

cucumbers

dandelion leaves

eggplant

Belgian endive

escarole

kale

Bibb, Boston and iceberg
lettuce

mushrooms

mustard greens

green peppers

radishes, white and red

sauerkraut

sorrel

spinach

yellow squash

tomatoes

watercress

zucchini

B. Low-calorie vegetables:

The vegetables in this second list produce approximately 36 calories per serving with 7 grams of carbohydrate, and a good portion of each of them is ½ cup.

artichokes

beets

carrots

onions

red peppers

white turnips

yellow turnips (rutabagas)

Notice that all vegetables containing starches have been eliminated. You will find them as a relief and reward in your special celebration dinners.

Whenever you can, use fresh vegetables. Be alert to their seasons; it will vary with your geographical location. I am certain that every cook will do as I do, notice the first of the new vegetables of a season with a little internal thrill. Where I live, for example, the appearance of asparagus at mid-March is a cause for jubilation since it coincides usually with the melting of dirty old snow.

As to frozen vegetables, everyone knows that although they are short of perfection they still brighten plates during the winter months and are as good as fresh ones as a source of vitamins. Canned vegetables have only one virtue: they reheat in seconds. Let us hope that they will always remain an emergency supply for most of us.

In modern light French cuisine, fruit is often used as a vegetable. In the translated recipes and in the celebration menus you will find apples, grapes, oranges for example. Beware, they obviously contain sugar; whenever you meet fruit slices or berries on your plate, be good to yourself, and end your meal with a small piece of one of the authorized cheeses rather than a dessert. The key to complete enjoyment of that cheese is to budget your wine and keep half of it to drink and enjoy with your cheese; let the flavor combination of the cheese and wine marriage linger on your palate.

FRUITS

That brings me almost naturally to the list of fruits that you can use safely and to their portioning. A portion, and you can have two portions per day, will yield 40 to 45 calories each with 10 grams of carbohydrate. The fruits that follow are listed in portions.

> 1 apple, or ½ cup sweet cider
>
> 2 fresh apricots, or 4 dried apricot halves soaked in water
>
> 10 cherries
>
> ½ grapefruit, or ½ cup grapefruit juice
>
> 12 grapes, that is 12 berries
>
> lemon as you like as a seasoning or with water as a drink
>
> lime as you like as a seasoning, or with water as a drink
>
> ⅛ honeydew melon
>
> ⅓ cantaloupe
>
> 1 peach
>
> ½ pear, not very ripe
>
> 1 slice, ⅓ inch thick, of fresh pineapple or pineaple canned without sugar in unsweetened pineapple juice
>
> 2 plums
>
> 1 small orange
>
> 1 tangerine

½ cup strawberries

½ cup raspberries

½ cup blueberries

½ cup blackberries

If you are really trying to lose a lot of weight, watch out for cherries, grapes and pears, for of all fruits they are the heaviest in sugar. Concentrate instead on melons and tart berries.

CHEESES

Cheese lovers will have to bid goodbye for a little while to the best and most satisfying cheeses: Camembert, Brie, Triple Crème, etc. They are simply too rich; you might as well be eating butter. It certainly is painful to look at those lovely cheeses and smell them without being able to enjoy them, but wait until your celebration meals, you will find them there and enjoy them twice as much. Meanwhile stay with those cheeses that are made of so-called "cooked pastes" and limit your daily intake of any of them to 4½ ounces. Also if you have 4½ ounces of cheese at lunch, for example, do not have any other source of protein such as eggs or meats at the same meal. The following cheeses can safely be enjoyed.

Emmentaler and Gruyère from Switzerland

Comté and Beaufort from France

Jarlsberg from Norway

Edam and Gouda from Holland

Port-Salut, Saint-Paulin, Saint-Nectaire and Tomme de Savoie from
France

Munster from Wisconsin

Monterey Jack from California

Cheddar from New York State

any of your local cheeses that are made from a cooked and pressed
paste, not from a soft fermented paste

OTHER DAIRY FOODS

You can also have a portion of low-fat cottage cheese or one of low-fat yogurt; each will amount to 60 to 70 calories. A portion is the following:

½ cup natural unsweetened yogurt

¼ cup cottage cheese

As milk use skim milk and have 1 cup per day at least; 2 cups would be better.

If you have a source of unpasteurized milk, do not hesitate to prepare your own homemade cottage cheese as follows:

First, let 2 quarts of milk stand until all the cream has come to the top. Lift off the cream gently with a large sauce spoon and donate it to a friend who can use it. Or arrange the cheese making to coincide with one of your celebration dinners and use the cream for that. Now, to prepare the cheese itself: heat the milk to 96°F. or 37°C. and add 1 small tablet of rennet dissolved in water or 3 drops of liquid rennet. Let stand at room temperature for 24 hours, and drip into a cheesecloth placed over a colander. Whip the curd to fluff it up and flavor it with fresh herbs and/or seasonings of your choice. The whey can be used instead of water to make a simple white diet bread with flour, water and salt, but no sugar.

SEASONINGS AND SPICES

Most of them are on your good list and you can use them freely. These spices will considerably pep up any dish:

allspice	curry powder
cayenne pepper	ginger
cinnamon	nutmeg
cloves	paprika
cuminseed	saffron

Also useful are all sorts of herbs:

basil	parsley
bay leaf	rosemary
chervil	sage
chives	savory
fennel, fresh	scallions or green onions
fennel seeds	tarragon
marjoram	

Everyone considers it a tremendous "downer" to have to read a long list of what one must not and cannot have, so let us put it this way: anything not mentioned above is not for you, wait for your celebration meal. I'll soothe your soul with cream and butter in those little interludes; they will do a lot for your morale and not much to your waistline.

REPLACEMENT FOODS

REPLACEMENT FOR OILS
In the chapter on salad dressing and salads, you will find a few recipes for aromatic oils. These oils will not be used to cook, but will be added in ever-so-tiny quantities to a finished dish or dressing to give it "slip." What makes all light slimming foods unattractive is the fact that they feel thin to the palate, since all the fat coating food preparations in normal diets is absent. You will be surprised to see how a teaspoon of oil, which will account for only 5 calories per person, will work miracles in many ways when combined with the cooking juices of vegetables or with aromatics in salad dressings.

REPLACEMENT FOR FATS USED FOR COOKING
You will replace butter, oil and margarine by very light, but very rich stocks called all through the book "meat stock" or "fish stock" for which the recipes are given in the next chapter. Please read carefully all the explanations given there on how to prepare those stocks. They may appear forbidding and difficult to make, but in reality they are simple and the true key to delicious satisfying light meals.

REPLACEMENT FOR CREAM
Of course there is absolutely no replacement for that lovely heavy cream, but . . .

1 egg yolk mixed with a tablespoon or so of evaporated skim milk or yogurt is most effective in giving the cooking juices of meats and fish not only the appearance of a lovely cream sauce but also its texture, and the "slip" needed to make the dish enjoyable to the palate.

WINES AND ALCOHOLS
A. As drinking wines the following would probably be the best.

RED: Cabernet Sauvignon or French Bordeaux. Beware of all red wines coming from warm climates where the natural sugar is abundant, and of all wines from northern climates which are chaptalized by vintners and thus contain quite a bit of sugar (Beaujolais).

WHITE: For everyday use, Muscadet and Bourgogne Aligoté will be fine and for celebration meals a dry natural Coteaux de Champagne will be excellent. These wines are not very expensive and they contain a reasonable amount of natural sugars. Of course, avoid all sweet white wines or all "cream" types of sherries (Oloroso sherries, cream Ports, Liebfraumilch, etc.).

B. As cooking wines:

A small amount of natural wine can be used in cooking to prepare sauces since the cooking process burns the alcohol off. Use the same wines already mentioned.

C. Liquors and Brandies:

Be very careful with the use of alcohols and liquors. Although three quarters of the alcohol is burned off during flambéing, some of it remains in the finished dish. A tablespoon or so of brandy will still do wonders for a fruit salad and a custard; used for 6 persons, it will not account for more than 10 to 12 calories per person.

REPLACEMENT FOR SUGAR

The sugar replacement problem remains one of the most important stumbling blocks of a slimming program. Try to do without sugar altogether, or to utilize the natural sugar of fresh fruits to satisfy your needs for a "sweet taste."

It is important that you remember that all sugar replacement products made with saccharin have a few health drawbacks. Their labels and packagings are very explicit. It will be up to you to decide whether the sweet taste that you may be craving is so very important that you must absolutely have it. We actually have no need for sugar in our diet, and only a little exercise in will is sufficient to "unsweeten" your palate forever. Whatever your decision, remember that many saccharin-based sweeteners are better added after a food is cooked; for example if you cook a custard, it will taste better if you thicken it first, then sweeten it off the heat. Some sugar substitutes have an unfortunate bitter aftertaste that cooking tends to accentuate.

There is a natural fruit sugar called *fructose,* the sweetness of which is so strong that one can use half as much of it as of regular cane sugar, which is sucrose. Adults should avoid fructose as all sugars, but children may have it without problem. One teaspoon of fructose will yield only 11 calories and 3 grams of available carbohydrate, and it will sweeten with as much potency as a teaspoon of cane sugar with its 18-calorie yield. Fructose is available in your supermarket.

REPLACEMENT FOR FLOUR

Since flour is on the forbidden list, you will want to replace its thickening power by a mixture of egg yolk and skim milk or stock, known as *liaison* in French, which simply means "thickener" or "binder." Use either 1 egg yolk plus 1 to 2 tablespoons of evaporated skim milk, or 2 tablespoons or so of meat or fish stock mixed with either 2 very finely mashed hard-boiled egg yolks or 1 raw egg yolk. Those mixtures added to the cooking juices of meats, fish or vegetables will give you very nicely bound sauces that will be light and pleasant.

THE BREAD PROBLEM

If you have no diagnosed health reason not to eat gluten bread or unsweetened zwieback, these are the two bread products that you should use. Every country has at least one brand available of each of these baked products. Two slices of this type of bread is all that you should allow yourself within a 24-hour period.

Investigate also the myriads of Melba toasts and Norwegian flat breads which contain a minimum of starch and can have as little as 12 calories per each very satisfying cracker or wafer.

If you need bread crumbs, toast gluten bread slices until very dry, and powder them finely in a blender or food processor.

COCKTAIL FOODS

Replace all nuts, crackers and cheeses by a nice platter of fresh vegetables with a thick dressing made of yogurt and low-fat cottage cheese, flavored with plenty of fresh herbs.

COOKING IMPLEMENTS

Now that we have discussed what the doctor recommends to cook, I would like to examine with you a few specialized cooking implements, that are most useful for light, almost fat-free cooking. All can be used either on your stove or as a separate electric appliance. You may want to invest in these:

■ One large rectangular so-called "buffet electric frying pan" with a nonstick surface and a lid with steam vents, You will use it for sautés and stews.

■ One or eventually 2 large 10-inch Teflon-lined skillets with lids. The thicker the material it is made of, the better. There are 2 specialized methods to cook in Teflon-lined pans and I will describe these later.

■ You will find a pressure cooker most helpful, and the savior of the busy woman. In it you can stew, steam, boil. You can even cook a meat dish at the bottom of the pot while you steam its accompanying vegetable in a basket placed over the meat.

■ For excellent red meat with good, almost outdoor flavor, acquire a cast-iron grill or a French heavy cast-iron skillet with ribs which can be used on any home stove burner. Sear the meat extremely fast with a lot of good caramelization on the outside; this accentuates the feeling of inside juiciness when the meat is tasted.

COOKING METHODS

Here is a list of all the cooking methods you can use with the diverse types of food you are recommended to cook; the method is listed on the left and suggestions to make each method more effective are listed on the right.

BAKING in baking dishes
You can bake meat, fish, poultry, skewered meats and vegetables.

Suggestions: Do not use butter. Follow the recipes, which are precise on how to proceed. Place all meats or fish on racks to allow the fat to drip off into the baking dish.

BOILING in large kettles
Also called blanching; this method can be used for meats and vegetables.

Suggestions: Add plenty of herbs and aromatics to the cooking water.

BRAISING in enameled cast-iron braising pots or in the pressure cooker
Excellent for tougher cuts of meat, fish and fibrous vegetables (fennel, celery, etc.).

Suggestions: See the method for browning the meat under "panfrying." Then transfer the meat to a large heavy pot with a cover, or to a pressure cooker. Rather than use water, use exclusively meat or fish stock as described in the next chapter; you will obtain excellent sauces that require barely any thickening.

BROILING on broiler pans fitted with a rack
For meats and fish.

Suggestions: Do not use oil on the surface of the food. Put the food on a rack. Sprinkle it well with herbs to enhance the flavor.

PANFRYING exclusively in skillets with nonstick lining or electric frying pans also with nonstick lining
For meats and fish as well as vegetables.

Suggestions:
A. For meats that are marbled and still contain some fat (stewing beef, stewing lamb). Put the meat in a Teflon-lined skillet over medium heat until the fat exudes out of the meat. Then raise the heat and brown the meat

well in its own fat; discard the fat carefully and pat the meat dry before adding any braising liquid, or deglazing liquid.

B. For meats that are not marbled but are extremely lean (filet steaks, chops, escalopes). Use the cooking juices of the aromatic vegetables to obtain a good browning. First, cook the onions and/or other aromatics in a bit of meat stock, then remove the aromatics to a plate and replace them by the meat. You will see the onion juice and meat stock glaze on the bottom of the skillet and around the meat. The meat will look nice and brown. When you dissolve or deglaze the cooking juices with meat stock the gravy will take on a beautiful deep brown color.

POACHING in special fish poachers or large pots
For both fish and poultry.

Suggestions: See individual recipes; the techniques for poaching may vary with the type of meat or fish.

SAUTÉING in skillets with nonstick lining with lids, or in electric frying pans also with nonstick lining and with lids
Sautéing refers here to cooking in a very small amount of stock; the technique is used for poultry, veal, lamb, and some fish such as monkfish.

Suggestions: First brown the meat as described under panfrying, then add a bit of meat or fish stock. When the meat or fish is done, thicken the sauce with an egg-yolk *liaison* (see Replacement for Flour).

STEAMING in a regular pot fitted with a steaming basket or in a pressure cooker
Excellent for meats and vegetables.

Suggestions: Place the pieces to steam in the basket of a pressure cooker or a vegetable steamer containing a minimum amount of water in the bottom section.

WEIGHTS AND MEASURES

All measures and temperatures are given in American (US), British (UK) and metric units, so that any American, British or Canadian cook can find measures in the system that he or she is used to.

OVEN TEMPERATURES

	Fahrenheit (F.)	Celsius (C.)	Regulo
very low	200° to 275°	95° to 135°	1 to 2
low	300° to 325°	150° to 165°	2 to 4
moderate	350° to 375°	175° to 190°	4 to 6
hot	400° to 425°	205° to 220°	6 to 8
very hot	450° to 500°	232° to 260°	8 to 9

These are not exact equivalents, but approximations, but they should offer you a reasonable guide. The Regulo figures are less accurate than those for exact temperatures, but if you are cooking on a Regulo stove you will soon discover whether 4 or 5, or 7 or 8, is better for a particular procedure. For roasting most meats, poultry or fish, or for baking vegetables, you can use a lower temperature for a longer time, or vice versa. The size and shape of your roast, as well as the age of the animal, and the heaviness of the pot can make considerable difference. The temperature is more critical for soufflé or cake. For best results in any oven, have it checked to be sure the controls are accurate according to whichever system you have.

Now let us look at the ingredients in a typical recipe, Beef Miroton (see Index). An ingredient usually purchased by weight, such as onions, will be listed by weight. American and British weights are the same, ¾ lb. onions, but the metric weight is listed in grams, and the gram weight, 375 g, is the last measure given. Next we have a liquid measure, US 3 cups, UK 2¾ cups. There is this difference because the British cup is larger than ours. The American cup contains 8 ounces, the British cup 10 ounces. The last measure is the metric volume, .75 L. Next we have an ingredient measured in tablespoons, US 3 TB, UK 1½ TB, metric 1½ TB. Both the British (BSI) and metric tablespoon have twice the volume of the American tablespoon. When one gets to larger volumes, the American quart contains 32 ounces, the British (or Imperial) quart contains 40 ounces. The metric measures are based on the liter (35 ounces), which contains 10 deciliters (dl), about 7 US tablespoons per deciliter. Ingredients purchased by the unit, as 1 egg or 6 leeks, are listed that way; a pinch is a pinch; salt and pepper and other ingredients added to your taste are listed without a measured amount.

Use the tables that follow as a general reference.

LIQUID MEASURES

US/AVP	UK/BSI	METRIC
1 teaspoon (1 tsp.)	½ teaspoon (½ tsp.)	½ tsp. (5 milliliters)
1 tablespoon (1 TB) (3 teaspoons)	½ tablespoon (½ TB)	½ TB (15 milliliters)
2 tablespoons (2 TB) (1 ounce)	1 tablespoon (1 TB)	1 TB (30 milliliters)
¼ cup (4 tablespoons)	2 tablespoons (2 TB)	2 TB
½ cup (8 tablespoons)	⅓ cup (4 oz.)	1 generous deciliter (dl)
1 cup (.25 liter) (16 tablespoons)	⁴/₅ cup (8 fluid ounces)	2.5 dl
1¼ cups	1 cup (10 fluid ounces)	3 dl
1 quart (1 liter)	⁴/₅ quart (32 ounces)	1 L
5 cups	1 quart (40 ounces)	1.25 L

SOLID MEASURES

There are variations in weight according to the ingredient, and even the same ingredient can vary in weight according to the humidity of the day or the length of time the food has been stored. These equivalents are based on the weight of all-purpose flour.

US/AVP	UK/BSI	METRIC
1 teaspoon (1 tsp.)	½ teaspoon (½ tsp.)	3 grams (3 g)
1 tablespoon (1 TB)	½ tablespoon (½ TB)	9 grams (9 g)
¼ cup	2 tablespoons (2 TB)	36 grams (36 g)
⅓ cup	3 tablespoons (3 TB)	46 grams (46 g)
½ cup	4 tablespoons (4 TB)	72 grams (72 g)
1 cup	8 tablespoons (8 TB)	144 grams (144 g)

Some reminders: Vegetables bought fresh, in bulk, to be cleaned at home will yield only about one third of the original weight in prepared edible portions. Meats that are broiled or roasted lose one fifth of their weight during cooking.

COMPOUND BUTTERS, STOCKS AND SAUCES

(Les Beurres Composés, les Bouillons, les Sauces)

SLIM COMPOUND BUTTERS

In Classic French Cuisine, a compound butter is made by creaming plain butter and flavoring it with all kinds of herbs, spices and seasonings to change the taste. Compound butters are usually added to sauces to change or augment their flavors, or they are used in pats over grilled meats.

The mixture called compound butter in this book is a paste of hard-boiled egg yolks and raw egg yolks that can be thinned with skim milk or stock as needed or desired. The butter, plain, is spread on a variety of cold meats and vegetables. For hot or warm foods, the butters are more often than not added to the cooking juices of those foods to form a small sauce.

The mixture will keep refrigerated but for the sake of best possible taste and flavor, it is recommended always to make these butters fresh as needed.

COMPOUND BUTTER BASE
(Base pour Beurre Composé)

■ Easy
   15 minutes

4 servings
   2 hard-boiled egg yolks
   1 raw egg yolk
   skim milk to thin
   salt and pepper

6 servings
   3 hard-boiled egg yolks
   2 raw egg yolks
   skim milk to thin
   salt and pepper

8 servings
   4 hard-boiled egg yolks
   3 raw egg yolks
   skim milk to thin
   salt and pepper

• Hard-boil the eggs in boiling water for 10 minutes. Rinse the eggs under cold water and peel immediately. Cool completely and separate yolks from whites.

• Remove the yolks to a fine-mesh conical strainer; one by one, push the yolks through, letting them fall through the strainer into a small bowl.

• Add the raw egg yolk(s) and mix very well until a smooth paste is obtained. If you wish, or need to, thin with a bit of skim milk. Season with salt and pepper in moderate amounts only.

• Keep stored in the refrigerator, well covered with plastic wrap, until ready to use. Use the same day.

NOTE
The leftover egg whites are a good source of proteins. Chop them and mix with chopped fresh herbs to use as a garnish.

BASIL AND GARLIC BUTTER
(Beurre de Pistou)

- **Easy**
  6 servings
  25 minutes
  Best season: July through September

  **US 1 cup, UK 1 scant cup, packed fresh
    basil leaves**
  1 garlic clove
  Compound Butter Base for 6 servings
  salt and pepper
  **US 2 TB, UK 1 TB, grated Parmesan
    cheese**

- Pack the basil leaves and the garlic in the bowl of a food processor and process until puréed, approximately 15 seconds.

- Gradually blend the base into the basil purée and process for another 15 seconds, until homogenous.

- Add salt and pepper to taste and the Parmesan. Give a last 15 seconds of processing.

- Should the butter be too liquid, add 1 raw egg yolk.

NOTE

This butter can be served with boiled vegetables, especially green beans; broiled fish and white meat of chicken; broiled and panfried veal steaks; panfried and broiled beef, especially steaks.

The basil purée alone is excellent on poached eggs and omelets.

GARLIC BUTTER
(Beurre d'Ail)

- **Easy**
  6 servings
  20 minutes

  12 garlic cloves
  Compound Butter Base for 6 servings
  salt and pepper
  skim milk to thin

- Crack the garlic cloves open with the flat of a knife blade; slip the skins off. Drop the garlic cloves into a small pot of boiling water and blanch for 2 to 3 minutes. Drain.

- Put the garlic and the compound butter base in the bowl of a food processor, add salt and pepper to taste, and process for 15 seconds.

- Repeat processing in small 15-second bursts until the mixture is perfectly smooth. If too thick for your taste, thin with a little skim milk.

NOTE
This butter can be served with cold fish and cold meats (pork, lamb); as an enrichment for soups and certain sauces; as an appetizer spread on thin wafers.

ANCHOVY BUTTER
(Beurre d'Anchois)

- **Easy**
  6 servings
  20 minutes

  US and UK 2 oz. anchovies preserved in
  ** oil**
  Compound Butter Base for 6 servings
  pepper
  salt only if needed

- Rinse the anchovies under running cold water and pat them very dry.

- Cut the anchovies into small pieces and put them into the bowl of a food processor. Add the compound butter base and pepper to taste. Process for 15 seconds.

- Taste the butter and add salt if necessary. Process for 15 seconds more if you have added salt.

NOTE
This butter can be served with broiled fish and meats, and it can also be used as a cold appetizer spread on thin crackers.

SHALLOT BUTTER
(Beurre d'Echalotes)

■ **Easy**
6 servings
20 minutes

US ¼ cup, UK 2 TB, chopped shallots (4 TB)
US 1½ cups, UK 1⅓ cups, dry white wine (3.5 dl)
Compound Butter Base for 6 servings
salt and pepper

- Mix shallots and white wine in a small saucepan and reduce the mixture by two thirds. Cool completely.

- Pour the shallot reduction into the bowl of a food processor and add the compound butter base. Process for 15 seconds.

- If not smooth enough, process for another 15 seconds, at the same time adding salt and pepper to your taste.

NOTE
This butter can be served with broiled meats and fish, or can be spread on wafers as an appetizer.

SHRIMP BUTTER
(Beurre de Crevettes)

■ **Easy**
6 servings
20 minutes

¼ lb. shelled shrimps (125 g)
clam juice
pepper
Compound Butter Base for 6 servings
salt

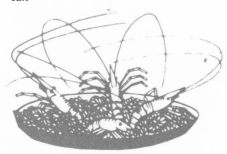

- Purée the shrimps in a food processor with a dash of clam juice.

- Add pepper to taste and the compound butter base, and process for 15 seconds.

- If the mixture is not smooth enough process for another 15 seconds, at the same time adding salt and pepper if needed.

NOTE
This butter can be served with cold or broiled fish and shellfish; it can also be spread on wafers for canapés.

LEMON AND PARSLEY BUTTER
(Beurre Maître d'Hôtel)

- Easy
  6 servings
  25 minutes

  ¼ cup parsley sprigs
  Compound Butter Base for 6 servings
  US 1 TB, UK ½ TB, lemon juice (½ TB)
  salt and pepper
  1 raw egg yolk (optional)
  skim milk (optional)

- Put the parsley sprigs into a food processor bowl and break them up with 15 seconds of processing.
- Add the compound butter base, the lemon juice, and salt and pepper to taste. Process until smooth.
- If the butter becomes too liquid, add a raw egg yolk. If it becomes too thick again, add a few drops of skim milk.

NOTE
This butter can be served with broiled meats and fish and with some boiled vegetables, such as cauliflower, asparagus, green beans, carrots, etc.

PROVENÇAL HERB BUTTER
(Beurre aux Herbes de Provence)

- Easy
  6 servings
  15 minutes, plus time to infuse the herbs

  1 TB mixed Provençal herbs (½ TB)
  US 3 TB, UK 1½ TB, skim milk (1½ TB)
  Compound Butter Base for 6 servings
  salt and pepper
  1 raw egg yolk (optional)

- Crumble the herbs as finely as possible. Bring the milk to a boil in a small pot and add the herbs. Let cool completely.

- Place herb infusion and compound butter base in a food processor bowl. Add salt and pepper to taste and process for 15 seconds.
- If the butter is too thin, add another raw egg yolk.

NOTE
This butter can be served with broiled fish; white meat of chicken or turkey; veal steaks; beef steaks; all boiled vegetables, especially zucchini, green beans and spaghetti squash.

RED-WINE AND SHALLOT BUTTER
(Beurre Marchand de Vin)

■ Easy
   6 servings
   25 minutes

US 2 cups, UK 2 scant cups, dry red wine
   (.5 L)
6 shallots, finely chopped
salt and pepper
Compound Butter Base for 6 servings
⅓ tsp. commercial meat extract, or US 2
   TB, UK 1 TB, reduced Meat Stock
   (see Index) (1 TB)
lemon juice
1 raw egg yolk (optional)
US 2 TB, UK 1 TB, chopped parsley (1
   TB)

• Put the wine, shallots, and salt and pepper to taste in a saucepan over moderate heat. Reduce by two thirds. Remove from the heat and cool to barely lukewarm.

• Whisk the reduction into the compound butter. Add the meat extract and lemon juice to suit your taste.

• If the butter is too liquid for your taste, add a raw egg yolk. You may reheat the butter if you wish, but do not let it boil. Add parsley and use immediately.

• To obtain an even better taste, dissolve the meat juice in the broiler pan in which you broiled your steak, with a dash of hot water or meat stock, and add the mixture to the butter.

NOTE
This sauce or butter is especially good for broiled steaks.

CURRY BUTTER
(Beurre de Kari)

■ Easy
  6 servings
  15 minutes

  1½ tsps. fresh curry powder, or more or less
  US ¼ cup, UK 2 TB, Meat Stock (see Index) or water (2 TB)
  Compound Butter Base for 6 servings

● Strain the curry powder into a small pot. Gradually add the stock or water. Bring to a boil and simmer for a few minutes.

● Put the compound butter on a plate. Using a rubber spatula, scrape the curry over it. Mash butter and curry very well together.

NOTE
This compound butter can be served with broiled veal or chicken; steamed mussels; poached trout, or fillets of any white fish.

WATERCRESS BUTTER
(Beurre de Cresson de Fontaine)

■ Easy
  6 servings
  15 minutes

  ½ cup loosely packed watercress leaves
  Compound Butter Base for 6 servings
  salt and pepper
  prepared mustard (optional)

● Bring a small pot of water to a boil. Add the watercress, turn the heat off, and let the pot stand for 2 minutes. Drain and pat the leaves dry.

● Place the watercress leaves in the bowl of a food processor. Add the compound butter base and salt and pepper to taste. Process for 15 seconds, or until well homogenized.

● If you wish, you can add a bit of prepared Dijon mustard.

NOTE
This compound butter can be served with shrimps, lobster, poached fillets of white fish, cold or warm, broiled fatter fish such as mackerel or bluefish; white meat of chicken, poached or broiled, broiled chicken parts; veal, broiled, panbroiled or panroasted.

MEAT AND FISH STOCKS

This is the most important part of this book. Please read the following pages and recipes with great attention. This book is different from books written by other "diet cooking" authors, because of these particular recipes.

The recipes are those for meat and fish stocks. The modern woman faced with the chore of making a stock usually gives up even before starting, because it is too time-consuming, or why not use leftover soup bouillon or leftover vegetable broth and strengthen those with a little bouillon cube here or a bit of meat extract there? There is almost nothing wrong with that if you work with butter, cream, and all the goodies that a regular diet lets you afford, but we are here in a special situation.

No butter, no cream, a few egg yolks here and there but not really enough to give your preparations and concoctions that "slip" that makes regular sauces, rich with butter and cream, go down like silk on the palate. So, something had to replace cream and butter and the authors of the book went to that other natural "slip" giver: gelatin. Gelatin you make yourself when you cook meat so that its connective tissues break down to a sticky material. For example, the more you cook a broth, the more the connective tissues of the meat break down and the more gelatinous the stock will be.

The French use the term *gelée*, or jelly, for this type of stock which, once strained and cooled completely will turn into a stiff gel. The stiffer the gel, the better the stock.

There are two basic "jellies." Fish jelly, which cooks very fast, and meat jelly, which takes a little longer to cook. The pressure cooker is not necessary for fish jelly, but you will find it the greatest help to minimize work and save energy and time when you prepare meat jelly.

Yes, you certainly can continue using bouillon cubes, canned bouillon, etc., but however good the ideas and the ingredients you will know that you are eating diet food. With the stocks or jellies, you truly will not.

One bit of advice: You will find recipes for Fish and Beef Consommé in the Soup chapter. These two products can replace any jelly at any time. So if you have some left over, save it for cooking.

MEAT STOCK
(Gelée de Viande)

- Easy
  Medium expensive
  3 hours, 1 hour in pressure cooker

  3 lbs. veal shank (1.36 kg)
  2 lbs. veal bones or trimmings (.9 kg)
  3 carrots
  1 turnip
  2 large onions
  3 to 6 cloves
  3 or 4 leeks
  bouquet garni
  salt and pepper
  4 quarts water (4 L)
  US 1 cup, UK 1 scant cup, dry white wine
      (2.5 dl)

- Wash the shank and bones well. With a cleaver, cut the shank into several pieces, or have your butcher shop do it for you.

- Peel the carrots, turnip and onions. Stick the onions with 2 or 3 whole cloves per onion. Put all the ingredients in a large all-purpose pot and bring to a boil. Add very little salt. Simmer for 3 to 6 hours.

- Strain through a fine strainer or a regular strainer lined with cheesecloth. Let cool at room temperature and refrigerate overnight.

- The next day defatten the stock by lifting off the sheets of fat on top. Discard fat.

- This stock will keep in the refrigerator for about 10 days. Like the fish *fumet* in the next recipe, it may be frozen in containers of various sizes to accommodate your needs as they arise.

Other Stocks: Proceed exactly as described to make stocks with chicken wings and bones, game and game-bird bones. Keep the veal shank at all times; it is your best source of gelatin.

NOTE
Use this stock to replace butter and cream when panfrying meats, broiling meats, preparing small sauces, or seasoning vegetables, either blanched or steamed.

FISH STOCK
(Fumet ou Gelée de Poisson)

■ Easy
Inexpensive
45 minutes

1 quart cold water (1 L)
3 lbs. fish heads and bones (no skins, no
    fins please) (1.36 kg)
1 large onion, sliced
bouquet garni
juice of 1 lemon
1 carrot, sliced
salt and pepper

● Put all ingredients in a stainless-steel pot. Bring to a boil; turn heat down to a simmer, and cook for no more than 40 minutes. With a wooden spoon, crush the fish heads and bones at regular intervals while simmering.

● Strain the mixture through a fine strainer or a regular strainer lined with cheesecloth. Let cool at room temperature, then refrigerate.

● Under refrigeration the fish stock will become gelatinous. It will keep in the refrigerator for several days, and you may also freeze it.

● To save time, you can make a larger quantity of *fumet* and freeze containers of varying sizes to accommodate unexpected needs or planned needs.

NOTE
Use this stock to replace butter or cream when baking fish, panfrying fish, poaching fish, preparing small fish sauces.

EGG-YOLK BINDING OR ENRICHMENT
(Liaison au Jaune d'Œuf)

- Very delicate, needs all your attention
  4 minutes

Proportions for 1 cup US or BSI or 2 generous deciliters
   3 raw egg yolks
   US 3 TB, UK 1½ TB, evaporated skim
      milk, yogurt or plain skim milk
      (1½ TB)

- Due to the impossibility of using either a *roux*, cream, starch or butter to thicken sauces and gravy, the obvious remaining method of thickening is the *liaison* or enrichment with egg yolks.

- The principle consists in coagulating the yolk in a hot sauce no further than the poaching stage, so that the liquid will eventually be thickened by the poached egg yolk gel.

- The liquid thickened may be a gravy, a sauce, a broth, plain or mixed with lemon juice.

METHOD

- Mix the egg yolks and liquid with one quarter of the sauce in a small bowl.

- Remove the pan of sauce from the heat. Gradually whisk in the lightened egg yolks.

- Return saucepan to the heat and stir over medium-low heat until the sauce thickens.

- Positively do not boil, or the egg yolks overpoach and hard-boil, pitting the sauce with millions of hard yellow flakes.

NOTE

The rule about boiling or not boiling a *liaison*: If the *liaison* is mixed with a plain liquid and not combined with any type of starch such as flour, cornstarch, potato starch, arrowroot, *never boil*, for even the slightest little boil will bring on curdling.

If the *liaison* is mixed with a liquid already thickened with a starch, a few boils must be given to the sauce or it will liquefy on standing.

MODIFIED SAUCES

How about your favorite sauces, perhaps Duxelles or the Béarnaise sauce to top your steak or fish? You could even make a Bordelaise sauce of sorts by reducing red wine and shallots in the nonstick saucepan in which you just broiled a steak. Here they are, all modified to produce a minimum amount of calories.

DUXELLES
(Duxelles de Champignons)

- Relatively easy
  6 servings
  15 minutes by hand, 7 to 8 minutes with
      food processor

  ½ lb. mushrooms (227 g)
  1 large onion, chopped
  2 shallots, chopped
  salt and pepper
  US 2 TB, UK 1 TB, Meat Stock (see Index)
      (2 TB)
  grated nutmeg

- Clean mushrooms and trim the stem ends. Chop mushrooms finely. Also chop the onion and shallots.
- Put the mushrooms in a skillet over medium heat. Salt and pepper them and cover immediately. As soon as the juices run out of the mushrooms, add the meat stock and both the onion and shallots. Add a dash of nutmeg.

- Continue cooking until all vegetables are tender and the mushroom hash is still slightly moist, not dry or brittle.
- Store in a glass preserving jar. The mixture keeps well in the refrigerator for several days, or it can be frozen in small jars for later use.

NOTE
Duxelles can be used with all white meats, broiled, panfried, or panroasted; eggs, poached or scrambled; sautéed vegetables, étuvéed vegetables.

SLIM BÉARNAISE SAUCE
(Sauce Béarnaise de Régime)

- Requires care
  6 servings
  Inexpensive
  30 minutes

  US ½ cup, UK ⅓ cup, wine vinegar (1 generous dl)
  US ½ cup, UK ⅓ cup, dry white wine (1 generous dl)
  3 shallots, finely chopped
  4 tsp. dried tarragon
  1 tsp. dried chervil
  1 bunch of parsley stems, chopped
  ¼ tsp. cracked white peppercorns
  ¼ tsp. salt
  boiling water
  US ⅓ cup, UK ¼ cup, Meat Stock (see Index) (1 scant dl)
  3 egg yolks
  1 tsp. olive oil

- Place vinegar, white wine, shallots, 1 teaspoon of the tarragon, the chervil, chopped parsley stems, cracked white peppercorns and a pinch of salt in a thick pot over medium heat. Bring to a boil, turn the heat down, simmer, and let reduce until the aromatics look dry.

- Meanwhile put remaining 3 teaspoons dried tarragon in a small bowl; moisten it barely with boiling water to mellow and revive the herb.

- Bring the meat stock to a boil. Set aside and let cool to warm.

- As soon as the mixture of aromatics is reduced properly, combine with the warm stock and gradually mix into the egg yolks. Put back over heat; treat it like a custard: let it thicken, *stirring constantly with a wooden spoon, but do not boil.*

- As soon as sauce is thickened, remove pot from the heat and whisk the sauce heavily and quickly so as to trap air into the poached egg protein. The sauce will have the look of a regular Béarnaise sauce. Strain into a clean saucepan.

- Whisk in the oil, add the revived tarragon, and correct the salt and pepper.

FOLLOWING THE SAME TECHNIQUE

Hollandaise Sauce: In the reduction, replace the wine by water and the vinegar by lemon juice. Use ¼ to ⅓ cup water and 1 tablespoon lemon juice. Use meat stock in the same quantity as for the Béarnaise sauce.

Use with all poached fish, asparagus, cauliflower, broccoli.

Orange Hollandaise or Mikado Sauce: Add the grated rind of ½ orange in the reduction prepared as for Hollandaise, and use half orange juice, half meat stock, as liquid.

Use with asparagus and broccoli.

NOTES

Use fresh herbs if you have them.

The main use of Béarnaise is as a sauce for broiled steaks, broiled white meat of chicken, broiled and panfried veal.

HUNTER'S SAUCE
(Sauce Chasseur)

■ Easy
6 servings
Inexpensive
40 minutes

US 2 TB, UK 1 TB, vinegar (2 TB)
US 2 cups, UK 1¾ cups, Meat Stock (see Index) (4.5 dl)
US ⅓ cup, UK ¼ cup, tomato purée (1 scant dl)
3 shallots, chopped
2 large garlic cloves, chopped
bouquet garni
salt and pepper
1 tsp. dried tarragon
3 raw egg yolks
1 oz. Cognac or brandy of your choice

● In a saucepan, combine the vinegar, stock, tomato purée, chopped shallots and garlic, the *bouquet garni*, salt and pepper to taste, and the tarragon. Bring to a boil and simmer together until reduced by one third.

● Strain into a small saucepan. Add the egg yolks, proceeding according to the rules of the *liaison* (see Index).

● Heat the Cognac in a small pan, ignite it, and pour it flaming into the sauce. Stir well.

NOTE
Make sure that the alcohol in the brandy has completely evaporated.

Serve with game birds, boiled beef, broiled beef, poached chickens, broiled fish.

CURRY SAUCE
(Sauce au Curry)

- Easy
  6 servings
  Inexpensive
  1 hour

  3 large onions
  US 1 cup, UK 1 scant cup, Meat Stock
     (see Index) or bouillon (2½ dl)
  salt and pepper
  US 1½ TB, UK ¾ TB, curry powder (¾
     TB)
  4 fresh tomatoes, about 1 lb., or 2 cups
     canned Italian pear-shaped tomatoes
  2 garlic cloves
  bouquet garni
  2 egg yolks
  US 3 TB, UK ½ TB, evaporated skim milk
     (½ TB)
  juice of 1 lemon

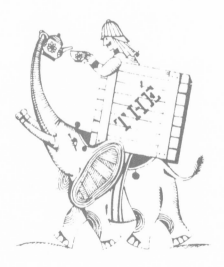

- Place the onions and half of the meat stock in a saucepan. Add salt and pepper to taste and the curry powder. Cook gently until the onions have softened and start to take on some color.

- Add the remainder of the stock, the tomatoes, peeled, seeded and chopped, the garlic cloves mashed to a purée with the tip of your knife blade, and the *bouquet garni*. Cover, leaving the pot lid askew by ¼ inch, and let cook for 30 to 40 minutes.

- Strain the sauce through a fine conical strainer.

- Mix the egg yolks and evaporated skim milk. Add some of the tomato curry sauce to the *liaison*, then whisk this mixture into the bulk of the sauce. Reheat without boiling.

- Correct the seasoning with salt, pepper and lemon juice, all added to suit your taste.

NOTE
This sauce can be used on poached eggs and poultry; poached and broiled fish; boiled meats, panfried meats.

LEMON SAUCE
(Sauce Froide au Citron)

- **Easy**
  6 servings
  Inexpensive
  5 minutes

  US 2 TB, UK 1 TB, lemon juice (1 TB)
  US 2 TB, UK 1 TB, natural yogurt (1 TB)
  US ⅔ cup, UK ½ cup, ricotta cheese, very
  fresh (250 g)
  salt and pepper
  US 2 TB, UK 1 TB, finely grated horserad-
  ish (1 TB), or more
  freshly chopped herbs

- Place lemon juice, yogurt, ricotta, and salt and pepper to taste in a blender container or in the bowl of a food processor. Process until smooth. Add more salt if needed.
- Add as much horseradish as you like and as many chopped fresh herbs as you have available (see Notes).

NOTES

The cheese used in France would be Petits Suisses. A few cheese stores have them; look for them for best flavor.

This sauce can be used on cold asparagus, cucumbers, tomatoes, hard-boiled eggs.

Fines herbes in France are always chopped parsley, tarragon, chives and chervil. But consider anything else growing in your area.

SHALLOT VINEGAR
(Vinaigre d'Echalotes)

- **Easy**
  6 servings
  Thrift recipe
  5 minutes

  US 1 cup, UK 1 scant cup, vinegar (2.5
  dl)
  US ¼ cup, UK 2 TB, finely chopped shal-
  lots (2 TB)
  salt and pepper

- Mix vinegar, chopped shallots, and salt and pepper to taste. Let steep for several hours before serving.

NOTES

Use on oysters and other raw shellfish.

The longer this vinegar sits, the better it tastes, so prepare a larger amount and let it ripen in the refrigerator. It does not spoil.

MUSTARD SAUCE
(Sauce Moutarde)

- Easy
  6 servings
  Inexpensive
  5 minutes

  3 egg yolks
  US 3 TB, UK 1½ TB, prepared Dijon mustard (1½ TB)
  US ½ cup, UK ⅓ cup, natural yogurt (1 generous dl)
  salt and pepper

- Mix egg yolks and mustard in a small bowl. Using an electric mixer, whip them until very foamy.
- Gradually whisk in the yogurt. Season with salt and pepper to taste.
- Use cold as a salad dressing. To use as a binding, add some of this mixture to the pan gravy of meats to obtain a hot mustard sauce.

NOTE
Use on poached fish; raw vegetables; blanched vegetables, cold or hot.

TOMATO SAUCE
(Sauce Tomate)

- Easy
  6 servings
  Inexpensive
  45 minutes

  3 lbs. tomatoes, or 6 cups canned Italian pear-shaped tomatoes (1.5 kg)
  2 large onions, chopped
  2 garlic cloves, mashed
  1 bay leaf
  1 small bunch of parsley stems, chopped
  5 basil leaves
  salt and pepper

- Wash the tomatoes and cut them crosswise into halves. Remove all the seeds and water.
- Cut up the tomatoes and put them in a saucepan. Add the onions, garlic and herbs. Cook over medium heat, uncovered, for about 45 minutes.
- Purée the sauce and strain it. Add salt and pepper to taste.

SOUPS

(Les Potages)

BEEF CONSOMMÉ
(Consommé de Bœuf)

- Easy
  6 servings
  Affordable
  30 minutes for preparation, 3½ hours for cooking, 1 hour in pressure cooker

  2 whole veal shanks, cut into 1-inch slices
  3 quarts cold water (3 L)
  3 carrots
  3 turnips
  3 leeks, white part only
  1 small celery rib
  3 onions, each stuck with 2 cloves
  bouquet garni
  salt
  1½ lbs. lean beef, ground (750 g)

- Put the pieces of veal shank in a large stewing pot. Cover them with cold water and slowly bring to a boil. Cook for 10 minutes.

- After these 10 minutes, skim the broth very carefully. Let cook for another 10 minutes, then skim again. Add the vegetables, the *bouquet garni* and a pinch of salt and let cook for 2½ hours.

- After this time, put the ground beef in another pot. Cover it with cold water and very slowly bring to a boil. As soon as the mixture boils add both water and beef to the main pot.

- Continue cooking on slow simmer for another hour.

- Strain the consommé into a large bowl, using a colander lined with several layers of cheesecloth.

- Cool at room temperature, then refrigerate overnight. The next day lift off the solid layer of fat and discard it.

NOTES

You will extract a lot more taste out of the ground beef by letting it leach its juices first in cold water and adding both water and beef to the broth during the last hour of cooking.

A similar consommé can be prepared with any type of meat. When using chicken, a good old stewing hen will do best and must be put to cook with the veal shanks from the onset of the cooking.

Would you prefer a deeper browner color? Then brown the veal shanks in a hot oven before putting them to cook in the water.

Are you out of meat stock? Then, keep any leftover consommé and use it instead.

FISH CONSOMMÉ
(Consommé de Poisson)

■ Easy
6 servings
Thrift recipe
30 minutes for preparation, 40 minutes
    for cooking, 20 minutes in pressure
    cooker

6 sole heads
1 haddock head
backbones of 6 soles
US or UK 1½ quarts water (1.5 L)
US ½ cup, UK ⅓ cup, dry white wine (1
    scant dl)
salt and pepper
3 onions
2 carrots
2 leeks
1 small sprig of celery
bouquet garni

GARNISH
1 lb. fish fillets (.45 kg)
chopped parsley
1 lemon

• Put the fish bones in a large pot with the water, wine and only a little salt and pepper. Bring to a boil over medium-low heat. Skim as soon as some scum has accumulated on the surface of the water.

• Add the onions, carrots, leeks and celery, all sliced, and the *bouquet garni*. Cover, leaving the lid askew. Bring to a boil, then let simmer for no more than 35 minutes.

• Strain the broth through a colander lined with cheesecloth into another pot.

• To garnish, cut the fresh fish fillets into ½-inch cubes. Chop the parsley; squeeze the lemon juice. Bring the consommé to a high boil, add the fish and parsley. Remove immediately from the heat and let stand for 4 minutes before turning into a soup tureen. Add lemon juice to your taste.

NOTE
The broth plain, before addition of the fish garnish, can replace fish stock. Keep any leftover broth.

SHELLFISH CONSOMMÉ
(Consommé aux Fruits de Mer)

■ Easy
6 servings
Expensive
30 minutes

1 recipe Fish Consommé (preceding recipe)
½ lb. mushrooms, sliced (227 g)
salt and pepper
½ lb. bay scallops (227 g)
½ lb. shrimps, shelled (227 g)
chopped parsley
lemon juice

• Have the fish consommé ready the day before. *Do not use the garnish of fish fillets.*

• Slice the mushrooms. Put them in a pot with a few tablespoons of the fish consommé, and salt and pepper to taste. Cover and steam until the mushrooms have exuded their moisture and are cooked.

• Add the remainder of the consommé and bring to a boil.

• Wash and dry the bay scallops and shrimps. Add the shrimps to the boiling soup. Then immediately afterwards, add the scallops. Reheat for 1 minute.

• Remove soup from the heat. Add chopped parsley and lemon juice to taste and adjust the salt and pepper. Serve immediately.

Variation: Instead of the mushrooms, you could use 24 mussels. Steam them and add their well-filtered steaming juices to the soup. Then finish with a *liaison* of 2 egg yolks and a few tablespoons of evaporated skim milk.

PROVENÇAL FISH SOUP
(Soupe de Poisson à la Provençale)

- Easy
  6 servings
  Medium expensive
  1 hour

  1 recipe Fish Consommé (see Index)
  1 envelope whole saffron, .045 oz. (1.5 g)
  US 6 TB, UK 3 TB, Parmesan cheese (3
    TB)

  ROUILLE
  1 recipe Slim Mayonnaise (see Index)
  1 large garlic clove, or more
  large pinch of cayenne pepper
  US 1 TB, UK ½ TB, paprika (½ TB)

- The day before you plan to serve this, prepare the fish consommé, but *do not use the garnish* of fish fillets.

- Heat the consommé and simmer it for 10 minutes. Add the saffron and turn the heat off.

- Prepare the slim mayonnaise. Do not let the mayonnaise cool since it will be added to a hot soup. Put the garlic clove, cayenne and paprika in the bowl of a food processor. Add the mayonnaise and process until the garlic is completely puréed. The mayonnaise has become a *rouille*.

- Put the *rouille* into a soup tureen and gradually whisk in the fish soup. Serve in warmed bowls.

- Sprinkle 1 tablespoon cheese over each bowl and serve.

EGG SOUP
(Potage aux Œufs)

- Easy
  6 servings
  Inexpensive
  14 minutes

  US and UK 1½ quarts bouillon, chicken
    or beef (1.5 L)
  5 eggs
  salt and pepper
  US ½ cup, UK 4 to 5 TB, grated Gruyère
    cheese (5 TB)
  chopped parsley

- Bring the bouillon to a boil.

- Meanwhile, lightly beat the eggs in a bowl with a little salt and pepper. Be careful with the salt since the bouillon should already be salted.

- When the bouillon reaches the boiling point, slowly pour the eggs through a coarse-meshed strainer into the soup. Then turn the heat down and continue stirring and cooking for 2 minutes.

- Put the grated cheese in a soup tureen. Pour the soup over it and sprinkle with chopped parsley.

JULIENNE OF VEGETABLE SOUP
(Potage Julienne)

■ Easy
6 servings
Inexpensive
30 minutes for preparation, 40 minutes
for cooking, 15 minutes in pressure
cooker

2 onions
½ lb. carrots (250 g)
½ lb. turnips (250 g)
2 leeks
½ lb. cabbage (250 g)
½ lb. celery (250 g)
US and UK 2½ quarts water (2.5 L)
chopped parsley and chervil
salt and pepper

• Peel all the vegetables and cut them
into ⅛-inch julienne strips by knife,
or better in a food processor. Bring
the water to a boil.

• As soon as the water boils, add all
the vegetables. Bring back to a boil,
add salt and pepper to taste, and
turn down to a simmer. Cook for 40
to 45 minutes.

• Just before serving the soup, add
freshly chopped parsley and chervil
and correct the seasoning.

Variation: For a richer texture, put the
vegetables through a food mill or
purée them; in this case you need not
julienne them before cooking. Or you
may finish the soup with a *liaison* of
2 egg yolks mixed with a few tablespoons of evaporated skim milk. Or
you can even do both: purée and enrich. It tastes almost like a rich cream
soup full of butter.

GARLIC AND BASIL SOUP
(Soupe à l'Ail et au Basilic)

■ **Easy**
  6 servings
  Thrift recipe
  1 hour

2 heads of garlic
US and UK 1½ quarts cold water (1.5 L)
salt and pepper
1 cup packed basil leaves
2 baby zucchini (marrows or courgettes)
US 6 TB, UK 3 TB, grated Parmesan
    cheese (3 TB)

- Crush the garlic cloves with the flat of a knife blade but do not peel them. Put them in a soup pot.

- Cover with the cold water and slowly bring to a boil. Add salt and pepper to taste. Simmer for 55 minutes.

- Meanwhile sort, wash, and pat dry the basil leaves. Roll them in a towel. Cut the zucchini into fine julienne either with a knife or in a food processor.

- After 45 minutes check if the soup is tasty enough. If not, continue cooking. If it is ready, strain it, pushing well with a spatula against the side of the strainer to extract the garlic pulp out of the skins.

- Put the basil leaves in a blender container or food processor bowl. Add 1 cup of the soup and process until very smooth. Season with salt and pepper to taste.

- Return basil purée, julienne of zucchini and remainder of the soup to the saucepan. Simmer for another 5 minutes together. Serve in warm bowls, topped with Parmesan cheese.

COUNTRY-STYLE SOUP
(Potage Paysan)

- Easy
  6 servings
  Inexpensive
  25 minutes for preparation, 1½ hours for cooking, 35 to 40 minutes in pressure cooker

2 chicken giblets
1 gelatinous veal bone
US and UK 2½ quarts water (2.5 L)
salt and pepper
¾ lb. carrots (375 g)
¾ lb. turnips (375 g)
4 leeks, white part only
1 celery rib

- Clean the giblets and veal bone very well. Blanch them.

- In a large soup pot, put giblets and veal bone and cover with water. Bring to a boil, add salt and pepper to taste, and turn heat down to a simmer. Simmer for 1 hour.

- Meanwhile, peel the vegetables and cut them into small cubes. Add them to the pot and cook for another 30 minutes.

- Remove the chicken parts and bones and serve the soup.

NOTE
Any leftover cooked chicken carcass will do well in this soup; any leftover chicken meat may be diced and added as yet another garnish.

ONION SOUP
(Soupe à l'Oignon)

- Easy
  6 servings
  Inexpensive
  25 minutes, 15 minutes in pressure cooker

2 lbs. onions (1 generous kg)
US and UK 2 quarts water or bouillon (2 scant L)
½ lb. Gruyère cheese, grated
salt and pepper
nutmeg

- Peel the onions and cut into thin slices, using a food processor.

- Put onions in a large saucepan. Add one quarter of the liquid, and salt and pepper to taste. Cook gently without browning.

- Add the remainder of the liquid; bring to a boil. Add nutmeg to taste and let simmer for 20 minutes.

- Correct the final seasoning of the soup. Ladle it into 6 heatproof soup bowls and sprinkle it with cheese. Pass the bowls under the broiler to melt and gratiné the cheese. Serve piping hot.

PUMPKIN SOUP
(Soupe au Potiron)

- Easy
  6 servings
  Inexpensive
  25 minutes, 15 minutes in pressure cooker

  3 lbs. pumpkin meat (1.5 kg)
  US 3 cups, UK 2¾ cups, skim milk (.65 L)
  salt and pepper
  bouillon (optional)
  chopped parsley

- Peel the pumpkin and cube it. Put it into a pot with 1½ cups water. Cover and cook over moderate heat for approximately 30 minutes.

- If there is too much liquid in the pot, cook without a cover to allow evaporation.

- When the pumpkin is cooked, whisk it with a hand whisk to purée it. It will fall apart readily.

- Scald the skim milk. Add it to the pumpkin purée. Season with salt and pepper to taste. If you think the texture is too thick for your taste, dilute it with enough bouillon to bring it to the consistency you are pleased with.

- Turn into a soup tureen and sprinkle with parsley. Serve promptly.

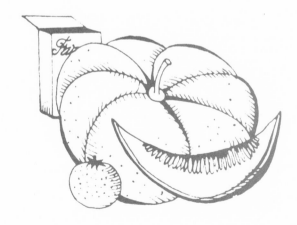

TOMATO SOUP
(Soupe à la Tomate)

■ Easy
  6 servings
  Inexpensive
  15 minutes for preparation, 30 minutes
      for cooking, 15 minutes in pressure
      cooker

  US ⅓ cup, UK ¼ cup, Meat Stock (see
      Index) (1 scant dl)
  3 onions, chopped
  3 lbs. tomatoes, peeled, seeded, and
      chopped, or 6 cups canned Italian
      pear-shaped tomatoes (1.5 kg)
  3 garlic cloves, mashed
  US and UK 1½ quarts water (1.5 L)
  salt and pepper
  2 raw egg yolks
  chopped parsley

● In a large pot, combine meat stock and onions. Cook slowly and without browning.

● When the onions are translucent, add the tomatoes. Cook for a few minutes, then add the garlic, water, and salt and pepper to taste. Cook uncovered for about 25 minutes.

● Mix the egg yolks and parsley in a soup tureen and let them steep together while you purée the soup, through a food mill, in a blender, or in a food processor.

● Return the soup to the pot; reheat well. Correct the seasoning and gradually beat the soup into the egg yolks and parsley mixture. Serve immediately.

Variation: Use 3 more tomatoes. Cook the soup as in the basic recipe, but do not purée the soup. Finish it in exactly the same manner.

SALAD DRESSINGS, SALADS AND HORS-D'ŒUVRE

(Les Assaisonnements, les Salades,
les Hors-d'Œuvre)

SLIM SALAD DRESSINGS

OIL:

The oils you can use in your dressings, by the teaspoon only, are corn oil, regular olive oil, virgin olive oil, walnut oil, hazelnut oil. Corn and olive oils are available, and so is walnut oil sometimes in regular markets, but hazelnut oil is difficult to find most of the time.

You can prepare hazelnut or any other nut oil yourself by mixing 1 ounce of any given nut, blanched and chopped, with 1 cup of regular corn oil. Blend both ingredients together in a blender and let steep for several days. Then, transfer the mixture to a bottle, leaving the nuts at the bottom of the bottle. Positively keep refrigerated. In this slim cooking you will not be using much oil, and you want to keep the oil you have prepared from becoming rancid.

VINEGARS:

Be creative and try all kinds of vinegars: regular red- or white-wine vinegar, Champagne vinegar from France, cider vinegar, pineapple vinegar from Hawaii, sherry vinegar from Spain. All these are available on the market, plain or aromatized.

You can prepare herb or fruit vinegars, using white-wine vinegar as a base. All you have to do is slip herbs into the bottle of vinegar. Use the following herbs, preferably fresh and on their stems: tarragon, basil, chives, mint, dill, and a delicious fruit vinegar can be made with raspberries.

CREAM:

There is no possibility of using any cream; you will have to limit yourself to plain natural yogurt, skim-milk ricotta cheese, evaporated skim milk.

KEEPING DRESSINGS:

Slim dressings are better made fresh each time they are needed, no more than 2 hours before being used. Dried herbs should be added when the dressing is being made; fresh herbs should be added at the last minute.

SLIM VINAIGRETTE
(Vinaigrette de Régime)

■ Easy
6 to 10 servings
4 minutes

US 3 TB, UK 1½ TB, vinegar (1½ TB)
salt and pepper
US ⅔ cup, UK ½ cup, water (2 scant dl)
1 tsp. cornstarch
2 tsps. oil of your choice

- Mix vinegar and salt and pepper to taste. Bring to a boil; turn down to a simmer.

- Mix water and cornstarch. Add mixture, stirring, to the simmering vinegar and continue to stir until thickened.

- Add the oil of your choice.

- To vary this dressing, here are a few ideas that you can use. Be creative and try all kinds of things, but adapt the seasonings and aromatics to the food used.

Variation 1: Add 1 chopped shallot, 1 tiny garlic clove also chopped, 1 tablespoon chopped parsley to basic vinaigrette. *Use on any grated carrot salad.*

Variation 2: Add 1 chopped shallot, 1 teaspoon basil, 1 teaspoon anchovy paste to basic vinaigrette. *Use on red peppers, tomatoes, artichokes.*

Variation 3: Add 1 chopped garlic clove, ½ teaspoon orégano, a pinch of grated lemon rind, and a dash of red pepper flakes to basic vinaigrette. *Use on cold meat salad, eggplant salad, heart of palm salad.*

Variation 4: Add 1 teaspoon tarragon, 1 teaspoon prepared Dijon mustard, 1 tablespoon snipped fresh chives to basic vinaigrette. *Use on any salad containing ham, white meat of chicken, celery.*

Variation 5: Cook 1 teaspoon curry powder in the oil for 1 minute, then finish the dressing as in basic recipe. *Use on shellfish salads, especially mussels.*

Variation 6: Add ½ teaspoon grated orange rind, 1 teaspoon prepared Dijon mustard, 1 teaspoon Sercial Madeira. *Use on all bitter salads (endive, escarole).*

SLIM CREAM-STYLE DRESSING
Sauce Crème de Régime pour Salade)

- Easy
  6 to 10 servings
  3 minutes

  US 2 TB, UK 1 TB, plain natural yogurt (1 TB)
  US 2 TB, UK 1 TB, evaporated skim milk (1 TB)
  US 1½ TB, UK ¾ TB, vinegar (¾ TB)
  salt and pepper

- Put all the ingredients in a bowl and mix together well. Add salt and pepper to taste.
- To vary this dressing, here are a few ideas that you can use; be creative and try all kinds of things, but adapt the seasonings and aromatics to the food used.

Variation 1: Add 1 artichoke bottom, cooked and mashed; 2 anchovies, rinsed in water and mashed; 2 tablespoons minced basil to a basic cream dressing. *Use on cold boiled artichokes, a salad of artichoke bottoms, or any meat or fruit salad.*

Variation 2: Add ½ red onion, chopped (salted and rinsed in water first if very strong); 1 tablespoon or more green Madagascar peppercorns; and chopped Italian parsley. *Use on all hard-boiled egg salads, shellfish salads, pepper salads.*

Variation 3: Add grated lemon rind to your taste. *Use on asparagus.*

Variation 4: Add grated lime rind to your taste and a dash of lime juice. *Use on salad made with permitted fruits.*

Variation 5: Add chives and serve on plain green French-style salads served after dinner.

Variation 6: Add 1 teaspoon anchovy paste and 3 dashes of Worcestershire sauce plus chives. *Use on cucumbers and tomatoes.*

SLIM MAYONNAISE
(Mayonnaise de Régime)

■ Easy
  6 servings
  15 minutes, plus 20 minutes for cooling

  US 4 tsp., UK 2½ tsp., cornstarch (2½ tsp.)
  US ¾ cup, UK ⅔ cup, bouillon (2 scant dl)
  ⅓ tsp. salt
  pepper from the mill
  1 egg yolk
  US 1 TB, UK ½ TB, prepared Dijon mustard (½ TB)
  US 1 TB, UK ½ TB, vinegar (½ TB), or more
  US 1 tsp., UK 1 scant tsp., olive oil (1 scant tsp.)

● Mix cornstarch, bouillon, salt, pepper to taste and the egg yolk in a saucepan. Bring to a boil.

● As soon as the sauce boils, remove from the heat and cool to warm.

● Add mustard and vinegar; mix well. Add oil, mix well again.

● Let cool completely, covered with clear plastic wrap to prevent formation of a skin.

Aïoli: Place 2 garlic cloves, finely chopped, in the bowl of a food processor. Add 1 recipe of Slim Mayonnaise and process until smooth. Strain into a bowl and refrigerate again. *Use on poached fish, poached and hard-boiled eggs, fish soups, vegetable salads.*

Andalusian Mayonnaise: Place US 2 tablespoons, UK 1 tablespoon, tomato paste in a bowl and whisk in 1 recipe of Slim Mayonnaise. *Use on poached fish and shellfish.*

Mayonnaise d'Artagnan: Cook together 6 ounces dry white wine and 2 chopped shallots. Reduce by two thirds. Strain into a bowl. Add 1 tablespoon or more of snipped chives and black pepper. Add to 1 recipe of Slim Mayonnaise. *Use on cold meats.*

Mousseline Mayonnaise: Fold 1 beaten egg white into a recipe of Slim Mayonnaise. *Use on eggs, asparagus, poached fish.*

Tartar Sauce: Add to 1 recipe of Slim Mayonnaise, chopped pickles, capers, and herbs of your choice and in the quantity that you like. *Use on fish, shellfish, poached eggs, cold pork, cold lamb.*

Green Mayonnaise: Blanch a cup of combined tarragon, chives, parsley, chervil, spinach and watercress in boiling water. Drain the greens. Pat them dry. Put the greens in the bowl of a food processor and process until smooth and unformly green. Add to 1 recipe of Slim Mayonnaise. *Use on fish, shellfish, poached eggs, asparagus.*

Hot Pepper Mayonnaise: To 1 recipe of Slim Mayonnaise, add 2 chopped shallots, squeezed in the corner of a towel to extract the bitter juices. Also add 1 small hot red pepper, fresh or dried, finely crumbled or chopped; 1 tablespoon each of chopped tarragon and capers, and salt and pepper to taste. *Use on all cold meats, poached fish, poached eggs.*

Rémoulade Sauce: To 1 recipe of Slim Mayonnaise, add 2 tablespoons or more of capers, anchovy paste to taste, chopped fresh herbs to taste, and 2 chopped pickles. *Use on fish, shellfish, soft-boiled eggs, leftover boiled beef.*

SALADS AND HORS-D'ŒUVRE

RAW VEGETABLE SALAD
(Assiette de Crudités)

- Easy
  6 servings
  40 to 50 minutes

  7 eggs
  1 cauliflower
  1 small red cabbage
  2 celery ribs, peeled
  2 medium-size red beets
  6 carrots
  ¾ lb. mushrooms
  1 bunch of fresh radishes
  1 recipe Vinaigrette Variation 3 (see Index)

- Hard-boil the eggs. Rinse them under running cold water, peel them, and set them to wait in a bowl of cold salted water.

- Meanwhile cut the cauliflower into small flowerets; peel the stems. Remove the ribs from the red cabbage. Roll the leaves and cut them across into ⅛-inch strips.

- Cut the celery and beets into ⅓-inch cubes. Grate the carrots. Clean, trim, and slice the mushrooms.

- Arrange the vegetables attractively on one large platter.

- Cut a small slice of egg white from the larger end of 5 eggs. Stand the eggs all around the dish and surround them with the radishes.

- Remove the yolks from the remaining 2 eggs. Mash them well and gradually add them to the salad dressing.

- Serve the dressing separately in a sauceboat.

NOTE
For a good cocktail plate, put out small plates and forks for the convenience of your guests; serve this platter with tomato juice during cocktail hour.

VEGETABLE SALAD WITH RED PEPPER DRESSING
(Crudités, Sauce Poivron)

- Easy
  6 servings
  Inexpensive
  45 minutes

  2 cucumbers
  salt
  4 eggs
  4 tomatoes
  1 celery rib
  1 jar (4 oz., 113 g) red pimientos
  1 recipe Slim Mayonnaise (see Index)
  1 TB chopped parsley
  1 TB chopped chervil
  pepper

- Wash the cucumbers and dry them well. Do not peel them. Cut them into ⅙-inch slices. Sprinkle the slices with salt and let them stand to render their juices for approximately 1 hour. After that, rinse the cucumbers and dry them well.

- Hard-boil the eggs. Cut the tomatoes and the celery into thin slices.

- Drain the pimientos, rinse off any seeds, and put pimientos into a blender container or the bowl of a food processor with the hard-boiled eggs. Process until smooth. Adjust the texture with just enough mayonnaise to make a fine smooth pâté-like mixture.

- Mix parsley and salt and pepper to taste into the paste, and arrange the paste attractively at the center of a serving platter.

- Arrange the sliced vegetables all around. Serve the remainder of the mayonnaise flavored with the chervil in a sauceboat.

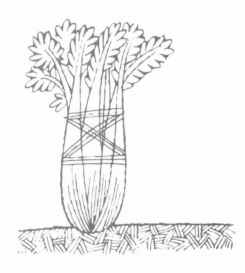

ARTICHOKE BOTTOMS VINAIGRETTE
(Fonds d'Artichauts Vinaigrette)

■ Easy
  6 servings
  Inexpensive
  20 minutes for preparation
  40 minutes to cook artichokes, 15 minutes in pressure cooker

  6 large artichokes
  6 eggs
  1 recipe Slim Vinaigrette (see Index)
  2 TB finely chopped herbs of your choice (1 TB)
  1 lemon
  6 tomatoes
  2 celery ribs

- Cook the artichokes in boiling salted water. Remove from the pot and cool them. Remove the leaves. Trim the bottoms, making sure that you keep them whole.

- While the artichokes cook, add the eggs to the pot during the last 10 minutes so they hard-boil while the artichokes finish cooking.

- Scrape the pulp from the artichoke leaves and add it to the vinaigrette. Put in a blender container and process until you have a smooth dressing.

- Sprinkle the artichoke bottoms with approximately half of the herbs and a few drops of lemon juice each; fill each bottom with some of the dressing and sprinkle more herbs on top.

- Slice tomatoes, celery ribs and eggs, and prepare 6 salad plates as follows: Put 1 artichoke bottom on each plate. Surround it with tomato, celery and egg slices. Put the remainder of the sauce in a sauceboat.

ARTICHOKE BOTTOMS MOUSSELINE
(Fonds d'Artichauts Mousseline)

- **Easy**
  6 servings
  Affordable
  15 minutes

  3 medium-size tomatoes
  salt
  6 large lettuce leaves
  6 large artichokes, cooked
  lemon juice
  12 oz. plain natural yogurt (360 g)
  pepper
  3 TB snipped chives (1½ TB)

- Cut the tomatoes horizontally into halves. Scoop out seeds and water without piercing the skin. Lightly salt the inside of each tomato half and invert the halves on a platter to drain the excess moisture.

- Wash the lettuce leaves, dry them completely, roll them upon themselves, and cut them across into chiffonnade. With this chiffonnade prepare a bed of lettuce on a serving platter.

- Remove the leaves of the artichokes. Trim the bottoms and place them on the bed of lettuce. Squeeze lemon juice over them.

- Set 1 tomato half into each artichoke bottom.

- Season the yogurt with salt and pepper to taste and fold in the chives. Fill the tomatoes with equal amounts of the yogurt mixture.

NOTE

Think of seasoned yogurt as a dressing with diverse raw vegetables. Keep those artichoke leaves to add to a salad dressing for ham or chicken salad.

STUFFED RED CABBAGE LEAVES
(Paupiettes de Chou Rouge)

- **Easy**
  6 servings
  Inexpensive
  40 minutes, plus 4 hours for marinating

  6 herring or skipper fillets
  skim milk to cover fillets
  US ⅓ cup, UK ¼ cup, prepared horserad-
  ish (2 TB), or more
  3 sour dill pickles, chopped
  1 jar (3 oz., 90 g) capers in vinegar,
  drained
  chopped parsley
  1 recipe Slim Mayonnaise (see Index)
  1 small red cabbage
  US 1 cup, UK 1 scant cup, vinegar (2.5
  dl)
  US 1 TB, UK ½ TB, olive oil (½ TB)

- Soak the herring or skipper fillets in milk for approximately 30 minutes to lessen the salt content.

- Meanwhile mix the prepared horseradish, chopped pickles, capers, and chopped parsley to taste. Dry the fish fillets very well in paper towels and cut them into small dice. Bind the mixture with mayonnaise; it will be up to you to decide how much mayonnaise you want to use. The whole recipe will probably be needed.

- Remove the 6 best leaves of the cabbage; blanch them in boiling water, salted and lightly vinegared (1 tablespoon or so vinegar is enough to prevent discoloration of the leaves to bluish red), until they are soft and pliable, 8 to 10 minutes.

- Drop the leaves into a bath of cold water to cool them. Remove the rib portion. Dry on a tea towel.

- Fill each leaf with some of the herring mixture, and roll into those small packages known in French as *paupiettes*. Trim the ends of the *paupiettes* if need be for the sake of uniformity of size. Put the bundles to marinate in vinegar for approximately 4 hours.

- When ready to serve, brush extremely lightly with 1 tablespoon olive oil for all 6 cabbage rolls. (Please be strict on the quantity of oil.)

GRATED CARROTS WITH CHEESE
(Carottes Râpées au Fromage)

- Easy
  6 servings
  Inexpensive
  10 minutes

  6 carrots
  Vinaigrette Variation 1 (see Index)
  1 recipe Slim Mayonnaise (see Index)
  1 small red onion, finely chopped
  6 oz. Gruyère cheese (200 g)
  1 head of Boston lettuce
  chopped parsley

- Grate the carrots and toss them with the vinaigrette.

- Prepare the mayonnaise and add the chopped onion to it.
- Cut the cheese into ¼-inch julienne strips or into ⅓-inch cubes. Add the cheese to the mayonnaise.
- Wash and dry the lettuce leaves very well. Arrange several leaves on a serving platter.
- Place the cheese mayonnaise in the center of the platter and surround it with the grated carrots. Sprinkle wth chopped parsley.

CURRIED CARROT SALAD
(Salade de Carottes au Curry)

- Easy
  6 servings
  Inexpensive
  10 minutes

  1½ lbs. carrots (750 g)
  Curry Vinaigrette, Variation 5 (see Index)
  chervil or chives
  1 small shallot, chopped (optional)

- Peel the carrots and grate by hand or in a food processor.
- A few minutes before serving, pour the vinaigrette sauce over the carrots and mix well.
- Sprinkle with chopped chervil or chives, and the chopped shallot if you like.

WITH THE SAME METHOD
The same method may be used for any other raw vegetable. You could use celery root, diced or cubed artichoke bottoms, asparagus tips, beets, celery ribs, endives, fennel bulbs, cauliflower.

NOTE
Adapt the basic dressing to your personal taste.

CAULIFLOWER SALAD
(Chou-Fleur en Salade)

- Easy
  6 servings
  Inexpensive
  30 minutes

  2 heads of cauliflower
  salt

- Peel the cauliflower and cut into large bouquets. Cook them in boiling salted water.
- While still warm, mix with any of the following ingredients:

Peppers: Wash and remove the seeds from 4 peppers; cut them into strips. Mix them with the cauliflower. Pour over them a mustard vinaigrette (Variation 4), and sprinkle with finely chopped herbs. Let steep for a few hours before serving.

Shrimps: Arrange the cauliflower on a bed of lettuce leaves in the center of a round platter. Coat with Mayonnaise and sprinkle salad with finely chopped herbs. Garnish all around with cooked shelled shrimps or cooked mussels, sliced tomatoes, hard-boiled eggs and lemon wedges.

Tomatoes: Slice tomatoes and place them on lettuce leaves with the cauliflower and quartered hard-boiled eggs. Season and dress with mayonnaise or vinaigrette, or even serve both sauces in separate bowls.

NOTE
All of these salads are particularly well-suited partners for fish or cold meats.

BELGIAN ENDIVE SALAD
(Salade d'Endives)

■ **Easy**
  6 servings
  Expensive
  **10 minutes, plus 30 minutes for boiling
    beets**

  3 **Golden Delicious apples**
  3 **Belgian endives**
  1 **celery rib**
  2 **beets, cooked**
  1 **recipe Slim Mayonnaise or Slim Vinai-
    grette (see Index)**
  tomato paste
  chopped parsley

• Wash the apples and endives and cut them into thin slices. Cut the celery rib into fine julienne and the beets into ¼-inch cubes.

• Prepare the mayonnaise and season it well; color it with a bit of tomato paste to your taste. Or prepare vinaigrette instead.

• Toss dressing with vegetables; mix well. Sprinkle with chopped parsley.

EXOTIC SALAD
(Salade Exotique)

■ **Easy**
  6 servings
  Medium expensive
  15 minutes

  1 **can (16 oz.) hearts of palm (454 g)**
  1 **can (14½ oz.) artichoke bottoms (410
    g)**
  4 **tomatoes**
  1 **grapefruit**
  juice of 1 lemon
  1 **recipe Slim Vinaigrette (see Index),
    made with cider vinegar and mustard**

• Rinse the hearts of palm and artichoke bottoms well under lukewarm water.

• Slice the tomatoes and the hearts of palm. Cube the grapefruit and artichoke bottoms. Mix these ingredients well and add lemon juice.

• Prepare the mustard vinaigrette.

• Present the salad this way: Top each slice of tomato with a slice of heart of palm; arrange those around the platter. Pile the mixture of artichokes and grapefruit at the center of the platter.

• Serve the vinaigrette in a sauceboat.

EGGPLANT MAYONNAISE
(Mayonnaise d'Aubergines)

■ Easy
6 servings
Inexpensive
35 minutes

4 medium-size eggplants
3 garlic cloves
3 raw egg yolks
salt and pepper
double recipe of Slim Mayonnaise (see Index)
1 lemon
6 large lettuce leaves

- Preheat oven to 500°F., 270°C. or 8 Regulo.
- Wash the eggplants very well. Prick them with a skewer and place them on the middle oven rack. Bake until a skewer in the center of the largest eggplant comes out clean and feels hot to the top of the hand.
- Cool the vegetables, cut them into halves, and scoop out the pulp. Let the pulp cool completely.
- Place the coarsely cut garlic cloves and the eggplant pulp in the bowl of a food processor. Process until smooth.
- Add the raw egg yolks, salt and pepper to taste, and gradually the mayonnaise. Process until homogenous. Finish with lemon juice to taste.
- Line a plate with lettuce leaves and pile the eggplant mayonnaise on it. Serve well chilled.

BEEF SALAD
(Salade de Bœuf)

■ Easy
  6 servings
  Thrift recipe
  10 minutes

  ¾ lb. cooked beef from any leftover roast
    (375 g)
  3 shallots
  parsley
  1 recipe Mustard Vinaigrette, Variation 4
    (see Index)
  6 lettuce leaves
  2 hard-boiled eggs

● Trim the fat off the meat and cut meat into large cubes. Mince the shallots and parsley.

● Prepare the mustard vinaigrette and add shallots and parsley to it.

● About 1 hour before serving, toss the meat with the dressing.

● Garnish a plate with lettuce leaves, pile the meat salad at the center, and decorate all around with slices of hard-boiled eggs.

● Sprinkle with more chopped parsley.

HAM SALAD
(Salade de Jambon)

■ Easy
  6 servings
  Affordable
  20 minutes

  3 Red Delicious apples
  1 bunch of radishes
  ¾ lb. ham in 1 thick slice (360 g)
  6 celery ribs
  finely chopped herbs of your choice
  1 recipe Slim Cream-Style Dressing, Vari-
    ation 1 or 3 (see Index)

● Wash the apples; do not peel them. Cut them into thin slices.

● Cut the radishes into thick slices. Cut the ham into ¼-inch julienne strips and cut the celery into ¼-inch cubes.

● Mix these 4 ingredients together. Add the chopped herbs.

● Pour the dressing over the salad; mix well. Let the ingredients steep for 15 minutes.

BAKED APPLES STUFFED WITH HAM AND PEPPERS
(Pommes Fourrées au Jambon)

- Easy
  6 servings
  Affordable
  25 minutes, 30 to 40 minutes for baking

  2 onions
  1 red pepper
  1 green pepper
  salt and pepper
  ¼ lb. boiled ham, in 1 thick piece (120 g)
  finely chopped herbs of your choice
  6 Golden Delicious apples

- Preheat oven to 350°F., 180°C. or 4 to 5 Regulo.

- Peel and finely chop the onions. Cut the peppers open, seed them, and dice them.

- Put onions and peppers in a non-stick pan over medium heat. Add a dash of water and salt and pepper to taste. Cook until the vegetables have softened noticeably but remain firm. Remove from the heat.

- Cut the ham into ⅓-inch cubes and add them to the pan. At the end mix in the herbs.

- Cut off the top of each apple and carefully scoop out the core, leaving about ⅓ inch of pulp attached to the skin. Fill the apples with the prepared mixture.

- Bake in the preheated oven for 30 to 40 minutes. Serve either warm or cold.

WITH THE SAME METHOD
Baked Stuffed Tomatoes: Use the same filling, but do not bake the tomatoes longer than 20 to 25 minutes.

ISLAND CHICKEN SALAD
(Salade de Volaille des Iles)

- Easy
  6 servings
  Medium expensive
  1 hour

1 recipe Slim Mayonnaise (see Index)
3 double chicken breasts
salt and pepper
1 pineapple
1½ tsps. curry powder
1 bunch of watercress
1 lime
1 garlic clove
1 TB coconut flakes, fresh or toasted

- Prepare the mayonnaise. Cool and store in the refrigerator.

- Skin and bone the chicken breasts to obtain 6 fillets. Trim them of all fat and gristle.

- Put the chicken fillets on a nonstick skillet over medium heat and cook, turning often, until the meat is just tender. Test often. Salt and pepper halfway through the cooking.

- Cool the chicken. Cut across into ¼-inch-thick slices. Remove to a plate.

- Peel the pineapple and cut into slices. Cut each slice into 4 pieces.

- Use the same skillet in which the chicken was cooked. Drop in the pineapple pieces and all the juices that escaped from the fruit during cutting. Cook over medium heat first to let all the juices escape. Add the curry powder, then let the juices evaporate. Remove the skillet from the heat. Cool pineapple completely.

- When pineapple is cold, mix the chicken with the pineapple.

- Clean the watercress well and separate it into tiny bouquets. Arrange them on a round platter; salt and pepper them lightly.

- Grate approximately 1 teaspoon lime rind into the mayonnaise. Chop and mash the garlic clove and add it also to the mayonnaise. Mix well. Correct the seasoning of the dressing with salt, pepper and a dash of lime juice.

- Toss the chicken and pineapple mixture into the mayonnaise. Again correct the seasoning very well. Be generous with pepper.

- Arrange the chicken salad on the bed of watercess. Leave a 1-inch border of the green leaves around the edge of the dish for better appearance. Sprinkle salad with the coconut flakes.

DUCK SALAD WITH ORANGE SLICES
(Salade de Canard à l'Orange)

- Easy
  6 servings
  Medium expensive
  20 minutes, plus 3 hours to roast the duck

  1 duck, 4 lbs. (2 kg)
  1 recipe Slim Vinaigrette, Variation 6 (see Index)
  3 oranges
  1 large head of chicory
  chopped parsley

- Roast the duck. Let it cool.

- Empty the gravy and fat into a measuring cup. With a baster, remove the lean gravy. Discard the fat.

- Prepare the vinaigrette.

- Cook the gravy of the duck down to a few teaspoons, and add them to the vinaigrette. The dressing will be quite salty, but the acid of the oranges and the bitterness of the chicory will take care of the excess salt and tamper it.

- Peel and section the oranges.

- Remove the meat from the duck carcass and cut it into small chunks about 1½ inches long.

- Clean the head of chicory, wash it, and pat it dry. Arrange the chicory on a platter. Arrange the duck meat and the orange sections attractively on top.

- Pour the dressing evenly over the whole salad. Sprinkle with parsley and serve immediately.

SMOKED TROUT SALAD
(Salade de Truites Fumées)

■ Easy
   6 servings
   Medium expensive
   35 minutes

   6 smoked trout, or other small smoked
      fish of your choice
   1 recipe Slim Cream-Style Dressing (see
      Index)
   prepared horseradish
   salt and pepper
   ½ head of white cabbage
   3 carrots
   3 beets
   chopped parsley

- Lift off the fillets of the smoked trout; try to keep them whole. Remove all the visible bones.

- Prepare the dressing. Add to it as much horseradish as your taste dictates. Season with salt and pepper to taste.

- With a food processor, cut the cabbage into a "slaw." Cut the carrots into ¼-inch julienne strips and the raw beets into strips of the same size. Keep the vegetables separated.

- While you prepare the vegetables, bring a pot of water to a boil. Add salt. Blanch the vegetables; first blanch the cabbage for 1 minute, then the carrots for 2 minutes, finally the beets for 2 minutes.

- Rinse each vegetable under running cold water and pat dry in paper toweling.

- Mix all the vegetables and as much chopped parsley as you like. Season the vegetable mixture very carefully.

- Arrange the mixed vegetables on a round platter and spoon one third of the dressing over them.

- Place the trout fillets over the vegetables and spoon the remaining dressing over them. Sprinkle with chopped parsley.

CRAB SALAD
(Salade de Crabe)

- **Easy**
  6 servings
  30 minutes

  3 eggs
  2 grapefruits
  4 artichokes, cooked
  1 lemon
  1 head of soft-leaf lettuce
  1 can (6½ oz.) crab meat, picked over
     (184 g)
  1 recipe Slim Mayonnaise (see Index)

- Hard-boil the eggs. Peel them. Cut the grapefruits into sections, working over a bowl to save the juice.

- Cut the artichoke bottoms into small cubes and squeeze lemon juice over them.

- Put the lettuce, grapefruit sections, artichoke hearts and crab meat in a salad bowl.

- Add 1 or more tablespoons of the reserved grapefruit juice to the mayonnaise. Slice the hard-boiled eggs and place them as a garnish on top of the salad.

- Pour a small amount of dressing over the salad and serve the remainder in a sauceboat.

MUSSEL SALAD
(Salade de Moules)

- **Easy**
  6 servings
  Inexpensive
  20 minutes

  3 quarts mussels (3 L)
  1 large red onion
  parsley
  1 recipe Slim Mayonnaise (see Index) (see
     Note)
  lettuce leaves

- Steam the mussels open. Shell and chill them. Filter all the juices and reserve them.

- Chop the onion and parsley. Toss the mussels, onion and parsley together. Bind the mixture with the mayonnaise.

- Arrange mussels on a bed of lettuce leaves and serve sprinkled with more parsley.

NOTE

When you prepare the mayonnaise, use half mussel juice and half water to give it better taste.

Keep the rest of the mussel juices for a fish dish.

SHRIMP SALAD
(Salade de Crevettes)

- Easy
  6 servings
  Medium expensive
  15 to 20 minutes

  1½ lbs. shelled cooked shrimps (680 g)
  2 celery ribs
  3 Golden Delicious apples
  1 recipe Rémoulade Sauce (see Index)

- Rinse the shrimps under running cold water. Pat them dry. Cut each shrimp lengthwise into halves.
- Cut the celery and apples into ⅓-inch cubes.
- Mix shrimps, celery and apples, and bind with rémoulade sauce. Let ingredients steep together for 15 minutes (no more) before serving.

Variation: For a more substantial salad, add cooked flaked fish fillets, hard-boiled eggs, diced cooked mushrooms.

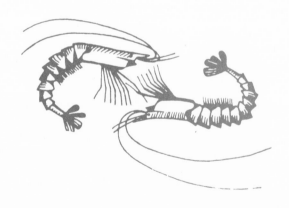

EGG DISHES

(Les Œufs)

EGGS STUFFED WITH SHRIMPS
(Œufs Farcis aux Crevettes)

■ Easy
   6 servings
   Medium expensive
   30 minutes

   6 eggs
   ¼ lb. cooked shelled shrimps (120 g)
   1 recipe Slim Mayonnaise (see Index)
   cayenne pepper
   lettuce leaves

● Hard-boil the eggs; remove them to a bath of cold water.

● Peel the eggs and cut them lengthwise into halves. Remove the yolks without damaging the whites.

● Finely chop half of the shrimps. Work chopped shrimps into the egg yolks with a fork. Add 2 tablespoons or so of mayonnaise and a pinch of cayenne pepper.

● Line a serving platter with several lettuce leaves. Fill the egg white boats with the shrimp mixture.

● Arrange them attractively on the lettuce leaves. Use the remaining shrimps and mayonnaise as a garnish.

NOTE
This dish can make an excellent appetizer; if you double the proportions, you will have an equally pleasing main course for the summer.

PEPPER AND EGGS
(Œufs au Poivron)

■ Easy
   6 servings
   Medium expensive
   15 minutes

   6 eggs
   ¼ lb. cooked shrimps (120 g)
   1 red pepper
   1 recipe Slim Vinaigrette (see Index)
   lettuce leaves
   finely chopped herbs of your choice

● Hard-boil the eggs and cool in a cold water bath. Shell the eggs and cut them lengthwise into halves.

● Cut the shrimps into ¼-inch cubes.

Cut the red pepper into pieces the same size as the shrimp cubes.

● Separate the egg yolks. Put them on a plate, mash them, then add the pepper cubes and shrimps. Add the vinaigrette and mix well.

● Fill the egg-white boats with the mixture, and arrange them on a serving platter lined with lettuce leaves. Sprinkle with herbs.

NOTE
You may replace the vinaigrette with a mixture of ketchup and mayonnaise, plain ketchup, or any other commercially prepared sauce.

SPICY EGGS
(Œufs Épicés)

- Easy
  6 servings
  Inexpensive
  35 minutes

  6 eggs
  2 onions
  2 green peppers
  ¼ tsp. dry mustard
  ½ tsp. curry powder
  lemon juice
  salt and pepper
  lettuce leaves
  1 TB snipped chives

- Hard-boil the eggs, cool them completely in cold water, and shell them. Finely chop the onions and green peppers.

- Cut the eggs lengthwise into halves and remove the yolks. The yolks will not be used in this recipe (see Note). Add mustard, curry powder, lemon juice and salt and pepper to taste to the onions and peppers. Mix well. Fill the egg whites with the vegetable mixture.

- Line a serving platter with lettuce leaves and arrange the stuffed eggs on top. Sprinkle with freshly snipped chives.

NOTE
To put the cooked yolks to use, see Compound Butter Base (see Index) and Mimosa Eggs (following recipe).

MIMOSA EGGS
(Œufs Mimosa)

- **Very easy**
  6 servings
  Inexpensive
  40 minutes

  6 eggs
  2 tomatoes
  lettuce leaves
  chopped herbs of your choice
  1 recipe Slim Mayonnaise (see Index)
  salt and pepper

- Hard-boil the eggs and immerse them in a cold water bath to cool them. Cut 6 slices out of each tomato.

- Line a serving platter with the lettuce leaves. Arrange the tomatoes on the lettuce.

- Shell the eggs and cut them lengthwise into halves. Remove the yolks and reserve 2 yolks for the "mimosa."

- Mix the other yolks with the finely chopped herbs and blend in the well-seasoned mayonnaise, tablespoon by tablespoon, until you obtain the proper consistency for your taste. Season with salt and pepper to taste.

- Fill the egg whites with the mixture and arrange them on the tomatoes.

- To make the "mimosa," press the reserved egg yolks through a strainer, and as you strain them, sprinkle the yolks over the entire platter.

NOTE
This dish is usually served as an appetizer; it is a good companion to any fish or shellfish. You may also use these mimosa eggs to garnish a salad of grated carrots or turnips, or sliced green beans.

HAM AND EGGS
(Œufs au Jambon)

■ Easy
  6 servings
  Medium expensive
  10 to 15 minutes

  6 slices of smoked ham
  12 eggs
  salt and pepper

- Preheat oven to 425°F., 220°C. or 6 Regulo.
- Trim the ham of its natural fat. Rub a nonstick frying pan with a piece of ham fat and lightly color the meat.
- Place 1 slice of ham in each of 6 ovenproof baking dishes. Carefully break 2 eggs over each slice. Proceed gently so as not to break the yolks. Season with salt and pepper.
- Bake on the lower oven rack for 7 to 8 minutes. Serve in the baking dishes.

EGGS IN RAMEKINS
(Œufs en Cocotte)

■ Easy
  6 servings
  Inexpensive
  15 minutes

  US ¾ cup, UK 6 TB, liquid skim milk (6 TB)
  6 eggs
  salt and pepper
  3 TB finely chopped parsley or tarragon
  paprika

- Preheat oven to 325°F., 165°C. or 4 Regulo.
- Put 1 tablespoon skim milk into each of 6 ramekins or custard cups. Break 1 egg into each cup. Spoon another tablespoon skim milk over each egg. Sprinkle with salt and pepper to taste, finely chopped parsley or tarragon, and a pinch of paprika.
- Cover each ramekin with a silicone parchment paper. Set ramekins in a roasting pan. Pour enough boiling water into the pan to reach halfway to the rim of each cup. Slide the pan into the oven, and bake for 6 to 7 minutes.

Variation: Before adding the eggs to the ramekins, you may also add small pieces of ham, cooked mushrooms, spinach or green beans to each cup as a garnish.

SPANISH-STYLE EGGS
(Œufs Espagnols)

- **Medium difficult**
  6 servings
  Inexpensive
  50 minutes

  2 onions, finely chopped
  1 green pepper, chopped
  3 garlic cloves, finely chopped
  ½ lb. mushrooms, chopped (250 g)
  2 lbs. tomatoes, coarsely chopped and
      seeded (1 kg)
  celery salt and pepper
  salt
  wine vinegar
  6 eggs
  1 TB chopped herbs of your choice

- Put the onions, pepper, garlic, mushrooms and tomatoes in a pot. Add celery salt and pepper to taste. Cover and simmer for about 20 minutes.

- Meanwhile, bring 1 quart water to a boil and add 2 teaspoons salt and 1 tablespoon or so of wine vinegar. Simmer for 3 minutes.

- Break each egg into a cup and let it slide into the poaching bath. Cook for 4 to 5 minutes, then immerse the eggs in cooler but still warm salted water.

- Empty the vegetables into a shallow serving dish. Lift the eggs from their water bath with a slotted spoon and drain them on the paper towels. Trim the eggs, then arrange them on top of the vegetables.

- Sprinkle them with finely chopped herbs of your choice. Serve immediately.

NOTE
The poached eggs may be replaced by soft-boiled eggs if you prefer. Immerse the eggs in shells in boiling water for 6 minutes, rinse them under cold water, and shell them immediately. Set them on the vegetables.

POACHED EGGS IN TOMATO SHELLS
(Œufs des Alpilles)

- Medium difficult
  6 servings
  Medium expensive
  25 minutes

  1 recipe Aïoli (see Index)
  6 eggs
  1 small eggplant, cubed
  3 tomatoes
  6 large lettuce leaves
  chopped parsley
  1 dozen brine-cured black olives, pitted
       and chopped

- Prepare a stiff aïoli, using 5 teaspoons cornstarch instead of 4.
- Poach the eggs (see Spanish-Style Eggs, preceding recipe), and drain them thoroughly on paper towels. Trim the eggs for better appearance.
- Blanch the eggplant cubes in boiling salted water. Cook until tender, drain, and let cool to room temperature.
- Wash the tomatoes, cut them horizontally into halves, and remove the center pulp and seeds. Arrange the tomato halves on the lettuce leaves.
- Mix the eggplant cubes and aïoli, and fill the tomatoes with the mixture.
- Set 1 egg into each tomato. Sprinkle with a mixture of chopped parsley and chopped olives.

POACHED EGGS AVIGNON STYLE
(Œufs Pochés d'Avignon)

- Easy
  6 servings
  Inexpensive
  30 minutes

  2 quarts water (2 L)
  vinegar
  salt
  12 eggs
  6 baby zucchini (marrows or courgettes)
  pepper
  US ⅓ cup, UK ¼ cup, chopped basil (4 TB)
  US 1 TB, UK ½ TB, anchovy paste (½ TB)
  Parmesan cheese

- Bring 2 quarts of water to a boil; add vinegar and salt to taste. Turn heat down to a simmer.
- Slide 3 eggs, one at a time, into the poaching bath and cook for 2½ minutes. Remove to a salted warm water bath. Repeat with the other eggs in 3 more batches.
- Cut the zucchini into very thin slices. Put them into a nonstick skillet, sprinkle with salt and pepper, and cover for a few minutes, or until their natural juices start oozing out. Toss, and finish cooking, still covered.
- As soon as the vegetables are translucent green, add the basil and anchovy paste and toss well. Transfer to a baking dish.
- Remove the eggs from their water bath; pat them dry; trim them and set on the zucchini bed.
- Sprinkle with Parmesan and broil for 1 minute to "gild" the top of the cheese.

EGGS IN JELLIED STOCK
(Œufs en Gelée)

■ Requires care
6 servings
Medium expensive
35 minutes

US 1½ cups, UK 1⅓ cups, Meat Stock
(see Index) (4 to 4.5 dl)
chopped tarragon
chives
4 thin slices of ham
white-wine vinegar
12 eggs
lettuce leaves

- Bring the stock to a boil. Remove from the heat and cool to lukewarm. Pour about ½ inch (1 cm) of the stock into each of 12 ramekins. Chill the ramekins to set the stock. Sprinkle with freshly chopped tarragon.

- Meanwhile, snip the chives and cut the ham into 12 diamonds.

- Pour 4 inches (10 cm) water into a large pot and add 1 cup vinegar. Bring to a boil, then turn down to a simmer. Slide the eggs into the poaching bath and cook for 3 to 4 minutes. Remove the eggs to a cold water bath. Dry them well, and trim the edges.

- Add a piece of ham and some chives to each ramekin. Top with an egg and cover with the rest of the stock. Refrigerate for at least 4 hours.

- To serve, unmold the eggs on a platter garnished with lettuce leaves.

NOTE
You will be able to unmold the eggs with more ease if you quickly dip the bottom of the ramekins into very hot water before inverting them onto the serving platter.

POACHED EGGS ROYAL PRINTEMPS
(Œufs Pochés Royal Printemps)

- Easy
  6 servings
  Inexpensive
  30 minutes

  2 carrots
  2 white turnips
  1 red pepper
  1 green pepper
  2 small zucchini (marrows or courgettes)
  salt and pepper
  1 garlic clove, mashed
  pinch of crumbled dried marjoram
  US 2 TB, UK 1 TB, tomato paste (1 TB)
  US ½ cup, UK ⅓ cup, Meat Stock (see Index) (.5 dl)
  4 oz. Gruyère cheese, grated (120 g)
  2 quarts water (2 L)
  vinegar
  12 eggs

- Peel carrots and turnips. Cut them into ⅛-inch julienne strips, using a food processor. Bring a small pot of water to a boil, add both vegetables, and blanch for 2 minutes. Drain. Set aside.

- Cut peppers and zucchini into ¼-inch julienne, also using a food processor.

- Put those 3 vegetables in a nonstick skillet, add salt and pepper to taste, cover, and cook until the juices have run out of the vegetables.

- Mix in the carrots and turnips, the mashed garlic clove and the dried marjoram. Finish cooking together for another 5 minutes.

- Dissolve the tomato paste in the meat stock. Blend into the vegetables and let cook together for 1 more minute. Correct the seasoning.

- Empty this vegetable mixture into a baking dish. Cover with an ⅛-inch layer of Gruyère. Keep warm.

- In a large skillet, bring the water to a boil. Add vinegar and salt and turn down to a simmer. Slide 3 eggs, one at a time, into the poaching bath. Cook for 2½ minutes. Remove to a salted warm water bath. Continue the same procedure with the remaining eggs.

- Remove the eggs from the water bath. Trim them. Set them on the vegetables and sprinkle a good pinch of Gruyère over each. Broil for 1 minute, just long enough to "gild" the cheese.

SCRAMBLED EGGS WITH ASPARAGUS
(Œufs Brouillés aux Asperges)

- Easy
  6 servings
  Medium expensive
  40 to 45 minutes

  2 bunches of asparagus, about 48 stalks
  12 eggs
  salt and pepper
  chopped parsley

- Peel the asparagus. Cut off 2-inch-long tips. Slice the remainder of the stalks into ½-inch-long pieces.

- Drop the pieces of stalk into boiling salted water; bring back to a boil. Immediately add the tips; bring back to a boil again, and cook for no more than 3 or 4 minutes. Drain. Turn both tips and stalks into a bowl. Cover and let stand.

- In a bowl, lightly beat the eggs with salt and pepper to taste. Turn them into a nonstick pan, set it over medium-low heat, and stir constantly with a wooden spoon until the eggs have reached the desired consistency.

- Remove pan from the heat, but continue stirring the eggs for another minute to prevent hardening on the bottom of the pan. Add the pieces of asparagus stalks.

- Mound the eggs on a warm serving platter and arrange the asparagus tips attractively on top. Sprinkle with chopped parsley.

NOTE
In the winter you can prepare this dish with frozen asparagus.

BASIC OMELET
(Omelette Nature)

- Easy
  1 serving
  Inexpensive
  2 minutes

  2 eggs
  salt and pepper

½ lb. mushrooms (250 g)
salt and pepper
chopped garlic
chopped parsley

- Beat the eggs lightly in a bowl with salt and pepper. Pour the eggs into a nonstick pan over moderately high heat. When the eggs begin to set, continue beating, bringing the batter steadily toward the center of the pan. Shake the pan back and forth to make sure that the omelet does not stick. When there is no liquid left, roll the omelet upon itself and invert it onto a plate.

WITH THE SAME METHOD
Mushroom Omelet (Omelette aux Champignons): Clean and slice the mushrooms. Cook them with salt, pepper, chopped garlic and parsley to taste. As soon as the juice has run out of the mushrooms, raise the heat and let juices evaporate. Prepare the omelets. Add one sixth of the mushrooms before rolling each omelet. Makes enough filling for 6 individual omelets.

**6 medium-size onions, thinly
    sliced
salt and pepper**

**3 or 4 medium-size tomatoes
1 onion, finely chopped
chopped parsley
bay leaf
salt and pepper**

Onion Omelet (Omelette aux Oignons):
Cook the onions gently, season them
with salt and pepper so they lose their
juices and cook in their own moisture.
Onions are done when translucent.
Add them to the omelet just before
rolling. Makes enough filling for 6 individual omelets.

Tomato Omelet (Omelette aux Tomates):
Peel, seed, and coarsely chop the tomatoes. Cook the tomatoes with the
finely chopped onion, some chopped
parsley, and a bay leaf until tomatoes
acquire a custardlike consistency.
Season the sauce and remove the bay
leaf. Spoon the tomato cream into the
omelets just before serving. Makes
enough filling for 6 individual omelets.

NOTES
It is easier and quicker to prepare six 2-
egg omelets rather than a big 12-egg
omelet.

A few drops of vinegar sprinkled on any
of the omelet variations does wonders for
their final flavor.

GRAPE-NUTS OMELET
(Omelette Croquante)

- Easy
  1 serving
  Inexpensive
  1 to 2 minutes per omelet

  2 eggs
  salt and pepper
  1 garlic clove
  US 2 TB, UK 1 TB, Grape-Nuts (1 TB)

- Break the eggs into a small bowl. Add salt and pepper to taste. Beat with 30 strokes of a fork.

- Rub a nonstick skillet with the garlic clove, pressing hard to extract the juice.

- Add the Grape-Nuts and toss over medium-high heat until the cereal particles are very hot.

- Pour the eggs over and beat into an omelet, cooking for only 15 seconds. Invert on a plate.

GASCONY-STYLE OMELET
(Omelette de Gascogne)

- Easy
  6 servings
  Medium expensive
  10 minutes

  12 eggs
  salt and pepper
  6 slices of ham, trimmed well, ½ inch
      thick (1 cm)
  1 bunch of chives, coarsely snipped

- Beat the eggs lightly with salt and pepper to taste.

- In a nonstick pan, cook the ham slices slowly, then raise the heat to high to brown them. Shake the pan so that the ham will not stick. Remove ham from the pan and keep warm.

- Prepare six 2-egg omelets. Invert each omelet into a slice of ham, and sprinkle with snipped chives.

NOTE
An idea: While the omelet is bright hot, heat a small amount of Armagnac in a pan and flambé the omelet just before serving.

HADDOCK OMELET
(Omelette au Haddock)

- Easy
  6 servings
  Medium expensive
  20 minutes

  ¾ lb. smoked finnan haddie (375 g)
  2 cups skim milk (.5 L)
  ¼ lb. green beans (120 g)
  12 eggs
  salt and pepper

- Put the haddock in a pan and cover it with a mixture of half milk and half water. Bring to a boil, turn off the heat, and let stand for 10 minutes.
- Cook the green beans. Flake the fish. Mix fish flakes with the green beans.
- Beat the eggs lightly with salt and pepper to taste.
- Cook six 2-egg omelets as usual. Spoon one sixth of the haddock and green beans into each omelet just before serving.
- Accompany with a simple green salad.

BAKED TOMATO OMELET
(Omelette au Plat à la Tomate)

- **Easy**
  6 servings
  Inexpensive
  20 minutes

  7 eggs
  salt and pepper
  finely chopped herbs of your choice
  ¼ lb. Gruyère cheese, grated (120 g)
  4 to 5 TB milk
  3 medium-size tomatoes

- Preheat oven to 450°F., 230°C. or 6 Regulo.
- Beat the eggs lightly with salt and pepper to taste, finely chopped herbs, the cheese and the milk.
- Peel, seed, and slice the tomatoes; arrange them in an ovenproof dish.
- Pour the beaten egg mixture over the tomatoes and bake in the preheated oven for 15 minutes. The omelet should not color too much.

Variation: Use the same method to prepare ham omelet; line the baking dish with tiny pieces of well-defattened ham.

FISH AND SHELLFISH

(Les Poissons et les Fruits de Mer)

PORTUGUESE-STYLE COD
(Cabillaud à la Portugaise)

- Easy
  6 servings
  Affordable
  40 minutes

  6 slices of fresh cod
  salt
  12 baby onions
  5 tomatoes, peeled, seeded and chopped
  3 garlic cloves, finely chopped
  2 green peppers
  2 red peppers
  thyme, rosemary
  US ⅔ cup, UK ½ cup, dry white wine (2 scant dl)
  pepper

- Purchase slices of cod 1 to 1¼ inches thick. Wash and dry the fish, and salt it on both sides. Set slices on the broiler pan and sear 4 inches from the source of heat for 2 minutes on each side. Set aside.

- In a nonstick skillet, gently cook the onions until golden; set aside on a plate. In the same skillet, cook the chopped tomatoes and the garlic for a few minutes.

- Meanwhile, put the peppers under the broiler and char them on all sides. Peel them and cut them into thin strips.

- Put onions, tomatoes and peppers into a sauteuse pan. Add 1 small teaspoon thyme, a few rosemary leaves, the white wine, and salt and pepper to taste. Mix well. Bring to a boil. Add the fish steaks to the pan and spoon some of the vegetables over them. Cover, reduce the heat, and simmer for 12 to 15 minutes.

- Remove the steaks to a platter; keep them warm. Bring the sauce to a high boil and reduce for 3 to 4 minutes to blend flavors well. Correct seasoning and spoon over the fish.

COD ROAST
(Cabillaud Rôti)

- **Easy**
  6 servings
  Affordable
  55 minutes

  2½ lbs. cod fillets (1 kg)
  3 tomatoes
  ¾ lb. mushrooms (375 g)
  US ⅔ cup, UK ½ cup, dry white wine (2 scant dl)
  salt and pepper
  2 small onions
  parsley
  2 lemons

- Preheat oven to 425°F., 220°C. or 6 Regulo.

- Stack the cod fillets on top of one another to obtain a rectangular-shaped roast. Loosely tie the fillets together, as you would a meat roast; put the "roast" in a baking dish.

- Cut the tomatoes into halves; quarter the mushrooms. Arrange both vegetables around the cod. Pour the white wine over the fish, and season with salt and pepper. Bake on the middle rack of the oven for 10 minutes, basting the cod often with its cooking juices.

- Meanwhile, chop the onions and parsley, and sprinkle over the cod. Let cook for another 10 minutes.

- Remove the string. Squeeze the juice of 1 lemon over the fish. Garnish with lemon slices cut out of the second lemon.

NOTE
Any leftover fish can be used in a salad dressed with mayonnaise.

HADDOCK IN SAFFRON SAUCE
(Colin au Safran)

■ Easy
6 servings
Affordable
40 minutes

2½ lbs. haddock fillets (1 kg)
salt and pepper
3 onions
½ lb. mushrooms, sliced (250 g)
US ½ cup, UK ⅓ cup, Fish Stock (see Index) (1 generous dl)
US ½ cup, UK ⅓ cup, clam juice (1 generous dl)
grated rind of ½ orange
1 TB dried basil
juice of 1 lemon
US ¼ cup, UK 2 TB, dry vermouth (2 TB)
1 envelope whole saffron, .045 oz. (1.5 g)
2 egg yolks
US ¼ cup, UK 2 TB, evaporated skim milk (2 TB)
chopped parsley

- Wash and dry the fillets; salt and pepper them.

- Preheat oven to 350°F., 180°C. or 5 Regulo.

- Slice the onions; salt and pepper them. Put them into a nonstick skillet over medium-low heat, and cover. Toss at regular intervals.

- As soon as the onions have softened, add the mushrooms. Toss well together, cover again, and let the mushrooms lose all their juices.

- Place fish stock, clam juice, orange rind and basil in a blender container. Process together, then add to the skillet and cook for 10 minutes.

- Pour half of this mixture into a baking dish. Add the fish fillets; cover with the remainder of the mixture and a parchment paper. Bake in the preheated oven for 15 to 20 minutes.

- As soon as the fish is done, remove the fillets to a platter. Keep warm.

- Empty the cooking juices of the fish into a large sauteuse pan and reduce them by half. Add a dash of lemon juice. Mix vermouth and saffron, and add to boiling sauce. Boil hard for 1 to 2 minutes.

- Mix egg yolks and skim milk and enrich the sauce with this *liaison without boiling*. Spoon the sauce over the fish and sprinkle with parsley.

MARINATED MACKEREL
(Filets de Maquereaux Marinés)

■ Easy
  6 servings
  Inexpensive
  45 minutes

3 onions
3 shallots
US 1 cup, UK 1 scant cup, tarragon vine-
    gar (2.5 dl)
US 2 cups, UK 1¾ cups, water (4 to 5 dl)
2 bay leaves
8 peppercorns
3 whole cloves
parsley
1 carrot, finely sliced
salt and pepper
1 tsp. dried thyme, or 1 sprig of fresh
    thyme
6 medium-size mackerels, filleted

NOTE
When cooking fish in a vinegary broth, do not use an aluminum container but an earthenware, glass or enamel baking dish.

• Peel the onions and shallots and chop them coarsely. Gently cook them in a nonstick pan until they are translucent. Add tarragon vinegar, water, bay leaves, peppercorns, cloves, parsley, carrot, salt and pepper to taste and thyme. Bring to a boil, turn heat down, and keep at a simmer for 30 minutes; cool. Remove the bay leaves.

• Preheat oven to 475°F., 250°C. or 7 Regulo.

• Ask the fish store to dress the fish but not to remove the skin. Wash the fish and drain very well. Arrange them in a baking dish and cover completely with the marinade.

• Put the mackerel to bake, and as soon as the liquid boils turn the oven off. Baste with the marinade and let them remain in the oven for 10 minutes. Remove the dish from the oven and let mackerels cool completely. Cover with aluminum foil; refrigerate.

• Let the mackerels marinate for at least 4 days. They will keep for about 2 weeks if stored properly, that is, with enough marinade to cover the fish completely.

• Turn the fillets over at regular intervals during marination.

• Since the fish keeps well, cook more than 6 fish at a time; you will have another meal ready.

MACKEREL IN WHITE WINE
(Maquereaux au Vin Blanc)

- Easy
  6 servings
  Inexpensive
  25 minutes

6 medium-size mackerels
US 1 cup, UK 1 scant cup, Fish Stock (see Index) (2.5 dl)
US 2 cups, UK 1¾ cups, dry white wine (4 to 5 dl)
2 onions, finely sliced
3 carrots, finely sliced
1 lemon, sliced
salt
6 peppercorns
3 whole cloves
US 2 cups, UK 1¾ cups, water (4 to 5 dl)

- Ask the fish store to dress the fish through the gills.

- Wash the fish very well and put them in an ovenproof baking dish or a large pot. Add the fish stock, wine, onions, carrots, lemon, salt to taste, peppercorns, cloves and enough water to cover the fish completely. Cover. Place over medium heat and simmer for 5 to 12 minutes, depending on the size of the fish. The liquid must not boil, but only barely simmer.

- Take the pot off the heat and let the fish cool in the cooking liquid.

- Put the fish on a serving platter and garnish with slices of lemon, carrot and onion.

- Reduce the cooking liquid over moderate heat and strain the warm juices through a fine strainer. Pour over the fish. Serve the dish either hot or cold.

WITH THE SAME METHOD
Using the same method, you can prepare monkfish, cut into large pieces, conger eel or skate.

BAKED RED MULLET
(Rougets au Four)

- Easy
  6 servings
  Medium expensive
  20 minutes

  12 red mullets (see Note)
  salt and pepper
  thyme
  fennel seeds
  1 lemon

- Have the fish store dress the fish but leave the heads attached.

- Preheat oven to 400°F., 200°C. or 5 Regulo.

- Put salt, pepper, thyme and crushed fennel seeds in the cavity of each fish. Place the fish in a baking dish and squeeze lemon juice over them. Bake for 10 minutes. Should the skin dry out too quickly, squeeze more. lemon juice over it.

- A natural accompaniment would be étuvéed spinach or endive.

NOTE
Mediterranean red mullets are to be found frozen in Italian markets under the name of *triglia*. They are 7 inches long and 1½ inches wide.

BARBECUED RED MULLET WITH FENNEL
(Mulets Flambés au Fenouil)

- Easy
  6 servings
  Inexpensive
  25 to 35 minutes

  12 red mullets, about 6 oz. each (180 g each)
  salt
  dried fennel twigs
  1 recipe of Aïoli (see Index)

- Ask the fish store to dress the fish through the gills without removing the scales. Fresh mullets are coated with a body slime which should be washed off only when the fish is about to be cooked.

- Salt the fish on both sides and in the cavity. Let stand for about 1 hour.

- Meanwhile, start the barbecue fire. Wipe the fish very well without removing the scales. Place the fish on the grill 4 inches above the coals so that the fish will cook slowly and without burning.

- When the fish are ready to serve, place the fennel twigs directly on the hot coals so that the fish become flavored with the fennel aroma. Serve with aïoli sauce.

NOTE
If you cannot find fennel twigs in any specialty store, you can remove the fish to a platter and pour over each a little flaming Pernod or Pastis.

RED MULLETS EN PAPILLOTES
(Rougets en Papillotes)

■ Easy
  6 servings
  Medium expensive
  35 minutes

  4 medium-size onions
  Provençal herbs (see Glossary)
  salt, pepper
  12 red mullets, ¼ lb. each (120 g each)

- Preheat oven to 425°F., 220°C. or 7 Regulo.

- Cut 12 heart-shape sheets of aluminum foil each large enough to accommodate a fish.

- Chop the onions finely and place some in one side of each foil heart along with a good sprinkle of Provençal herbs, and salt and pepper to taste.

- Put the fish on top. Put remaining onions on top of fish, with more herbs and salt and pepper. Now close the foil over the fish, twisting the edges together to seal the fish tightly within.

- Bake in the preheated oven for 12 minutes. Serve immediately in the foil *papillotes*, giving each person 2 packages.

RED SNAPPER AND FENNEL
(Daurade au Fenouil)

■ **Easy**
  6 servings
  Affordable
  45 minutes

  **2 red snappers, 2½ to 3 lbs. each (1 to
     1.5 kg)**
  salt and pepper
  US 1 TB, UK ½ TB, fennel seeds (½ TB)
  2 bulbs of fresh fennel, thinly sliced
  **US 1 cup, UK 1 scant cup, Fish Stock (see
     Index) (2.5 dl)**
  2 lemons

● Ask the fish store to dress and scale
  the fish.

● Preheat oven to 425°F., 220°C. or 6
  Regulo.

● Wash and dry the snappers. Sprinkle
  the cavities with salt and pepper and
  put half of the fennel seeds into each
  cavity. Line the baking pan with the
  fresh fennel slices. Salt the fish.

● Slash 2 small incisions on each side
  of the fish with a paring knife, and
  set the fish on the bed of fennel. Add
  the stock; top each fish with several
  lemon slices. Bake for 30 to 35 minutes, basting often with the juices in
  the dish.

● Serve the fish in its baking dish, garnished with fresh lemon wedges. A
  vegetable suggestion: étuvéed whole
  tomatoes.

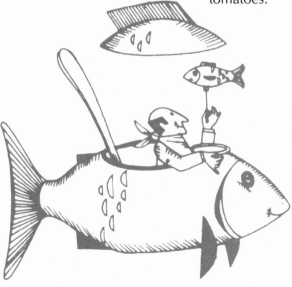

RED SNAPPER IN WHITE WINE
(Daurade au Vin Blanc)

- ■ Easy
  6 servings
  Inexpensive
  45 to 50 minutes

  2 red snappers, 2½ to 3 lbs. each (1 to
      1.5 kg each)
  salt and pepper
  2 onions
  6 tomatoes
  US 1½ cups, UK 1⅓ cups, dry white wine
      (3.5 dl)
  chopped parsley
  juice of ½ lemon

- ● Ask the fish store to dress and scale the fish.
- ● Preheat oven to 425°F., 220°C. or 6 Regulo.
- ● Salt and pepper the fish in the cavities. Place them in a baking dish.
- ● Slice the onions and quarter the tomatoes. Add them to the baking dish, with salt and pepper to taste and the white wine.
- ● Bake in the preheated oven; as soon as the juices begin to bubble, baste the fish with them every 10 minutes. Do not let the fish brown too fast. Let cook for 20 minutes, then add chopped parsley and the lemon juice. Finish baking for another 10 minutes. Serve immediately.

NOTE
The use of wine for cooking and in sauces is permitted as long as it is reduced quickly, to allow the alcohol to evaporate. The same principle applies to natural wines or fortified wines such as Port and Madeira.

BROILED SALMON STEAKS
(Darnes de Saumon Grillées)

- Easy
  6 servings
  Expensive
  10 to 15 minutes

  6 salmon steaks, ¾ inch thick (2 cm thick)
  salt and pepper
  6 lettuce leaves
  2 lemons

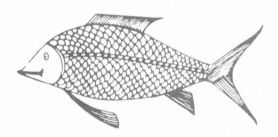

- Broil the salmon steaks 4 inches from the heating element or coals until tender, or approximately 4 minutes on each side.

- Please do not overcook the steaks. Place them on a warm serving platter, season with salt and pepper, and garnish with lettuce and lemon wedges.

- You may also serve them with a mayonnaise and a green salad.

NOTE
You may broil almost any fish of your choice. Be sure to wait until the fish is sufficiently broiled on one side before turning it. Use either a metal spatula or forks to turn the fish.

SALMON STEAKS IN ANCHOVY SAUCE
(Darnes de Saumon aux Anchois)

■ **Easy**
6 servings
Expensive
20 minutes

salt
6 salmon steaks, ¾ inch thick (2 cm thick)

SAUCE
US 1 TB, UK ½ TB, red-wine vinegar (½ TB)
US ½ cup, UK ⅓ cup, excellent red wine (1 generous dl)
salt and pepper
1 garlic clove, mashed
1 TB dried basil
US 1¼ cups, UK 1 generous cup, Fish Stock (see Index) (3.5 dl)
3 egg yolks, beaten
snipped fresh chives
1 teaspoon anchovy paste, or more
parsley

- Bring a large amount of water to a boil in a fish poacher. Add 1½ teaspoons salt per quart (liter) of water. Put the fish steaks on the rack of the poacher but not in the water bath.

- Place vinegar, red wine, salt and pepper to taste, garlic and basil in a small pot. Reduce by half. Add the fish stock and simmer together for 5 minutes.

- At this point of your sauce making, immerse the steaks in the boiling water in the poacher. Bring back to a boil; as soon as the water boils again, remove the poacher from the heat. Let stand for 7 minutes. Drain fish and place on serving platter or plates.

- Meanwhile, finish the sauce: Add some of the sauce to the well-beaten egg yolks, then return the mixture to the bulk of the sauce.

- Place chives and anchovy paste in a sauceboat. Gradually strain and whisk in the egg sauce. Correct the pepper. Serve over the salmon steaks. Garnish with parsley.

BRAISED STRIPED BASS
(Loup Braisé)

- Easy
  6 servings
  Expensive
  40 minutes

  2 striped bass, 2½ to 3 lbs. each (1.5 kg
      each)
  salt
  US 1 cup, UK 1 scant cup, Fish Stock (see
      Index) (2.5 dl)
  ½ bottle of dry white wine
  20 peppercorns
  2 lemons
  2 tomatoes
  1 recipe Slim Vinaigrette (see Index), fla-
      vored with chives

- Preheat oven to 350°F., 180°C. or 5
  Regulo.

- Salt the fish in their cavities. Put the
  fish in a large oval baking dish. Add
  fish stock, white wine, salt to taste
  and peppercorns. Cover with parchment paper.

- Bake in the preheated oven for 30
  minutes.

- To serve, remove the skin, and arrange the fish on a serving platter.
  Garnish with quartered lemons and
  tomatoes.

- Reduce the cooking juices of the fish
  to a few tablespoons and add them
  to the vinaigrette. Serve the sauce
  with the fish.

BAKED SMELTS
(Eperlans au Four)

- Easy
  6 servings
  Inexpensive
  40 minutes

  36 smelts
  2 onions
  2 shallots
  salt and pepper
  2 garlic cloves, finely mashed
  US ½ cup, UK ⅓ cup, chopped parsley (4
      TB)
  2 cups Fish Stock (see Index), approxi-
      mately (.5 L)
  4 oz. Gruyère cheese, grated (120 g)

- Dress the smelts; remove the heads.

- Preheat oven to 400°F., 200°C. or 6
  Regulo.

- In a nonstick pan cook onions and
  shallots with salt and pepper to taste
  until translucent. Mix in garlic and
  parsley.

- Empty the mixture into a large baking dish and spread over the bottom
  of the dish in an even layer.

- Arrange the smelts on the mixture,
  packing them together well. Add
  enough fish stock to barely cover
  the fish. Season with salt and pepper.

- Bake in the preheated oven for 5 to
  6 minutes. Sprinkle with the cheese
  and finish baking for another 5 to 6
  minutes.

BLUE TROUT
(Truites au Bleu)

■ Easy
6 servings
Expensive
40 minutes

6 trout, ½ lb. each (250 g each)
US 1 cup, UK 1 scant cup, red-wine vinegar (2.5 dl)
1 large onion, thinly sliced
1 large carrot, thinly sliced
salt
10 peppercorns
parsley
lemon wedges

- Dress the trout by making a small incision under the stomach. Do not wash the fish. Tie each trout head to tail, using a trussing needle to sew through the fish head and tail. Arrange the trout in a dish.

- Heat the vinegar, pour it into a measuring cup, and slowly pour some of it on the back of each trout, which will turn blue because of the acid reaction of vinegar on the natural body slime.

- In a large fish poacher put 3 quarts water (3 L), the remainder of the wine vinegar, the onion, the carrot, salt to taste and the peppercorns. Bring the liquid to a boil and cook for about 10 minutes.

- Put the trout on the poacher rack and lower into the *court-bouillon*. When the *court-bouillon* comes to a second boil, remove the pot from the heat, cover, and let the trout poach for 10 to 12 minutes, depending on size.

- Serve on a platter garnished with parsley and lemon wedges.

INDIAN-STYLE TUNA
(Thon à l'Indienne)

- Easy
  6 servings
  Expensive
  2 hours

  3 lbs. fresh tuna (1.5 kg)
  US 1 cup, UK 1 scant cup, dry white wine
     (2.5 dl)
  2 bay leaves
  thyme
  salt and pepper
  4 carrots
  4 onions
  3 tomatoes, peeled
  1 to 2 TB curry powder
  1 envelope whole saffron, .045 oz. (1.5 g)
  cayenne pepper
  lemon juice

- At 1 hour before cooking, put the tuna to marinate in a dish with the white wine, bay leaves, crumbled, some thyme, salt and pepper.

- Cut carrots and onions into ⅓-inch cubes and place them in a pot over low heat. Increase the heat, and add the peeled tomatoes. Sprinkle with curry powder, saffron and cayenne pepper to taste.

- Remove the tuna from the marinade and place it on the vegetables. Add the marinade. Cover and simmer for approximately 1 hour, or until tender.

- Defatten the sauce carefully. Add lemon juice to your taste and serve.

WHITING IN WHITE WINE
(Merlans au Vin Blanc)

■ Easy
  6 servings
  Inexpensive
  50 minutes

  1 large onion
  1 large carrot
  US 2 cups, UK 1¾ cups, dry white wine
    (4 to 5 dl)
  1 bunch of parsley
  1 bay leaf
  6 whitings
  salt and pepper

● Peel and finely chop the onion. Peel the carrot and slice thinly. Cook both in a nonstick pan until the onion is translucent.

● Add the white wine and bring to a boil. Add parsley and bay leaf. Cover and simmer for 30 minutes.

● Preheat oven to 425°F., 225°C. or 6 to 7 Regulo.

● Dress the fish, wash them, season with salt and pepper. Arrange the fish in a baking dish.

● When the cooking liquid is ready, remove parsley and bay leaf. Add 1 cup cold water to the wine reduction and pour this over the fish. Put to bake on the middle rack of the oven. Baste frequently with the cooking juices, and cover the dish when the fish begins to take on some color. Cook for 20 minutes.

● Turn the oven off and leave the fish in the oven for a few minutes before serving.

NOTE
Using the same method, you can prepare fillets of cod, pollock, haddock, red snapper, etc.

AÏOLI FISH FILLETS
(Filets de Poisson Aïoli)

- **Easy**
  6 servings
  Inexpensive
  30 minutes

  2 lbs. fish fillets (1 kg)
  Fish Stock (see Index)
  2 TB chopped parsley
  1 recipe Aïoli (see Index)
  salt and pepper

- Preheat oven to 425°F., 220°C. or 6 Regulo.

- Arrange the fillets in a baking dish without overlapping them. Add enough fish stock to barely cover the fish. Place a parchment paper over the dish, and set it on the middle rack of the oven. Cook for 5 to 12 minutes, depending on size. The fillets are done as soon as the liquid is simmering.

- Prepare the *aïoli* while the fish is baking. It does not need to be cooled completely since it will be used to bind a hot sauce.

- Remove the dish from the oven and arrange the fillets on a serving platter. Sprinkle with chopped parsley.

- Season the cooking juices of the fish and blend the *aïoli* with these juices. Serve in a sauceboat.

  NOTE
  If you prefer saving energy, the fish can be poached in a large sauteuse on top of the stove.

COLD FISH SALAD IN SCALLOP SHELLS
(Coquilles de Poisson Mayonnaise)

■ Easy
  6 servings
  Inexpensive
  **20 minutes, plus 10 minutes to cool the
    mayonnaise**

  3 eggs
  6 lettuce leaves
  1 lb. cooked fish (500 g)
  3 tomatoes
  1 recipe Slim Mayonnaise (see Index)
  salt and pepper
  chopped parsley
  capers

- Hard-boil the eggs.
- Line 6 ramekins or scallop shells with a lettuce leaf each, and fill with pieces of fish.
- Slice the tomatoes and the hard-boiled eggs and add them to the mayonnaise. Season with salt and pepper.
- Add some of the mayonnaise mixture to each shell. Sprinkle with freshly chopped parsley and garnish with a few capers.

NOTE
This is a good recipe to use any leftover fish that you may have. Stretch whatever you have by adding shrimps, crab, or even tuna. You may also splurge and garnish each ramekin with 2 or 3 jumbo shrimps.

MUSSELS WITH ONION AND PARSLEY SAUCE
(Moules Marinières)

■ **Easy**
   6 servings
   Inexpensive
   35 minutes

   4 quarts mussels (4 L)
   1 large onion, finely chopped
   US 2 cups, UK 1¾ cups, dry white wine
      (4 to 5 dl)
   freshly chopped parsley
   salt and pepper
   lemon wedges

● Scrub the mussels very well. Let them soak in salted water. Rinse and drain.

● Meanwhile, cook the onion in a nonstick skillet until translucent.

● Pour the wine into a pot large enough to accommodate all the mussels; bring to a boil. Add the onion, parsley, and salt and pepper to taste. Add the mussels. Place the pot over high heat, cover, and shake it from time to time, grasping the lid and pot to do so every 2 or 3 minutes. The mussels are cooked when they are completely opened, in 7 to 8 minutes. Discard any unopened mussels.

● Serve the mussels with their cooking liquid and pass a dish of lemon wedges.

STEWED SQUID
(Encornets à la Sétoise)

■ **Easy**
   6 servings
   Inexpensive
   1½ hours

   2 onions, finely chopped
   2 garlic cloves, mashed
   3 tomatoes, seeded and chopped
   US 2 TB, UK 1 TB, tomato paste (1 TB)
   US ⅔ cup, UK ½ cup, dry white wine (2
      scant dl)
   1 bouquet garni
   1 small hot red pepper, finely chopped
   salt, pepper
   2½ lbs. squids (1 kg)
   chopped parsley

● In a nonstick pan, cook the onions and garlic together over medium-low heat for a few minutes. Add tomatoes, tomato paste, white wine, *bouquet garni,* hot pepper and salt and pepper to taste. Cook for 15 minutes.

● Meanwhile, dress and wash the squids. Cut them into thin strips. Add them to the pot, cover, and let simmer for 1 hour, or until tender.

● Correct the seasoning and sprinkle with chopped parsley before serving.

SHELLFISH MEDLEY IN LEMON SAUCE
(Fruits de Mer au Citron)

- Easy
  6 servings
  Medium expensive
  1 hour

1 onion, chopped fine
salt and pepper
2 dozen large shrimps in shells
2 dozen oysters in shells
2 dozen large mussels in shells
US ½ cup, UK ⅓ cup, dry white wine (1 generous dl)
2 carrots, peeled and thinly sliced
1 white turnip, peeled and thinly sliced
3 leeks, white part only, sliced
1 baby yellow squash, thinly sliced
2 baby zucchini (marrows or courgettes), thinly sliced
US 1 cup, UK 1 scant cup, Fish Stock (see Index) (2.5 dl)
5 egg yolks
US ½ cup, UK ⅓ cup, evaporated skim milk (1 generous dl)
lemon juice
freshly chopped herbs of your choice (dill, chives or tarragon)

- Prepare all shellfish and vegetables first.

- Place the onion in a nonstick pan, add a drop of water and salt and pepper to taste, and let the onion soften, covered, until translucent. Remove to a plate.

- In the same skillet, stir-fry the shrimps until their shells turn bright red. Shell the shrimps. Set aside both shells and shrimps.

- Shuck the oysters. Beard them, set them aside on a plate; gather their juices in a cup.

- Put the mussels in the same pan in which you stir-fried the shrimps; add the white wine. Steam the mussels open. Shell the mussels; add their juices to that of the oysters.

- Mix all the shellfish both cooked and raw (*do not precook the oysters*).

- Blanch carrots, turnip and leeks in salted boiling water. Put those vegetables, all wet from their bath, into a nonstick skillet. Add both squashes and season with salt and pepper. Toss well, and cover for a few minutes until the squashes soften.

- Mix fish stock and shellfish juices; reduce together by one third to one half.

- Mix the egg yolks and evaporated milk. Proceed as follows: Empty both the stock reduction and the egg-yolk *liaison* over the vegetables and shake the pan over medium-high heat until the sauce thickens. *Do not boil!*

- Last, add all the shellfish and reheat well. The heat of the sauce will be enough to poach the oysters. Add plenty of lemon juice. Correct the seasoning. Finally, add chopped fresh herbs.

BEEF

(Le Bœuf)

RIB ROAST
(Côte de Bœuf Rôti)

■ Easy
  6 servings
  Expensive
  15 minutes per pound for rare; 18 minutes per pound for medium rare; 20 minutes per pound for medium well done

  1 boneless, fat-free rib roast, 3 lbs. (1.5 kg)
  US ½ cup, UK ⅓ cup, Meat Stock (see Index) (1 generous dl)
  water
  salt and pepper

• Trim all traces of fat from the roast; do not hesitate to expose the bare muscle completely.

• Preheat oven to 400°F., 200°C. or 6 to 7 Regulo.

• Place the meat on a rack set over a roasting pan. Let sear for 20 minutes, turn over, and roast for another 20 minutes.

• During the last 15 minutes of cooking, baste with the meat stock. Deglaze the roasting pan with water. Salt and pepper both gravy and roast and serve with Provençal-style green beans.

BŒUF MODE

■ Easy
  6 servings
  Medium expensive
  3 hours, 2 hours in pressure cooker

  3 lbs. beef chuck (1.5 kg)
  US ½ cup, UK ⅓ cup, Meat Stock (see Index) (1 generous dl)
  3 lbs. carrots (1.5 kg)
  2 onions
  2 shallots
  1 large gelatinous veal bone (shank)
  salt, pepper
  1 bouquet garni
  US 1½ cups, UK 1⅓ cups, dry white wine (3.5 dl)
  US 1½ cups, UK 1⅓ cups, water (3.5 dl)

• Put the piece of beef in a nonstick skillet over medium heat. Cook on medium-low heat until the meat has seared lightly. Add meat stock and increase the heat to brown the meat. Transfer to braising pot.

• Meanwhile, slice the carrots and chop the onions and the shallots. Add to the braising pot the veal bone, carrots, shallots, onions, salt and pepper to taste, *bouquet garni*, wine and water. Bring to a boil. Cover, turn down to a simmer, and cook for 2 to 2½ hours.

• Serve beef on a heated platter and warmed dinner plates. This dish may also be served cold, since it gels beautifully.

BOILED BEEF AND VEGETABLES
(Pot-au-Feu)

- **Easy**
  6 servings
  Affordable
  3½ hours, 1½ hours in pressure cooker

  1 beef blade roast, 3½ lbs., tied (1.75 kg)
  2 veal bones without marrow
  salt
  4 leeks
  1 celery rib
  6 whole cloves
  2 onions
  8 carrots
  5 turnips
  bouquet garni
  peppercorns

- Fill a large pot with 4½ quarts (4 L) cold water. Add the meat, bones, and a large pinch of salt. Bring to a boil, reduce heat to a simmer, and remove the scum that forms at the top. Cover and continue simmering.

- Prepare the vegetables: Tie the leeks and the celery together and stick 3 whole cloves into each onion. Peel carrots and turnips.

- After the first hour of cooking, add carrots, onions and *bouquet garni*. Yet another hour later, add celery, leeks, turnips and a few peppercorns. If you are using a pressure cooker put all the vegetables in at the same time as you put in the meat.

- To serve, strain and completely de-fatten the cooking liquid. Slice the meat and arrange it on a serving platter with all the vegetables. Serve with mustard, pickles and ketchup.

NOTE

Any leftover beef can be used to prepare Beef Miroton, or Stuffed Tomatoes (see Index).

BEEF MIROTON
(Bœuf Miroton)

- Easy
  6 servings
  Thrift recipe
  1 hour

  ¾ **lb. onions, finely chopped (375 g)**
  US 3 cups, UK 2¾ cups, Meat Stock (see Index) (.75 L)
  US 3 TB, UK 1½ TB, vinegar (1½ TB)
  2 lbs. leftover or cooked beef (1 kg)
  1 egg yolk
  US 2 TB, UK 1 TB, evaporated skim milk (1 TB)
  prepared mustard
  3 TB sliced pickles (1½ TB)

- In a nonstick, deep sauté pan, gently cook the onions in some of the meat stock for about 5 minutes, until translucent.
- Add the vinegar and the remainder of the stock. Bring to a boil and boil hard for about 5 minutes more.
- Slice the beef and add it to the pan; cover. Cook over low heat for 10 minutes.
- Remove the meat to a serving platter. Mix egg yolk and milk and blend into the onion sauce. Add a bit of mustard and the pickles.

POT-ROASTED BEEF
(Bœuf en Cocotte)

- Easy
  6 servings
  Affordable
  3 hours, 1½ hours in pressure cooker

3 lbs. chuck roast, in 1 piece (1.5 kg)
4 shallots, finely chopped
2 garlic cloves, finely chopped
2 carrots, finely chopped
8 onions, finely chopped
½ lb. mushrooms, quartered (250 g)
1 bouquet garni
US 2 to 3 TB, UK 1 to 1½ TB, heavy Meat
    Stock (see Index) (1 to 1½ TB)
salt, pepper, nutmeg
US ½ cup, UK ⅓ cup, Madeira (1 gener-
    ous dl), or US 1 cup, UK 1 scant cup,
    red wine (3 dl)

- Have the meat tied and all the vegetables and *bouquet garni* prepared.

- Put a nonstick skillet to heat over medium-low heat. Add the meat and let cook on all sides until lightly seared. Gradually add the meat stock and increase the heat so the meat colors better.

- Remove the meat to a braising pot. Add the *bouquet garni*, salt, pepper and nutmeg to taste. Cover and cook over low heat for 10 minutes on each side.

- In the meantime, add the Madeira or red wine and the shallots to the pan in which you browned the beef, and scrape well to deglaze it. Add the garlic, carrots and onions. Pour the whole mixture into the braising pot and cook for 1½ hours.

- Finally add the mushrooms to the pot and continue to simmer for another 30 minutes.

- Test doneness with a skewer, which will come out easily if the meat is done. Correct the seasoning of the sauce. Slice the meat and spoon the sauce over it.

- Serve with spinach, celery root or green beans as a vegetable.

CHATEAUBRIAND WITH PEPPER AND MADEIRA
(Chateaubriands au Poivre et au Madère)

■ Easy
6 servings
Very expensive
15 minutes

freshly cracked peppercorns
1 Chateaubriand (heart of the tenderloin)
    2¼ lbs. (1 kg)
2 tsps. olive oil
salt
2 oz. Cognac (2 TB)
US ½ cup, UK ⅓ cup, dry Madeira (1
    generous dl)
US ½ cup, UK ⅓ cup, Meat Stock (see
    Index) (1 generous dl)
1 tsp. tomato paste

• Put the freshly cracked peppercorns on a sheet of wax paper. Coat both sides of the chateaubriand with the pepper, flattening the meat to 1½-inch thickness as you do so.

• Brush a large skillet with the oil and brown the piece of meat on both sides.

• Turn the heat down, salt the meat, and cook for 10 minutes. Heat and ignite the Cognac and very carefully pour the flaming Cognac over the beef.

• Transfer the roast to a heated serving platter. Deglaze the pan with Madeira and meat stock mixed. Add the tomato paste, correct the seasoning, and pour the sauce over the steak. Serve with zucchini.

NOTE
Due to the high cost of this piece of meat, make an exception and use the 2 teaspoons oil or the pepper will burn badly and damage the meat.

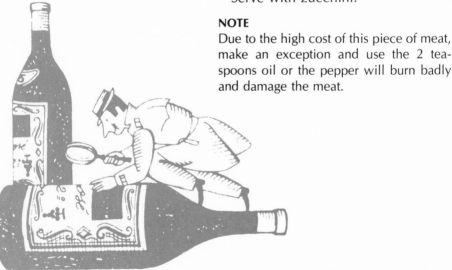

RIB STEAK BORDELAISE
(Entrecôte Bordelaise)

- Easy
  6 servings
  Expensive
  30 to 35 minutes

  2 rib steaks, each 1¼ inches thick (3 cm)
  10 medium-size shallots, finely chopped
  US 1½ cups, UK 1¼ cups, heavy Meat
    Stock (see Index) (3.5 dl)
  US ⅔ cup, UK ½ cup, white or red wine
    (2 scant dl)
  salt and pepper

- Sear the steaks in a nonstick frying pan and cook to your taste. Transfer steaks to a serving platter and keep warm.

- Meanwhile, gently cook the shallots in a little meat stock until they are translucent. Remove to a plate.

- Add the remainder of the meat stock and the wine to the steak pan. Reduce and cook to taste. Return the shallots to the pan. Season the sauce well.

- Pour the sauce over the meat. Serve with étuvéed lettuce and cheese.

BROILED RIB STEAK
(Entrecôte Grillée)

- Easy
  6 servings
  Expensive
  10 minutes

  2 rib steaks, each 1¼ inches thick (3 cm)
  US ½ cup, UK 4 TB, Meat Stock (see Index) (4 TB)
  ½ tsp. ground ginger
  2 hard-boiled egg yolks
  1 raw egg yolk
  salt and pepper
  green scallion rings

- Trim as much fat as possible from the steaks. Place the steaks 4 inches from the source of heat and broil to your taste.

- With the meat stock, deglaze the broiler pan. Add ginger, hard-boiled egg yolks and raw egg yolk to the gravy. Mash and mix well. Correct the seasoning.

- Serve the meat topped with the egg sauce and garnished with scallion rings.

PAPRIKA RIB STEAK
(Entrecôte Paprika)

- Easy
  6 servings
  Expensive
  15 to 20 minutes

  8 medium-size onions, thinly sliced
  US ⅔ cup, UK ½ cup, Meat Stock (see
      Index) (2 scant dl)
  salt and pepper
  US 2 TB, UK 1 TB, paprika (1 TB)
  2 rib steaks, each 1¼ inches thick (3 cm)
  US 1 TB, UK ½ TB, vinegar (½ TB)
  chopped parsley

- Put the onions and half of the meat stock in a large nonstick skillet. Add salt and pepper to taste. Cover and cook gently until the onions have softened and are starting to take on some color. Remove them to a plate.

- Sprinkle some paprika on the steaks, then put the steaks to cook in the same pan in which you cooked the onions. Add salt and pepper to taste and cook to the degree of doneness you prefer. Remove steaks to a plate as soon as done.

- To the same pan add the vinegar, the remainder of the meat stock, the onions and the remainder of the paprika. Season well; if the mixture appears too thick, add a drop or so of water.

- Spoon the mixture onto the steaks and sprinkle with chopped parsley. As a vegetable, serve braised red cabbage.

MUSTARD STEAKS
(Entrecôte à la Moutarde)

- Easy
  6 servings
  Expensive
  10 to 15 minutes

  6 rib steaks, each ⅔ inch thick (1.5 cm)
  salt and pepper
  US ½ cup, UK ⅓ cup, Meat Stock (see
      Index) (1 generous dl)
  US 2 TB, UK 1 TB, prepared Dijon mus-
      tard (1 TB)
  2 TB chopped parsley

- Trim the outside fat layer off the steaks.
- Use a nonstick skillet. Do not pre-heat it, put the steaks in the cold pan over medium heat until the fat melts. It will take about 2 minutes on each side of the steak. Then increase the heat to seal the steaks, salt and pepper them, and cook them to the degree of doneness you prefer.
- Transfer to a warm serving platter. Over moderately high heat add meat stock; with a wooden spatula, scrape the caramelized steak juices from the bottom of the pan. Turn down the heat a bit and off the heat add the mustard. Mix very well, until homogenous. Reheat well, add parsley, and spoon over the steaks.
- Sprinkle steaks with more finely chopped parsley. Serve with a simple green salad.

NOTE
Remember never to use any cooking fats for panfried meats. Instead, rely on your nonstick pan. Always put on low heat to release the natural fats of the meats.

STEAKS AND GARLIC PURÉE
(Biftecks à la Purée d'Ail)

- Easy
  6 servings
  Medium expensive
  40 minutes

  2 heads of garlic
  salt and pepper
  US ½ cup, UK ⅓ cup, Meat Stock (see Index) (1 generous dl)
  2 small zucchini (marrows or courgettes)
  6 steaks, cut of your choice, each ½ inch thick (1.2 cm)
  ½ additional tiny raw garlic clove, mashed
  chopped parsley

- Separate the garlic cloves from the roots; drop them into a small pot of cold water. Bring to a boil, add a pinch of salt, and simmer until a large clove is soft enough to give under the pressure of 2 fingers.

- Push the garlic purée out of each clove peel and drop the purée into a small pot. Add the meat stock and heat together. Whisk well with a small sauce whisk until smooth. Season to taste.

- With a knife or the food processor, cut the zucchini into ⅛-inch julienne. Put the julienne in a nonstick skillet, salt and pepper it, cover, and cook until the juices run out of the vegetable. Remove to a plate, juice and all.

- Cook the steaks to the doneness you prefer; salt and pepper them. At once remove steaks to a platter.

- Add the garlic purée, the julienne of zucchini and the mashed raw piece of garlic to the steak pan and mix well.

- Top each steak with an equal amount of the mixture, and sprinkle with parsley. Serve promptly. As a vegetable, serve green beans in tomato sauce.

TENDERLOIN STEAKS WITH HAM AND MUSHROOMS
(Tournedos Garni)

■ Easy
  6 servings
  Expensive
  10 minutes

¾ lb. mushrooms (375 g)
1 slice of ham, about 3½ oz. (100 g)
salt and pepper
6 tenderloin steaks, 4 oz. each (110 to
    120 g each)
US ½ cup, UK ⅓ cup, Meat Stock (see
    Index) (1 generous dl)
finely chopped parsley
1 garlic clove, finely chopped

● Clean, trim, and slice the mushrooms. Cut the ham into small cubes. In a nonstick pan, cook the mushrooms with salt and pepper until their juices have evaporated. Add the diced ham. Remove to a plate and keep warm.

● In the same pan, cook the steaks to your taste.

● Deglaze the steak pan with the meat stock. Add parsley and garlic and the mixture of mushrooms and ham. Top each steak with an equal amount of the mixture.

TENDERLOIN WITH HERBS
(Tournedos aux Herbes)

■ Easy
  6 servings
  Expensive
  10 to 15 minutes

6 tenderloin steaks, 4 oz. each (110 to
    120 g each)
finely chopped herbs of your choice
1½ tsps. prepared mustard
1 raw egg yolk
salt and pepper
lemon juice
US ½ cup, UK ⅓ cup, Meat Stock (see
    Index) (1 generous dl)
parsley

● Cook the steaks to your taste.

● Mix the herbs, mustard, egg yolk, salt and pepper to taste and a dash of lemon juice.

● Deglaze the steak pan with the stock. Off the heat, add the herb mixture. Reheat without boiling.

● Spoon the sauce over the steaks. Garnish with parsley. Serve with summer squash or zucchini.

ANCHOVY STEAKS
(Entrecôte au Beurre d'Anchois)

- Easy
  6 servings
  Expensive
  15 minutes

  6 sirloin steaks, each ⅔ inch thick (1.5
     cm)
  ½ lb. wild mushrooms, or plain cultivated
     mushrooms (250 g)
  salt and pepper
  1 garlic clove, mashed
  1 tsp. anchovy paste
  US ½ cup, UK ⅓ cup, Meat Stock (see
     Index) (1 generous dl)
  chopped parsley and bouquets of parsley

- Trim the steaks of all traces of fat and connective tissues.

- Clean the mushrooms and slice into ¼-inch julienne. Mash the garlic; have the anchovy paste and the stock ready.

- Put the mushrooms in a nonstick skillet over medium heat; add salt and pepper. Let the moisture exude out of the vegetables. As soon as this happens, increase the heat, add the garlic and anchovy paste, and mix very well. Cook until the mushrooms are barely coated with a little of their own juices. Remove them to a plate. Do not clean the skillet.

- In the same skillet, still containing the last bits of mushroom juice, sear the steaks. Reduce the heat, salt and pepper the steaks, and cook them to the degree of doneness you prefer.

- As the steaks cook a nice glaze will build at the bottom of the pan. Remove the cooked steaks to a platter. Deglaze the pan with the stock, and reduce by half.

- Return the mushrooms to the skillet and toss them into the glaze. Add plenty of chopped parsley and correct the seasoning.

- Top each steak with an equal amount of mushrooms and serve promptly, garnishing with parsley bouquets.

NOTE
The best mushrooms are Boleti of all edible types, Marasmius Oreades, Chanterelles.

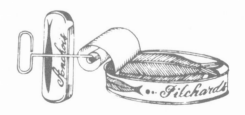

GOULASCH
(Goulash)

■ Easy
  6 servings
  Affordable
  2¼ hours, 1¼ hours in pressure cooker

3 lbs. beef stew meat, chuck or sirloin tip
  (1.5 kg)
US 1 cup, UK 1 scant cup, Meat Stock
  (see Index) (2.5 dl)
6 onions, finely chopped
salt and pepper
US 2 TB, UK 1 TB, sweet paprika (1 TB)
US 2 TB, UK 1 TB, hot paprika (1 TB)
1 tsp. cuminseed
1¼ lbs. tomatoes, chopped and seeded
  (625 g)
bouquet garni

- Preheat oven to 400°F., 200°C. or 6 to 7 Regulo.

- Cut the meat into 1½-inch cubes. Brown the meat in an ovenproof skillet in the oven for 15 to 20 minutes.

- Put some meat stock into a nonstick pan. Add the onions and salt and pepper to taste, and cook until onions are golden.

- Add both kinds of paprika. Add the meat cubes, cuminseed, tomatoes and *bouquet garni*. Deglaze the meat browning juices with a little boiling water, and pour into the pan. Cover and simmer for about 2 hours.

- Correct seasoning and serve with Swiss chard.

MINCED SIRLOIN
(Émincé de Bœuf)

- Easy
  6 servings
  Medium expensive
  35 minutes

  US ½ cup, UK ⅓ cup, Meat Stock (see
      Index) (1 generous dl)
  4 shallots, finely chopped
  salt and pepper
  2 lbs. top sirloin (1 kg)
  1 TB prepared mustard
  chives

- Put a few tablespoons of meat stock and the shallots in a nonstick pan, and cook gently with a pinch of salt and pepper.
- Meanwhile, trim the meat of all fat and cut it into thin slices, then into ¼-inch strips.
- Remove the cooked shallots to a plate. In the same pan sear the meat over high heat so it remains rare at the center. Remove the meat to a heated serving dish.
- Return the shallots to the pan, add the remainder of the stock, the mustard and chives. Correct the seasoning. Serve with an assortment of fresh vegetables.

NOTE
To obtain more sauce, increase the amount of meat stock after the meat is cooked and finish the sauce with an egg *liaison*.

HAMBURGERS BASQUE STYLE
(Bifteck Haché à la Basquaise)

- Easy
  6 servings
  Affordable
  40 minutes

  1½ lbs. ground beef, 14% fat (750 g)
  1 onion
  salt and pepper
  US ¼ cup, UK 2 TB, Meat Stock (see Index) (2 TB)
  2 red peppers, slivered
  2 green peppers, slivered
  2 garlic cloves, mashed
  1 tsp. anchovy paste
  6 slices of Pyrénées cheese (Doux de Montagne), 4 x 1½ inches, ¼ inch thick
  chopped parsley

- Shape the meat into 6 equal-size patties. Set aside.

- Slice the onion. Place it in a non-stick skillet. Salt and pepper it, and toss over medium heat for a few minutes. Add the meat stock, increase the heat, and let the onion cook until translucent.

- Add the red and green pepper slivers and garlic; toss well together. Add the anchovy paste and some pepper from the mill. Let cook until the peppers are nice and soft but not mushy. Remove the vegetable mixture to a plate. Keep warm.

- In the same skillet, still containing traces of the vegetable juices, sear the meat patties; salt and pepper them. Cook them to the doneness you prefer.

- When the hamburgers are three quarters done, top each one with an equal amount of pepper mixture and 1 slice of Pyrénées cheese.

- Cover the pan for 1 minute to melt the cheese. Sprinkle with parsley. Serve in the skillet.

STEAK TARTARE

■ Easy
  6 servings
  Medium expensive
  10 minutes

  2 lbs. finely chopped beef, sirloin strip or
      tenderloin (1 kg)
  6 egg yolks
  4 onions, finely chopped
  ½ cup mixed chopped fresh herbs
  prepared Dijon mustard
  2 small jars (2 oz., 60 g each) capers,
      drained
  salt and pepper
  garlic salt
  1 recipe Slim Vinaigrette (see Index)
  tomato ketchup

● Divide the meat into 6 portions and place on individual plates. Make a small hole in the center of the meat and place 1 raw egg yolk resting in half of its shell, in this hole.

● Place the onions, herbs, mustard and capers in separate serving dishes. Offer salt, pepper, garlic salt, vinaigrette sauce and ketchup on a tray. Let your guests prepare the raw meat to their own tastes. Serve with leeks prepared as a salad.

LAMB

(L'Agneau et le Mouton)

LEG OF LAMB WITH SPRING VEGETABLES
(Gigot aux Légumes Nouveaux)

- Easy
  6 to 8 servings
  Quite expensive
  1¼ hours

  1 leg of lamb, 3½ to 4 lbs. (1.5 to 2.0 kg)
  3 garlic cloves
  2 tsps. olive oil
  1 lb. white onions (500 g)
  US 1½ cups, UK 1⅓ cups, Meat Stock
      (see Index) (3.5 dl)
  1 lb. turnips (500 g)
  1 lb. carrots (500 g)
  ½ lb. fine green beans (250 g)
  2 celery ribs, cut into ¼-inch slices

- Preheat oven to 400°F., 200°C. or 6 Regulo.

- Trim leg to the bare muscle. Cut the garlic cloves into slivers and insert slivers into slits cut into the surface of the meat. Pour the olive oil into your hands and rub it all over the leg of lamb.

- Place the lamb in a brown earthenware dish and sear in the preheated oven for 20 minutes.

- Slice the onions and put them with half of the meat stock in a nonstick pan. Cook them until translucent.

- When the leg is seared, add the onions to the baking dish and continue roasting.

- Meanwhile cut turnips and carrots into small olive shapes. String the beans and cut them into 1½-inch pieces. Blanch each vegetable separately in boiling salted water; they should remain crunchy.

- At 15 minutes before the lamb is done mix the vegetables into the onions in the baking dish, and add the remainder of the meat stock. Baste the leg of lamb once or twice with these juices.

- To serve, slice the leg of lamb and surround it with the little vegetables.

LEG OF LAMB WITH HERBS
(Gigot d'Agneau)

■ Easy
6 servings
Quite expensive
1 hour to 1¼ hours

1 leg of lamb, 3½ lbs. (1.5 kg)
1 garlic clove
2 tsps. olive oil
Provençal herbs
salt and pepper

- Preheat oven to 400°F., 200°C. or 6 Regulo.
- It is essential that you remove all traces of fat from the top of the leg of lamb. Work all the way down to the bare muscle with a small paring knife.

- Mash the garlic, mix it with 2 teaspoons olive oil, and rub all over the leg of lamb. Sprinkle the leg with a mixture of Provençal herbs.
- Roast the leg of lamb for about 1 hour, or to the degree of doneness you prefer. Salt and pepper it when three quarters done.
- Serve with braised lettuce, or sautéed tomatoes sprinkled with parsley and garlic.

LAMB STEW
(Navarin de Mouton)

■ Easy
6 servings
Medium expensive
2 hours

3½ lbs. boneless lamb shoulder (1.5 kg)
½ lb. onions, sliced (250 g)
US ⅓ cup, UK ¼ cup, Meat Stock (see Index) (1 generous dl)
US ¾ cup, UK ½ cup, white wine (2 generous dl)
1 bouquet garni
salt, pepper, nutmeg
1½ lbs. carrots (675 g)
1 lb. green beans (500 g)

- Cut the meat into 1½-inch pieces, and remove all fat.

- Slice the onions. Cook them with the meat stock in a nonstick pan until translucent. Remove onions to a plate.
- In the same pan, brown the meat. Add white wine, *bouquet garni*, and salt, pepper and freshly grated nutmeg to taste. Cover and simmer for 45 minutes.
- Slice the carrots. Cut the green beans and blanch them in boiling salted water. Add them and the cooked onions to the pot for another 30 minutes of cooking.
- Correct the seasoning and serve the stew piping hot on hot plates.

SADDLE OF LAMB WITH KIDNEY SAUCE
(Selle d'Agneau aux Rognons)

- Requires care
  6 servings
  Expensive
  1 hour

  1 whole loin of lamb or saddle with both
      kidneys attached
  ½ oz. Cognac (½ TB)
  US 2 cups, UK 2 scant cups, Meat Stock
      (see Index) (4.5 to 5 dl)
  3 shallots, chopped
  US 2 TB, UK 1 TB, tomato paste (1 TB)
  US 2 TB, UK 1 TB, chopped fresh tarra-
      gon, approximately (1 TB)
  US 2 TB, UK 1 TB, chopped fresh basil,
      approximately (1 TB)
  salt and pepper
  tarragon mustard
  snipped chives

- Purchase a saddle of lamb. The saddle is the whole loin—both sides of the sirloin strip and the tenderloin attached to the backbone. Inside in heavy fat pads are the kidneys.

- Prepare the loin this way: Working on the bottom of the piece, remove the kidneys. Keep them for your sauce. Discard all the fat. Pull all the fat off until you see the tenderloins appear.

- Now, working on top of the piece, cut the fell open on each side of the backbone. With a very sharp knife lift the fell off the sirloin strips on each side until each strip of meat is exposed. *Do not cut off the fell,* but fold it back and cover the strips with it.

- Roll the "belly flaps" into a cigar on each side and tie the whole thing with kitchen string in 4 to 6 places. The rolled belly flap prevents the tenderloin from overcooking.

- Preheat oven to 400°F., 200°C. or 6 Regulo.

- Roast the saddle for 30 to 35 minutes. While the meat roasts, prepare the kidney sauce.

- Clean the kidneys; dice them. Put them in a nonstick skillet with a drop or so of water, and sauté them over very high heat *for 1 minute,* no more, until they turn gray. Ignite the Cognac and add it flaming to the kidneys. Shake the pan back and forth, then empty into a strainer placed over a bowl. Let the kidneys drip for 15 minutes.

- In the skillet put the meat stock, chopped shallots, tomato paste, tarragon and basil, and reduce by half. Add salt and pepper to taste and another drop of Cognac; cook for 1 more minute.

- When the meat is done, remove it from the oven and let it stand for 5 minutes during which you finish the sauce.

- Strain the reduction of the meat stock into the juices in the roasting pan. If there is any fat in the pan, first sponge it off lightly with a paper towel. Scrape pan well to deglaze. Strain the deglazing back into the saucepan.
- Add the kidneys, a smidgeon of tarragon mustard and the chives to the sauce. Reheat *without* boiling so the kidneys remain tender.

- To slice the meat: Lift both sirloin strips and both tenderloins from the bone with a thin-bladed knife. Cut the pieces of meat each lengthwise into ⅛-inch-thick slices. Serve topped with the kidney sauce. Season the meat well with salt and pepper before adding the sauce, so both are seasoned equally well.

BROILED LAMB STEAKS
(Grillades de Mouton)

- Easy
  6 servings
  Expensive
  15 minutes

  1 garlic clove
  1 tsp. olive oil
  6 lamb steaks, cut from the leg, all fat and sinews trimmed off
  salt and pepper

- Preheat the broiler.
- Rub the garlic clove on the broiler pan and spread the olive oil over the garlic juice.
- Broil the steaks 4 inches from the source of heat for 3 minutes on each side. Season with salt and pepper. Serve with Provençal-style green beans.

LAMB CHOPS WITH HERBS
(Côtelettes de Selle d'Agneau)

- Easy
  6 servings
  Very expensive
  15 minutes

  6 loin lamb chops, each ¾ inch thick (2 cm)
  herbs of your choice
  2 garlic cloves
  salt and pepper

- Trim all fat and gristle from the outside of the chops. Rub a nonstick pan with a piece of lamb fat. Heat the pan and cook the chops to the degree of doneness you prefer.

- Finely chop herbs and garlic together; season with salt and pepper. Spoon some of the mixture over each chop. Serve with celery hearts.

GARNISHED LAMB CHOPS
(Côtes d'Agneau Garnies)

- Easy
  6 servings
  Expensive
  1 hour, approximately

  5 eggplants
  salt and pepper
  3 garlic cloves, finely chopped
  chopped parsley
  4 tomatoes
  ground thyme
  6 well-trimmed lamb chops (cut of your choice)

- Peel the eggplants and cut them into ⅓-inch cubes. Salt them and let them stand for 30 minutes so they lose their bitter taste.

- Meanwhile finely chop the garlic and parsley. Peel the tomatoes, seed them, and chop them.

- Rinse the eggplant cubes, dry them well.

- Put tomatoes, garlic and parsley into a nonstick pan, and cook gently until a sauce forms. Add the eggplant cubes, cover, and cook over low heat. Season with salt, pepper and thyme.

- During the last few minutes of cooking the vegetables, broil the chops to the doneness you prefer, and serve them seasoned with salt, pepper and ground thyme.

- To serve, surround the chops with the vegetable ragout.

LAMB WITH TURNIPS
(Mouton aux Navets)

■ Easy
6 servings
Medium expensive
2 hours

3½ lbs. shoulder of lamb (1.5 kg)
4 large onions
US 1½ cups, UK 1⅓ cups, Meat Stock
   (see Index) (3.5 dl)
US 1½ cups, UK 1⅓ cups, dry white wine
   (3.5 dl)
bouquet garni
2 garlic cloves
salt and pepper
3 lbs. turnips (1.4 to 2 kg)

- Cut the lamb into 1½-inch cubes; completely defatten them. Set aside.

- Slice the onions. Cook them in a nonstick sauté pan with the meat stock. When onions are translucent, remove to a plate. Brown the pieces of lamb in the same sauté pan.

- Mix onions and meat; add white wine, *bouquet garni*, garlic, and salt and pepper to taste. Cover and cook for 40 minutes.

- Peel and quarter the turnips. Blanch them in boiling salted water and add them to the sauté pan. If there is not enough liquid in the pan, add a few tablespoons of meat stock or water. Season with salt and pepper. Simmer until the lamb is tender. Serve on warmed plates.

SAUTÉ OF LAMB
(Sauté d'Agneau)

- Easy
  6 servings
  Medium expensive
  1 hour

  BASIC PROPORTIONS
  1 boned shoulder of lamb, 3 lbs. (1.5 kg)
  4 onions, sliced
  6 garlic cloves, sliced
  US 1 cup, UK 1 scant cup, Meat Stock
    (see Index) (2.5 dl)
  salt and pepper
  chopped parsley

- The basic procedure is the following: Cut a shoulder of lamb into 1½-inch cubes and remove all the fat.

- Cut the onions and garlic into slices. Sauté those with some meat stock until translucent. Remove the vegetables to a plate. In the bit of sticky stock left, brown the lamb cubes. Salt and pepper them.

- Return the onions and garlic to the pan, mix well. Cover the pan and cook slowly. When two thirds done, add the vegetable garnish of your choice and a bit more meat stock if necessary. Serve topped with chopped parsley.

WITH THE SAME METHOD
Sauté of Lamb with Zucchini: To the basic recipe add 6 zucchini, cut into ¼-inch slices. Do not use sliced garlic at the beginning. Blanch 24 peeled garlic cloves instead, and add them to the pan at the same time as the zucchini. When done, sprinkle with several tablespoons of chopped basil.

Sauté of Lamb with Lemon-Dill Sauce: Increase the amount of meat stock to 2 cups. When the meat is done, bind the sauce with a *liaison* of 5 egg yolks and the juice of 1 lemon. Flavor with a large amount of chopped dill.

Sauté of Lamb with Green Beans: To the basic recipe, add 1 pound green beans (500 g), peeled and cut into 1-inch pieces. Finish the dish with a mixture of 2 tablespoons parsley, or parsley mixed with 1 raw garlic clove, chopped.

PORK

(Le Porc)

PORK ROAST
(Filet de Porc Rôti)

- Easy
  6 servings
  Affordable
  3 hours

  2 carrots
  2 onions
  4 shallots
  4 garlic cloves
  bouquet garni
  1 bay leaf
  salt and pepper
  3½ lbs. boneless pork roast (1 kg, 650 g)
  1 bouillon cube
  1 tsp. quatre-épices (see Glossary)

- Place the vegetables, the aromatics, salt and pepper to taste and the roast in a large pot. Add enough water to cover the roast by two thirds. Cover the pot. Bring to a boil; add the bouillon cube. Turn down to a simmer and cook for 15 minutes per pound.

- Turn the heat off and let roast stand for 5 minutes. Remove the meat from the water bath and pat dry.

- Meanwhile, preheat oven to 400°F., 200°C. or 7 Regulo.

- Sprinkle the pork well with *quatre-épices,* and put the meat in the oven to brown for about 30 minutes.

- As a vegetable fennel or turnips would be very complementary.

NOTE

Refrigerate the cooking water. Remove all fat. Reheat the liquid well. Purée the vegetables through the food mill and combine with the defattened cooking water; you will obtain a very good soup with no extra work.

PORK ROAST WITH GARLIC
(Filet de Porc à l'Ail)

- Easy
  6 servings
  Inexpensive
  3½ hours

  3½ lbs. boneless pork roast (1 kg, 650 g)
  3 garlic cloves, peeled and sliced thin
  salt and pepper
  3 onions
  5 unpeeled garlic cloves
  2 sprigs of thyme
  1 bay leaf
  US ½ cup, UK ⅓ cup, dry white wine (1 generous dl)
  US ½ cup, UK ⅓ cup, water (1 generous dl)

- Defatten the roast completely. Prepare the 3 garlic cloves. Insert the slivers of garlic into slits cut ¼-inch deep into the meat. Salt and pepper the meat. Let stand for 1 hour.

- Preheat oven to 325°F., 160°C. or 4 Regulo.

- Peel and quarter the onions. Put meat and onions in a roasting pan, with the unpeeled garlic cloves and the thyme, bay leaf, wine and water.

- Roast the pork for 2½ hours, basting often and turning it over several times.

ROAST PORK WITH MUSTARD
(Rôti de Porc à la Moutarde)

- Easy
  6 servings
  Medium expensive
  3 hours

  3½ lbs. boneless pork roast (1 kg, 650 g)
  prepared Dijon mustard
  US ¼ cup, UK 2 TB, dry gluten bread crumbs (2 TB)
  US ½ cup, UK ⅓ cup, dry white wine (1 generous dl)
  US ½ cup, UK ⅓ cup, Meat Stock (see Index) (1 generous dl)
  salt and pepper

- Preheat oven to 325°F., 160°C. or 4 to 5 Regulo.

- Set the roast in a roasting pan and put it to sear for approximately 1 hour.

- As soon as the roast has sealed and taken on a nice golden color, brush ⅛ inch of mustard over it and cover with bread crumbs. Continue baking until a skewer inserted into the roast comes out without resistance. Turn off the oven and let the roast stand for 5 minutes before carving.

- Remove the roast to a platter. Add the white wine to the roasting pan and deglaze the meat juices, scraping well. Empty into a large saucepan and quickly reduce by two thirds. Add the meat stock, correct the seasoning, and turn into a sauceboat.

ROAST PORK IN MILK
(Rôti de Porc au Lait)

■ Easy
  6 servings
  Medium expensive
  3 hours

  3½ lbs. boneless pork roast (1 kg, 650 g)
  16 unpeeled garlic cloves
  US and UK 1 quart skim milk (1 L)
  salt and pepper
  nutmeg
  1 egg yolk

- Trim the pork of all fat and gristle.

- Put the unpeeled garlic cloves and the meat in a large braising pot. Add enough milk to cover the roast by three quarters. Season with salt, pepper and freshly grated nutmeg. Bring the roast to a boil over low heat, taking care not to let the milk boil over. Cover and let simmer.

- Turn the meat several times while it is cooking; allow 20 minutes per pound of meat. The milk should reduce at least by half.

- About 20 minutes before the end of the cooking time, uncover the pot and let the sauce reduce. Turn off the heat and let stand for 10 more minutes.

- To serve the roast, slice the meat and serve with Swiss chard and grated Gruyère.

- The sauce must be homogenized, for milk sauces separate into curds. Defatten the sauce. Put the egg yolk into a blender container. Set the blender at medium speed and add the sauce, garlic and all.

- Strain the blended sauce into a warmed sauceboat. Correct the seasoning.

BROILED PORK STEAKS
(Grillades de Porc)

■ Easy
6 servings
Affordable
15 minutes

6 pork steaks, each ½ inch thick (1.3 cm),
    5 oz. each (150 g)
salt and pepper
ground allspice

- Trim the steaks of all fat and gristle. About 1 hour before cooking, salt and pepper both sides of the steaks.
- Preheat a heavy metal grill. Panbroil the steaks until just done, when the meat will resist under the pressure of a finger. *Do not overcook* to avoid stringiness.
- Remove steaks to a platter and sprinkle lightly with ground allspice.

CHOPS PORK-BUTCHER STYLE
(Côtes de Porc Charcutière)

■ Easy
6 servings
Affordable
30 minutes

6 pork loin chops
salt and pepper
3 onions
US 1 cup, UK 1 scant cup, dry white wine
    (2.5 dl)
US 1 cup, UK 1 scant cup, water (2.5 dl)
US 2 TB, UK 1 TB, prepared mustard (1
    TB)
US 2 TB, UK 1 TB, sliced cornichons (1
    TB)

- Trim the chops of all traces of fat. Save a piece of pork fat. Salt and pepper the chops. Set them aside.
- Peel and chop the onions. Cook them slowly in a nonstick skillet with salt, pepper and a dash of water until translucent.
- Add the wine and an equal amount of water, and bring to a boil. Reduce the heat and simmer for 30 minutes, reducing by one third. Correct the seasoning.
- Rub a skillet with the reserved piece of pork fat. Brown the chops on both sides. Reduce the heat and cook chops for 12 to 15 minutes. Remove to a warm serving platter.
- Empty the wine and onion reduction into the skillet in which you cooked the chops. Scrape well and boil for 1 or 2 minutes. Add mustard and pickles and spoon over the chops.
- For a vegetable consider cauliflower, plain or as a salad.

BURGUNDY-STYLE HAM
(Jambon à la Bourguignonne)

- Easy
  6 servings
  Medium expensive
  35 minutes

  **6 slices of cooked ham, each ⅓ inch thick
    (.8 cm)**
  4 shallots, finely chopped
  **US ⅔ cup, UK ½ cup, dry white wine (2
    scant dl)**
  **US ⅔ cup, UK ½ cup, Meat Stock (see
    Index) (2 scant dl)**
  US 2 TB, UK 1 TB, wine vinegar (1 TB)
  dried or fresh tarragon
  salt, pepper, freshly grated nutmeg
  US 2 TB, UK 1 TB, tomato paste (1 TB)
  1 egg yolk

- Trim the ham slices of all fat. Set aside.

- Put shallots, wine, meat stock, vinegar, and tarragon to taste in a small pot and slowly reduce by half. Add salt, pepper, a dash of nutmeg and tomato paste. Set aside.

- Panbroil the ham steaks rapidly over medium-high heat, and remove to a warmed platter.

- Add a few tablespoons of water to the skillet to dissolve the caramelized ham juices. Add this deglazing to the wine reduction.

- Mix the egg yolk *liaison* into the reduction (see Index). Reheat thickened sauce without boiling, and spoon unstrained over the slices of ham.

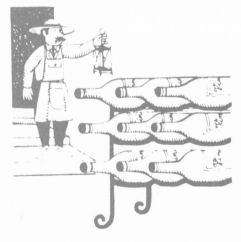

VEAL

(Le Veau)

ROAST VEAL
(Rôti de Veau en Cocotte)

■ Easy
  6 servings
  Expensive
  1¼ hours, 45 minutes in pressure cooker

  3½ lbs. veal roast from leg, loin or shoulder (1 kg, 650 g)
  US 6 TB, UK 3 TB, Meat Stock (see Index) (3 TB)
  3 onions
  bouquet garni
  salt and pepper

● Brown the veal roast on all sides, gradually adding the meat stock to make a good glaze.

● Add the onions, a few tablespoons of water, the *bouquet garni*, and salt and pepper to taste. Cover. Simmer for about 1 hour, turning the roast twice while cooking.

● Slice the roast. Serve the defattened sauce in a sauceboat. The best vegetable for accompaniment is a warm ratatouille.

JELLIED VEAL FILLET
(Noix de Veau en Gelée)

- Easy
  6 servings
  Expensive
  45 minutes

1 large slice of prosciutto
1 large veal "top," approximately 2½ lbs.
  (1 kg, 150 g)
3 carrots, peeled and sliced
3 whole onions, each stuck with 2 cloves
1 garlic clove
bouquet garni
3 veal bones, blanched, or 2 pig's feet,
  chopped into small chunks and
  blanched
US ½ cup, UK ⅓ cup, dry white wine (1
  generous dl)
US ⅔ cup, UK ½ cup, water (2 scant dl)
salt and pepper
tomato slices
hard-boiled eggs
1 recipe Slim Mayonnaise (see Index)
US ¼ cup, UK 3 TB, skim milk (3 TB)
fresh chopped herbs of your choice

- Wrap the slice of prosciutto around the cut of veal and tie. In a nonstick sauté pan, brown the meat on all sides.

- Add the sliced carrots, the onions stuck with cloves and the garlic clove. Add also the *bouquet garni* and the veal bones or pig's feet, the white wine, water, salt and pepper to taste. Cover, bring to a boil, then turn down to a simmer. Cook for 15 minutes per pound, turning the meat twice while cooking.

- Let the meat cool in the cooking juices. Then remove meat.

- Strain the cooking juices, and completely defatten them. The juices are very gelatinous and will gel in the refrigerator.

- Slice the meat and put it on a serving platter. Brush with the semijelled cooking juices. Repeat the operation several times to obtain a good coat of jelly.

- Garnish the platter with slices of tomatoes and hard-boiled eggs. Lighten the mayonnaise with the skim milk and flavor it with fresh herbs. Serve mayonnaise with the jellied veal.

BRAISED VEAL SHANKS
(Jarret de Veau à la Tourate)

■ Easy
6 servings
Moderately priced
2 hours, 30 minutes in pressure cooker

4 large onions, sliced
6 carrots, sliced
1 celery rib, sliced
3 tomatoes, peeled, seeded and chopped
1 garlic clove, mashed
US ¼ cup, UK 3½ TB, Meat Stock (see Index) (3½ TB)
6 veal shanks
US ½ cup, UK ⅓ cup, dry white wine (1 generous dl)
US ½ cup, UK ⅓ cup, water (1 generous dl)
bouquet garni
salt and pepper

• Clean, peel, and pare the vegetables. Put the meat stock in a large nonstick sauté pan and étuvé the onions, carrots, celery, tomatoes and garlic for about 30 minutes.

• Preheat oven to 350°F., 185°C. or 5 Regulo.

• Meanwhile, brown the veal shanks in the preheated oven. Deglaze the roasting pan with the wine and water.

• Transfer vegetables, shanks, *bouquet garni* and deglazing to a braising pot, season, and simmer for approximately 1 hour.

• Remove the *bouquet garni* before serving. Consider green beans as a vegetable.

VEAL STEAKS IN RED-WINE SAUCE
(Grenadins au Vin)

- Easy
  6 servings
  Very expensive
  40 minutes

  12 veal steaks, each ⅓ inch thick (.9 cm)
  no bone, no fat, cut out of the sirloin
  strip
  US ⅓ cup, UK ¼ cup, Meat Stock (see
  Index) (1 scant dl)
  6 white onions, sliced
  3 sun-ripened tomatoes, peeled, seeded,
  and finely chopped
  bouquet garni
  salt and pepper
  US 1 cup, UK 1 scant cup, dry red Côtes
  du Rhône wine (2.5 dl)
  chopped parsley

- Trim the meat very well. Using a meat bat, flatten it to ¼ inch thick. Set aside.

- Put the meat stock in a nonstick skillet. Add the onions and sauté slowly until translucent. Add the tomatoes, the *bouquet garni*, salt and pepper to taste and the red wine. Let cook gently until reduced by two thirds.

- Strain the sauce through a conical strainer. Keep the onions; discard the *bouquet garni*. Keep the sauce warm.

- Do not wash out the skillet. Quickly cook the veal steaks in the same skillet; salt and pepper them.

- Put the onions from the sauce on the bottom of a warm platter. Arrange the steaks over the bed of onions.

- Quickly add the wine sauce to the skillet and scrape well all the caramelized juices. Add parsley and spoon sauce over the meat. The perfect vegetable is a zucchini or green bean dish.

NOTE

You can use also the veal tenderloin and the top of the round for this dish. The cooked veal should be pink with juices running; dry white veal is overcooked. *Do not ever* simmer the meat in the sauce or it will become stringy.

FLAMBÉED VEAL CHOPS
(Côtes de Veau Flambées)

■ Easy
 6 servings
 Expensive
 10 minutes

6 loin veal chops
Meat Stock (see Index)
1 oz. Cognac or whisky
¾ lb. mushrooms (375 g)
salt and pepper
1 egg yolk
lemon juice
chopped parsley

- Trim the fat from the veal chops. Rub a large nonstick frying pan with a piece of veal fat, and brown the chops on both sides. Add a few tablespoons of meat stock.

- Heat the Cognac in a small saucepan, ignite it, and carefully pour it flaming over the veal chops.

- Add the mushrooms, season with salt and pepper, and cover. Cook the veal just until the mushrooms have lost their juices. Remove the chops to a warmed platter.

- Reduce the cooking juices, leaving the mushrooms in the pan. Bind with the egg yolk (see *Liaison*). Add a dash of lemon juice and some parsley. Correct seasoning, and spoon sauce over the chops.

- Any dish of zucchini would be very complementary.

STUFFED VEAL CHOPS
(Côtes de Veau Farcies)

■ Easy
  6 servings
  Expensive
  45 minutes

2 medium-size onions
½ celery rib
6 medium-size sun-ripened tomatoes
US ⅓ cup, UK ¼ cup, Meat Stock (see
     Index) (1 scant dl)
1 sprig of thyme
12 basil leaves, scissored
1 garlic clove, mashed
salt
pinch of cayenne pepper
6 loin veal chops
6 small slices of boiled ham
6 small slices of Gruyère cheese

- Chop onions and celery very finely by hand or food processor. Peel, seed, and chop the ripe tomatoes. Cook the onions and the celery slowly in the meat stock. When the onions are translucent, add the tomatoes and a sprig of thyme. Cook until smooth and tasty.

- Add the basil, garlic, salt to taste and cayenne pepper. Cook for a few more minutes. The sauce should be thicker. Turn the sauce into a baking dish large enough to accommodate all the veal chops.

- Trim the chops of all fat. In a non-stick frying pan, brown the chops, season them, then transfer them to the baking dish.

- Preheat oven to 375°F., 185°C. or 5 Regulo.

- Place a slice of ham, then a slice of cheese on each chop. Bake for approximately 10 minutes, until all is piping hot and the cheese has melted.

VEAL CUTLETS WITH PROVENÇAL HERBS
(Escalopes Grillées aux Herbes de Provence)

■ Easy
6 servings
Expensive
8 minutes, plus 2 hours for marinating

12 veal scallops, each ⅓ inch thick (.9 cm) (portion 5 oz. per person) (150 g each)
US 2 TB, UK 1 TB, lemon juice (1 TB)
1 tsp. olive oil
½ tsp. each of crumbled dried rosemary, thyme, majoram
¼ tsp. crumbled dried orégano
salt and pepper
2 lemons

- Completely defatten the veal and cut off all outside membranes.

- Mix lemon juice and olive oil. Using a pastry brush, coat both sides of each scallop with a very small amount of the mixture.

- Crumble all the herbs together. Sprinkle half of them on the bottom of 1 or 2 large baking dishes. Arrange the slices of veal flat in the dish(es) and sprinkle with the remainder of the herbs. Let marinate for 2 hours.

- Heat a grill to very hot. Sear the scallops for 2 minutes on each side. Salt and pepper them, and serve with lemon wedges.

QUICK VEAL ROLLS
(Paupiettes Rapides)

■ Easy
6 servings
Expensive
30 minutes (no pressure cooker, please, the meat is too delicate)

12 veal scallops, each ¼ inch thick
6 slices of boiled ham
US 3 TB, UK 1½ TB, dry gluten bread crumbs (1½ TB)
US 4 TB, UK 2 TB, chopped parsley (2 TB)
1 garlic clove, mashed
salt and pepper
US 1½ cups, UK 1⅓ cups, Meat Stock (see Index) (3.5 dl)

- Flatten the veal scallops to ⅛ inch. Set aside.

- Prepare a small filling with the ham, chopped, the bread crumbs, parsley and garlic mixed together. Season with salt and pepper. Bind the filling with 2 tablespoons of meat stock.

- Spread a small equal amount of the filling on each scallop. Roll and tie.

- In a nonstick pan, brown the veal *paupiettes*. Add the rest of the stock. Season with salt and pepper. Cover and simmer gently for 20 minutes.

- Present the rolls on a warmed serving platter and spoon the sauce over them. Garnish with cooked Swiss chard, if you like, or spinach.

VEAL PAUPIETTES WITH MUSHROOMS
(Paupiettes de Veau aux Champignons)

- Easy
  6 servings
  Expensive
  45 minutes

6 slices of boiled ham
¾ lb. mushrooms (375 g)
chopped parsley
thyme
¼ bay leaf
salt and pepper
1 raw egg
12 veal scallops, each ¼ inch thick
3 shallots, finely chopped
1 large onion, chopped
small bouquet garni
6 tomatoes, peeled, seeded, and coarsely
   chopped

- Trim the ham of any fat. Chop the ham, mushrooms and parsley very finely. Add crumbled thyme and bay leaf, salt and pepper to taste and the egg. Mix well.

- Spread some of this mixture over each veal scallop. Roll the scallops and tie them.

- In a nonstick skillet, brown the *paupiettes* gently. Add the shallots, onion, *bouquet garni*, tomatoes, and salt and pepper to taste. Cover and simmer for 20 minutes.

- Remove the rolls to a platter. Strain the sauce and spoon it over the *paupiettes*.

- You can make the dish more substantial by adding 6 sliced unpeeled zucchini to the pot while the meat is cooking.

PAUPIETTES, JURA STYLE
(Paupiettes Jurassiennes)

- Easy
  6 servings
  Expensive
  30 minutes (no pressure cooker, please)

  3 slices of ham
  6 slices of Gruyère cheese
  6 veal cutlets, about 4 oz. each (115 g
      each)
  pepper
  US ½ cup, UK ⅓ cup, Meat Stock (see
      Index) (1 generous dl)
  6 onions
  5 tomatoes, cut into halves
  1 bay leaf
  salt

- Place a half slice of ham and a thin slice of Gruyère on each cutlet. Sprinkle each one with pepper, roll, and tie.

- In a nonstick sauté pan, brown the *paupiettes*, adding some meat stock as you go along to build a good glaze.

- Add the onions, tomatoes, bay leaf, and a pinch of salt. Cover. Simmer for 5 to 20 minutes. Serve with braised lettuce.

VEAL ON SKEWERS
(Brochettes de Veau)

- Easy
  6 servings
  Very expensive
  20 minutes

  ½ lb. smoked shoulder of pork (Daisy
      Roll) (250 g)
  2 lbs. veal meat (1 kg)
  sweet paprika
  18 cherry tomatoes
  salt and pepper

- At 1 hour before cooking, remove all fat from the pork. Cut the pork and veal into cubes the approximate size of the tomatoes. Mix them in a shallow baking dish and season them with paprika. Add no salt yet since the salty pork will leach its salt into the veal.

- To cook, alternate pieces of veal and ham with tomatoes on 6 skewers.

- Grill on the barbecue or broil in the broiler for 10 to 12 minutes. Season. Serve with cabbage and caraway.

SAUTÉ OF VEAL AND ARTICHOKES
(Sauté de Veau aux Petits Artichauts)

■ Easy
  6 servings
  Medium expensive
  2 hours

  24 baby artichokes
  1 veal shoulder
  12 baby onions
  ½ lb. mushrooms (250 g)
  US ⅓ cup, UK ¼ cup, Meat Stock (see
      Index) (1 scant dl)
  US ⅔ cup, UK ½ cup, dry white wine (2
      scant dl)
  3 TB tomato paste (1½ TB)
  salt and pepper
  bouquet garni
  6 garlic cloves, crushed

● Clean, pare, and parboil the artichokes. Cut them lengthwise into
  halves. Set aside.

● Cut the veal shoulder into 1-inch
  cubes.

● Brown the onions, then the mushrooms, using some of the meat
  stock. Remove to a plate.

● Do not wash out the skillet, but
  brown the veal in the juices left from
  the vegetables.

● Transfer vegetables and meat to a
  sauteuse pan and add wine, tomato
  paste, salt and pepper to taste, the
  bouquet garni and the crushed
  garlic. Cook for 30 minutes.

● Add the artichokes and finish cooking until the meat is tender when
  tested with a skewer.

VEAL WITH PAPRIKA
(Veau au Paprika)

- Easy
  6 servings
  Very expensive
  20 minutes

  2 lbs. veal top (1 kg)
  salt and pepper
  US 2 TB, UK 1 TB, sweet paprika (1 TB)
  3 small onions
  US ¼ cup, UK 2 TB, Meat Stock (see Index) (2 TB)
  ¼ bay leaf
  lemon juice

- Cut the veal into 1-inch cubes and put them in a baking dish. Season with salt, pepper and paprika, and let stand for 30 minutes.

- Chop the onions finely and cook them with half of the meat stock until translucent.

- Add the meat to the pan with the ¼ bay leaf, finely crumbled. Cook uncovered over low heat, stirring often, until the meat is done. Veal should remain pink, juicy and soft as steak.

- Squeeze some lemon juice over the meat. Serve with sweet bell peppers.

VEAL MARENGO
(Veau Marengo)

- Easy
  6 servings
  Medium expensive
  1½ hours, 50 minutes in pressure cooker

1 veal shoulder, cut into 1-inch cubes
US ¾ cup, UK ⅔ cup, Meat Stock (see Index) (2 dl)
3 onions, chopped
6 tomatoes, coarsely chopped
3 garlic cloves, mashed
US ¾ cup, UK ⅔ cup, dry white wine (2 dl)
¾ lb. mushrooms, quartered (375 g)
US 2 TB, UK 1 TB, tomato paste (1 TB)
bouquet garni
salt and pepper
chopped parsley

- Brown the meat, using a few tablespoons of meat stock to obtain a good glaze.
- Remove the meat to a plate. In the same skillet place the onions, tomatoes and garlic. Simmer until the tomatoes are cooked.
- Add the white wine, the remainder of the meat stock, the mushrooms, tomato paste, the *bouquet garni*, and salt and pepper to taste.
- Finally add the veal, cover, and simmer for a scant hour.
- Remove the *bouquet garni*. Turn veal into a warmed deep serving dish. Sprinkle with chopped parsley.
- Serve with Spinach Gratin (see Index).

NOTE
If you use a pressure cooker, use half the amount of liquid indicated in the recipe; since there is no evaporation in the pressure cooker, there would be too much sauce if you used the whole amount.

VEAL STEW
(Blanquette de Veau)

- Easy
  6 servings
  Medium expensive
  1 hour and 40 minutes, 40 minutes in
      pressure cooker

  3 lbs. veal shoulder (1 kg, 500 g)
  2 carrots, sliced thick
  18 baby onions
  bouquet garni
  salt and pepper
  1 quart Meat Stock (see Index) (1 L)
  2 whole shallots
  ¾ lb. mushrooms (375 g)
  2 egg yolks
  juice of 1 lemon
  chopped parsley

- Remove all fat from the veal and cut it into ½-inch cubes.

- Put the veal, carrots, onions, *bouquet garni*, salt and pepper to taste in a large pot. Add enough stock to cover. Bring to a boil; add the whole shallots. Turn heat down to a simmer for 45 minutes.

- Clean and slice the mushrooms, and add them to the pot. Cook for another 10 minutes.

- When the meat is done, strain the solids into a colander placed over a bowl, and save all the cooking juices.

- Reduce the cooking juices to 1½ cups. Add the egg-yolk *liaison* (see Index), and thicken the sauce over medium heat. Return all the solids to the sauce, discarding only the shallots and the *bouquet garni*. Reheat well together.

- Add lemon juice to your taste and fresh parsley.

VARIETY MEATS

(Les Abats)

BRAISED VEAL HEART
(Cœur de Veau Braisé)

- Easy
  6 servings
  Thrift recipe
  1¼ hours

  3 veal hearts
  US ¼ cup, UK 2 TB, Meat Stock (see Index) (2 TB)
  1½ lbs. carrots (750 g)
  1 lb. onions (500 g)
  US 1⅓ cups, UK 1¼ cups, dry white wine (4 dl)
  US ⅔ cup, UK ½ cup, bouillon (2 scant dl)
  salt and pepper

- Clean the hearts of all membranes and sliver them.

- Brown the meat in a nonstick skillet, gradually adding half of the meat stock.

- Slice the carrots and chop the onions. Transfer meat and vegetables to a sauteuse pan. Add white wine and bouillon. Season with salt and pepper to taste. Cover and simmer for about 1 hour.

VEAL KIDNEYS WITH CURRY
(Rognons de Veau au Curry)

- Easy
  6 servings
  Affordable
  20 minutes

  3 large veal kidneys
  1 lb. mushrooms (500 g)
  US 1 TB, UK ½ TB, curry powder (½ TB)
  salt and pepper
  2 raw egg yolks

- Clean and trim the kidneys. Étuvé the mushrooms in a small braising pot for 7 to 8 minutes. Add curry powder and salt and pepper to taste.

- Add the kidneys. Cover and simmer for 5 minutes. Turn the kidneys over and cook for another 5 minutes.

- Slice each kidney lengthwise into halves. Remove to a warm serving platter.

- Bind the mushrooms and curry sauce with the egg yolks (see *liaison*). Correct the seasoning and spoon over the kidneys.

VEAL KIDNEYS IN BORDEAUX WINE
(Rognons de Veau au Bordeaux)

■ **Requires care**
6 servings
Affordable
1 hour

2 onions, chopped fine
4 shallots, chopped fine
1 garlic clove, mashed
US 1½ cups, UK 1⅓ cups, red Bordeaux
wine (use Pauillac) (3.5 dl)
bouquet garni
salt and pepper
dash of freshly grated nutmeg
3 large veal kidneys
US 1 cup, UK 1 scant cup, Meat Stock
(see Index) (2.5 dl)
1 oz. Cognac (1 TB)
1 tsp. tomato paste
3 raw egg yolks
US 1 TB, UK ½ TB, each of chopped fresh
tarragon, chives, parsley, chervil (½
TB)

• Put onions, shallots, garlic, red wine, the *bouquet garni*, a good pinch each of salt and pepper and the nutmeg in a small pot. Reduce together until only 1 tablespoon or so of liquid is left with the aromatics. Set aside.

• Cut the kidneys into cubes, removing all fat and connective tissues. Set aside.

• Reduce the meat stock by half.

• Heat a nonstick skillet. Add a drop or so of meat stock and sauté the kidneys quickly over very high heat, until they look uniformly gray. It takes only 1 minute.

• At the same time heat the Cognac in a small pan over medium heat. Ignite the Cognac and pour it flaming over the kidneys. Turn the kidneys into a colander placed over a mixing bowl.

• Mix the reduction of wine and aromatics with the tomato paste, egg yolks and hot reduced stock (see *liaison*). Thicken over medum-high heat as you would a custard. *Do not boil!* As soon as sauce is thickened, whisk very heavily to produce a lot of foam and strain into a small saucepan.

• To that final sauce, add the kidneys (discard their juices, please), the herbs and a final seasoning of salt and pepper. Reheat together until hot. *Absolutely no boiling*, please, or the sauce will curdle and the kidneys turn hard as leather.

CALF'S LIVER WITH HAM AND LEMON SAUCE
(Foie de Veau au Jambon et au Citron)

- Easy
  6 servings
  Medium expensive
  15 minutes

  1 tsp. olive oil
  6 slices of calf's liver, each 5½ oz. (165 g each)
  salt and pepper
  6 slices of prosciutto, defattened
  US ⅓ cup, UK ¼ cup, Meat Stock (see Index) (2 scant dl)
  lemon juice
  parsley

- Brush a nonstick skillet with the teaspoon of olive oil.

- Preheat the pan very well. Sear the slices of liver on both sides. Season them with only a bit of salt and a lot of pepper. Remove to a warmed serving platter.

- Top each slice of liver with a slice of prosciutto.

- Immediately pour the meat stock into the pan and add lemon juice to taste. Add salt, pepper and parsley, and spoon the sauce over the liver.

STEAMED CALF'S LIVER
(Foie de Veau à la Vapeur)

- Requires care
  6 servings
  Medium expensive
  1½ hours

  1 small calf's liver
  soy sauce of your choice
  US ⅔ cup, UK ½ cup, Meat Stock (see Index) (2 scant dl)
  1 lb. onions (500 g)
  1 tsp. dry mustard
  salt and pepper
  6 scallions, green tops only, cut into ⅛-inch-wide rings

- Keep the liver whole. Cut an incision approximately 1 inch long in the membrane. Passing your finger under it to loosen it, remove it from the whole surface of the liver.

- Brush a small stainless-steel steaming basket well with soy sauce. Set the liver in the basket. Brush the top of the liver with more soy sauce. Refrigerate for 1 hour.

- Cut the onions into very thin slices. With the help of half of the meat stock, cook them in a nonstick skillet until translucent.

- Transfer the onions to a deep braising pot. Add the remainder of the meat stock into which you will have mixed the mustard, a dash of salt and some pepper.

- Put the pot over low heat; arrange the steaming basket with the liver over the bed of onions. Cover and cook for 15 to 20 minutes. The liver should be pink at the center.

- Slice the liver; arrange the slices on a warmed platter. Spoon the onion mixture over. Top with scallions.

BRAISED BEEF TONGUE
(Langue Braisée)

■ **Fairly easy**
  6 servings
  Affordable
  2½ hours, 1½ hours in pressure cooker

  1 beef tongue, 4½ lbs. (2.25 kg)
  1 lb. carrots, sliced (500 g)
  3 onions, sliced
  3 garlic cloves, mashed
  bouquet garni
  salt and pepper
  ½ bottle dry white wine
  US 1 cup, UK 1 scant cup, blanching liq-
    uid (2.5 dl)
  US ⅓ cup, UK ¼ cup, Meat Stock (see
    Index) (1 scant dl)

• Blanch the tongue in boiling water for 15 minutes. Save the blanching liquid.

• In a large braising pot, put the tongue, carrots, onions, garlic, the *bouquet garni*, and salt and pepper to taste. Add also the white wine, the measured amount of blanching liquid and the meat stock. Cover the pot and simmer for 2 hours, *45 minutes in the pressure cooker*. Remove the tongue from the liquid and drain it well. Remove the skin, and slice the meat.

• Put the tongue slices on a serving platter; surround the meat with the vegetables. Keep warm.

• Correct the seasoning of the gravy and serve in a sauceboat.

BEEF TONGUE WITH SAUERKRAUT
(Langue de Bœuf à la Choucroute)

■ **Easy**
  6 servings
  Affordable
  2½ hours

  1 beef tongue, 4½ lbs. (2.25 kg)
  court-bouillon
  3 lbs. sauerkraut (1.5 kg)
  ⅔ bottle of dry white wine
  1 TB cuminseed
  salt
  coarsely cracked pepper

• Parboil the tongue in a well-seasoned *court-bouillon* for 30 minutes.

• Wash the sauerkraut. Pile it into a braising pot. Add wine and seasonings. Push the tongue into the sauerkraut. Cover the pot and simmer for 2 hours.

• To serve, remove the skin of the tongue and cut meat into ⅓-inch slices. Serve with the sauerkraut.

VEAL TONGUES WITH RAW TOMATO SAUCE
(Langues de Veau à la Tomate Fraîche)

- Easy
  6 servings
  Inexpensive
  1½ hours, plus 2 hours for soaking

  6 small veal tongues
  2 onions, sliced
  3 carrots, sliced
  US 1 cup, UK 1 scant cup, wine vinegar
     (2.5 dl)
  US 1 TB, UK ½ TB, dried tarragon (½ TB)
  bouquet garni
  US 1 TB, UK ½ TB, coriander seeds (½
     TB)
  3 sun-ripened tomatoes
  1 small red onion, chopped fine
  1 TB Madagascar green peppercorns, pre-
     served in water
  salt and pepper
  chopped fresh parsley

- Soak the tongues in cold water for 2 hours to discard dirt and blood.

- With onions, carrots, two thirds of the vinegar, the tarragon, *bouquet garni* and coriander seeds added to 1½ quarts (1.5 L) water, prepare a *court-bouillon*. Simmer it for 20 minutes before cooking the tongues.

- Add the tongues to the *court-bouillon*, bring to a boil, turn down to a simmer, and cook for approximately 1 hour, or until tongues are tender when tested with a skewer.

- Prepare the dressing while the tongues finish cooking. Peel, seed, and purée the raw tomatoes. Do not cook them. Mix them with the chopped red onion and the green peppercorns. Let stand.

- Mix the remaining vinegar with the same amount of the *court-bouillon* and reduce to 2 tablespoons. Add to the raw tomato sauce. Correct the seasoning and add a large amount of chopped parsley.

- Peel the tongues, cut them into ½-inch-thick slices, and spoon the dressing over them.

- As a vegetable consider small green beans cooked *al dente*; the raw tomato sauce will complement them well.

SWEETBREADS WITH VEGETABLES
(Ris de Veau aux Légumes)

■ Easy
6 servings
Expensive
1 hour, plus 2 hours for soaking

1¾ lbs. sweetbreads (875 g)
¾ lb. carrots (375 g)
¼ lb. turnips (125 g)
¾ lb. mushrooms (375 g)
¼ lb. celery (125 g)
salt and pepper
1 lemon
US 1 cup, UK 1 scant cup, Meat Stock
   (see Index) (2.5 dl)
chopped parsley

- Soak the sweetbreads in cold water for several hours. Blanch them; press them between 2 plates to extract the blood and flatten them to uniform thickness. Set aside.

- Preheat oven to 325°F., 165°C. or 4 Regulo.

- Cut the vegetables into ¼-inch julienne. Put the vegetables in a braising pot. Arrange the sweetbreads on top of the vegetables, season them, and squeeze a dash of lemon juice over them. Add just enough stock to cover the sweetbreads. Top with a parchment paper and the pot lid. Bake in the preheated oven for 45 minutes.

- Remove the sweetbreads to a platter. Drain the vegetables well. Reduce the cooking juices to a glaze. Mix glaze and vegetables again. Correct seasoning and spoon sauce over the sweetbreads. Sprinkle with chopped parsley.

SWEETBREADS EN PAPILLOTE
(Ris de Veau en Papillote)

■ Easy
6 servings
Medium expensive
45 minutes, plus 2 to 3 hours for soaking

2 lbs. sweetbreads (1 kg)
paprika
salt and pepper
6 lemon wedges

- Soak the sweetbreads in cold water for 2 to 3 hours. Change the water several times. Blanch the sweetbreads in salted water; press them between 2 plates to flatten them to uniform thickness.

- Cut the sweetbreads into large cubes. Toss these with paprika and salt and pepper. Divide into 6 portions. Wrap each portion tightly in a sheet of aluminum foil.

- Preheat oven to 400°F., 200°C. or 6 Regulo.

- Bake the sweetbread packages in the oven for 30 minutes. Serve with 1 lemon wedge and a good dish of leeks.

CHICKEN LIVERS IN RED-WINE SAUCE
(Foie de Volailles au Vin Rouge)

- Requires care
  6 servings
  Medium expensive
  30 minutes

  US ½ cup, UK ⅓ cup, Meat Stock (see Index) (1 generous dl)
  salt and pepper
  US ⅔ cup, UK ½ cup, dry red wine (2 scant dl)
  US 1 TB, UK ½ TB, tomato paste (½ TB)
  3 garlic cloves, mashed
  chopped parsley
  1 tsp. olive oil
  18 light-colored chicken livers
  US 2 TB, UK 1 TB, red-wine vinegar (1 TB)

- Put meat stock, a dash each of salt and pepper, the red wine, tomato paste and mashed garlic in a small pot, and cook until reduced by two thirds.

- Meanwhile, chop the parsley. Brush the olive oil on the surface of a non-stick skillet or electric frying pan.

- Remove the outside membrane of the livers, if any is visible, and all traces of the gall bladder. Salt and pepper the livers, and dip each of them into the chopped parsley.

- Preheat the skillet to 400°F., 200°C. or 6 Regulo. Add the livers, sear well on one side, then turn over and sear on the second side. Turn the heat down for 2 to 3 minutes, and continue cooking until livers are medium rare. Remove to a plate.

- Add the prepared stock and wine reduction and the vinegar to the skillet, and reduce again over high heat. Correct the seasoning with salt and pepper, and spoon sauce over the livers.

- For a vegetable, used braised endives or lettuce.

POULTRY AND GAME

(La Volaille et le Gibier)

POACHED CHICKENS FOR DIETERS
(Poulardes Pochées pour Régime Maigre)

■ Easy
  6 servings
  Affordable
  2 hours

2 chickens, 3½ lbs. each (1.75 kg each)
1 veal bone, meaty and gelatinous
3 onions, sliced
3 carrots, sliced
large bouquet garni
1 sprig of celery leaves
½ tsp. quatre-épices (see Glossary)
2 bouillon cubes
salt and pepper
4 raw egg yolks
juice of ½ lemon
chopped parsley
1 TB prepared Dijon mustard, or more or
  less

BASIC BROTH

- Remove the wingtips of the chickens. Put them in a pot with the necks, the veal bone and 3 quarts water (3 L). Bring to a boil, and skim. Add all the vegetables and cook for 30 minutes. Add the *quatre-épices* and the bouillon cubes.

TO COOK THE CHICKENS

- Truss the 2 chickens after seasoning them in the cavities. Add them to the boiling broth. Bring broth back to a boil and simmer for 1 hour. Turn off the heat. Put the chicken pot to one side.

- Put 2 cups (.5 L) of the cooking broth in a large flat-bottomed sauteuse. Quickly reduce it by half. Using the method described for *liaison* (see Index), bind the stock with egg yolks mixed with the lemon juice, without boiling. Add chopped parsley and the mustard.

- Correct the seasoning, carve the chicken, and serve with the vegetable of your choice. Zucchini, green beans, carrots, turnips, alone or in combination, are excellent.

POACHED CHICKEN WITH SHELLFISH AND CUCUMBERS
(Poularde Pochée aux Fruits de Mer)

- Difficult
  6 servings
  Expensive
  2 hours

1 recipe for Basic Broth (see preceding recipe)
2 chickens, 3½ lbs. each (1.75 kg each)
12 shrimps in shells
24 mussels, scrubbed
1 garlic clove
1 bunch of parsley stems, chopped
US ⅓ cup, UK ¼ cup, dry white wine (1 scant dl)
salt and pepper
4 raw egg yolks
juice of ½ lemon
½ lb. bay scallops (250 g)
US ⅓ cup, UK 3 TB, snipped fresh dill (3 TB)
3 cucumbers, sliced and seeded

- Prepare the basic broth and cook the chicken as described in the preceding recipe.

- Put a tablespoon or so of chicken cooking broth in a skillet. Add the shrimps and sauté over high heat until the shells turn red. Remove shrimps to a plate.

- In the same skillet put the scrubbed mussels, the garlic, chopped parsley stems, wine, and a pinch each of salt and pepper. Cover and steam for 3 to 4 minutes until mussels are opened.

- Shell shrimps and mussels. Put both to wait in a bowl. Put shrimp shells and mussel juices in a saucepan. Add the same amount of chicken broth and reduce by half. Strain.

- Using the method described for *liaison* (see Index), bind the reduced broth with egg yolks mixed with the lemon juice. Add the scallops.

- Heat both the *liaison* and the scallops without boiling. Add shrimps, mussels and snipped dill. Keep warm.

- Carve the chicken into serving pieces and spoon the shellfish stew over the portions.

- As a vegetable, sauté the cucumbers in a nonstick skillet for a few minutes and serve with the chicken and shellfish.

CHICKEN WITH SEA SALT
(Poularde au Sel)

- Easy
  6 servings
  Moderately priced
  1 hour and 40 minutes

  1 chicken, 3½ lbs. (1.75 kg)
  12 lbs. coarse salt (5.5 kg)

- Truss the chicken as you would to oven-roast it.

- Use only coarse salt, not fine kitchen salt. Line a large pot with aluminum foil and fill it with 1½ inches of salt. Place the chicken breast side down in the salt. Cover with more salt until the bird is covered with another 1½ inches of salt; it must be completely buried in the salt.

- Preheat oven to 400°F., 200°C. or 6 Regulo.

- Bake the chicken, uncovered, for 1½ hours.

- Turn the pot upside down on several layers of foil and remove the chicken from the block of salt. You may have to break the salt with a mallet. The chicken will be golden.

SPRINGTIME CHICKEN
(Poulet Printanier)

- Easy
  6 servings
  Inexpensive
  1½ hours, 40 minutes in pressure cooker

  2 small chickens
  salt and pepper
  2 small lettuce hearts
  2½ lbs. carrots, sliced (1.25 kg)
  3 lbs. green beans, cut into small slices
  **   (1.5 kg)**
  6 onions
  bouquet garni
  2 garlic cloves, mashed
  water

- Preheat oven to 375°F., 185°C. or 5 Regulo.

- Clean the chickens, salt and pepper the cavities, and truss them. Brown the chickens in the oven for 20 minutes.

- In a braising pot put chickens, lettuce hearts, carrots, green beans, onions, the *bouquet garni* and garlic. Season with salt and add barely enough water to cover the vegetables. Bring to a boil, lower the heat, and simmer for 45 minutes.

- Carve the chickens and serve them on a warmed platter surrounded by the vegetable garnish.

NOTE
In the pressure cooker do not use more than 1½ cups of water (.25 generous L) since there will be no evaporation.

CHICKEN WITH HOT SAUCE
(Poulet à la Diable)

■ Easy
6 servings
Inexpensive
40 minutes

3 chickens, 3 lbs. each (1.5 kg each)
salt and pepper
Dijon mustard
gluten bread crumbs
4 shallots, finely chopped
US 1½ cups, UK 1⅓ cups, dry white wine
    (generous 3.5 dl)
US 3 cups, UK 3 scant cups, hot ketchup
    (.75 L)

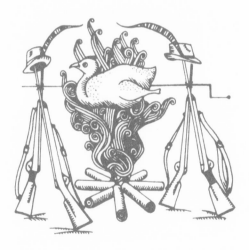

- Cut the chickens into halves and flatten each half. Season with salt and pepper.

- Preheat oven to 400°F., 200°C. or 5 to 6 Regulo.

- Place the chickens in a roasting pan and cook for 10 minutes. Brush with mustard, sprinkle with bread crumbs, and continue baking for another 15 minutes. Turn off the heat and leave the chickens in the oven for 5 minutes.

- While the chickens bake, mix shallots and wine and reduce by half. Add the ketchup, and salt and pepper to taste. As soon as the sauce comes to a boil, turn off the heat and pour into a sauceboat. Serve with the Vegetable Medley (see Index).

CHICKEN PACKETS
(Poulet Paquets)

■ Easy
6 servings
Medium expensive
50 minutes

2 chickens, 3 lbs. each (1.5 kg each)
pepper
Provençal herbs
12 slices of prosciutto, trimmed of all fat
1 tsp. olive oil

● Preheat oven to 400°F., 200°C. or 6 to 7 Regulo.

● Cut the chickens into serving pieces. Pepper each piece of chicken. Sprinkle it well with dried herbs, and wrap each piece in a slice of prosciutto to make little packets. Tie each packet with a kitchen string.

● Brush a baking dish with 1 teaspoon olive oil. Arrange the packets in the dish and bake for 30 minutes, turning once while baking.

● Transfer the chicken to a warm serving platter. Add ½ cup or so of warm water to the roasting pan to deglaze it. Scrape well. Strain the gravy into a sauceboat.

● As a garnish, consider slices of fresh pineapple broiled while you finish the chicken gravy.

BASQUE-STYLE CHICKEN
(Poulet à la Basquaise)

- Easy
  6 servings
  Inexpensive
  1 hour

  2 chickens, 3½ lbs. each (1.75 kg each)
  2 green peppers
  2 red peppers
  5 tomatoes
  4 large onions
  US 1½ cups, UK 1⅓ cups, dry white wine
  (3.5 generous dl)
  bouquet garni
  salt and pepper

- Cut each chicken into 4 or 5 serving pieces. Preheat the broiler, and sear the chicken pieces on both sides for 5 minutes.

- Meanwhile, place the peppers under the broiler and char them on all sides. Peel and seed them and cut into thin strips. Peel and seed the tomatoes. Peel and slice the onions.

- Gently cook the onions without letting them take on any color. Add the peppers and the tomatoes to the pot. Also add the wine and *bouquet garni* and cook the mixture for 15 minutes.

- Transfer the sauce and the chicken to a sauteuse pan. Correct the seasoning with salt and pepper. Simmer for about 20 minutes, or until the chicken is done.

- The nicest vegetable would be artichokes cooked in a bit of white wine.

CHICKEN WITH TARRAGON
(Poulet à l'Estragon)

- Easy
  6 servings
  Inexpensive
  40 to 45 minutes

  2 chickens, 3½ lbs. each (1.75 kg each)
  6 shallots
  2 carrots
  US ⅓ cup, UK ¼ cup, Meat Stock (see Index) (1 scant dl)
  1 oz. Cognac (1 TB)
  US ⅔ cup, UK ½ cup, dry white wine (2 scant dl)
  3 sprigs of fresh tarragon
  salt and pepper
  US 1 TB, UK ½ TB, chopped chervil (½ TB)
  US 2 TB, UK 1 TB, chopped tarragon (½ TB)

- Preheat oven to 400°F., 200°C. or 6 to 7 Regulo.

- Cut the chicken into pieces and brown them in the preheated oven for 10 minutes. Set aside.

- Slice the shallots and carrots and cook them in the meat stock for a few minutes. Add the chicken pieces to the pot. Heat the Cognac in a small pan, ignite it, and carefully pour it flaming over the chicken. Add the wine, tarragon sprigs, salt and pepper to taste. Simmer for 20 to 30 minutes.

- Sprinkle with the chopped chervil and tarragon. Serve with broiled tomatoes (see Index).

NOTE

This recipe may also be prepared with a whole chicken. Slip plenty of tarragon leaves under the skin and fill with more tarragon sprigs. Roast at 375°F., 185°C. or 5 Regulo for 1 good hour.

CHICKEN MARENGO
(Poulet Marengo)

- Easy
  6 servings
  Inexpensive
  1¼ hours

  2 chickens, 3 lbs. each (1.5 kg each)
  US ⅓ cup, UK ¼ cup, Meat Stock (see
      Index) (1 scant dl)
  4 very ripe tomatoes, peeled and seeded
  2 garlic cloves
  ¾ lb. mushrooms (375 g)
  US 1 cup, UK 1 scant cup, dry white wine
      (.25 L)
  US 2 TB, UK 1 TB, tomato paste (1 TB)
  salt and pepper
  chopped parsley

- Cut each chicken into 5 serving pieces. In a nonstick skillet, brown and cook the chicken parts, using a few tablespoons of meat stock to obtain a good glaze. Remove to a plate and prepare the sauce.

- Purée the tomatoes and garlic in a blender. Add this mixture to the pan in which the chicken was browned. Slice the mushrooms and add them to the pan with the wine and tomato paste. Correct the seasoning, cover, and simmer until the sauce reaches the consistency of light cream.

- Add the chicken to the sauce. Finish cooking together for another 20 minutes. Sprinkle with chopped parsley. Serve with either carrots or Swiss chard.

CHICKEN IN A HURRY
(Poulet Dernière Minute)

- Easy
  6 servings
  Inexpensive
  30 minutes

  2 chickens, 3½ lbs. each (1.75 kg each)
  salt and pepper
  2 garlic cloves, finely chopped
  chopped parsley

- Cut the chickens into pieces. Season with salt and pepper.

- Preheat oven to 500°F., 250°C. or 8 Regulo.

- Roast the chicken pieces for 10 to 12 minutes. Turn over and roast for another 10 to 12 minutes. Serve the chicken sprinkled with the chopped garlic and parsley.

- There will not be any gravy. If the chicken appears too "rare" for your taste, let it stand in the turned-off oven for 10 more minutes while you prepare some zucchini to accompany the dish.

CHICKEN CUTLETS FOR DIETERS
(Suprêmes de Volailles pour Régime Maigre)

■ Easy
  6 servings
  Medium expensive
  10 minutes, plus 2 hours or more for mar-
  inating

  6 chicken cutlets
  1 tsp. olive oil
  soy sauce of your choice
  US ½ cup, UK ⅓ cup, Meat Stock (see
      Index) (1 generous dl)
  pinch of ground ginger
  US ¼ cup, UK 3 TB, scallion rings (3 TB)
  pepper from the mill

● Marinate the cutlets in a mixture of
  the oil plus US ¼ cup, UK 2 tablespoons or so of soy sauce (2 TB),
  brushed on both sides of the cutlets.
  Let stand for at least 2 hours.

● Heat well a nonstick electric skillet
  to 325°F., 165°C. or 4 Regulo. Cook
  the cutlets in the pan until they are
  just resistant to the touch of the finger. Remove to a plate.

● Add meat stock and ginger to the
  skillet. Deglaze well and reduce the
  deglazing only a little so the gravy
  is not too salty. Spoon it over the
  chicken cutlets and sprinkle them
  with scallion rings and coarsely
  cracked pepper of your choice,
  black or white.

WITH THE SAME METHOD
Chicken Cutlets Camargue: Marinate the
cutlets in the juice of 1 lemon mixed
with 1 teaspoon of olive oil. Sprinkle
with rosemary and thyme. Cook as in
the basic recipe, and deglaze with the
same amount of meat stock. Add ½
garlic clove, finely mashed, and a few
pinches of freshly chopped parsley.

Chicken Cutlets Josefa: Marinate the cutlets in the juice of 1 lemon mixed with
1 teaspoon of olive oil. Sprinkle with
tarragon. Cook as in the basic recipe,
and deglaze the pan with a dash of
vinegar, the same amount of meat
stock and 1 teaspoon tomato paste.
Correct the seasoning carefully. Heat
a little Armagnac in a small pan and
pour it flaming into the gravy. Mix
well and spoon over the chicken cutlets.

CORNISH HENS WITH ONIONS
(Coquelets aux Oignons)

■ Easy
6 servings
Inexpensive
1¼ hours

3 Cornish hens or squab chickens
US ½ cup, UK ⅓ cup, Meat Stock (see
    Index) (1 generous dl)
2½ lbs. onions (1.25 kg)
salt and pepper
thyme, bay leaf

- Cut the hens into halves. Brown them in a nonstick pan with a few tablespoons of meat stock. Set aside when browned.

- Slice the onions thinly and cook them in the same pan over moderate heat for about 20 minutes. Stir often.

- When the onions begin to color lightly, return the hens to the pan. Add salt, pepper, thyme and bay leaf to taste, and the remainder of the meat stock. Cover and finish cooking the hens, for 20 to 25 minutes.

ROAST DUCK WITH TURNIPS
(Canard Rôti aux Navets)

■ Easy
6 servings
Expensive
3 hours

2 ducklings, 3½ to 4 lbs. each (1.75 to 2
    kg each)
salt and pepper
2 chicken livers
½ lb. mushrooms, diced (250 g)
3½ lbs. turnips, diced (1.75 kg)

- Preheat oven to 325°F., 165°C. or 4 Regulo.

- Remove the duck livers and set aside. Salt and pepper the cavity of the ducks.

- Dice the chicken and duck livers. Brown the mushrooms in a nonstick pan, then brown the livers. Mix livers and mushrooms. Stuff the mixture into the ducks. Truss the birds and roast them for 2½ hours.

- Meanwhile prepare the turnips. Blanch them in boiling salted water for 5 to 6 minutes.

- When the ducks are cooked, carve them and remove the stuffing from the cavities. Remove carved pieces to a serving platter and garnish with the stuffing.

- Using a baster, separate the lean gravy from the fat. Toss the turnips in one third of the gravy. Serve the remainder of the gravy in a sauceboat. Arrange the turnips around the duck portions.

DUCK WITH CHERRIES
(Canard aux Cerises)

- A bit difficult
  6 servings
  Medium expensive
  3 hours

  salt and pepper
  2 ducklings, 3½ to 4 lbs. each (1.75 to 2 kg each)
  1 lb. cherries (500 g)
  US 1⅓ cups, UK 1¼ cups, Ruby Port (3.5 dl)
  ground cinnamon
  4 whole cloves
  2 oranges

- Preheat oven to 325°F., 165°C. or 4 Regulo.

- Salt and pepper the cavity of the ducks. Roast them for 2½ hours.

- Meanwhile, pit the cherries and put them in a small pan.

- To prepare the sauce, combine the Port, cinnamon to taste, cloves, and the grated rinds of the oranges in a small saucepan. Reduce over low heat by one third. Add the juice of the oranges and let steep for 10 minutes. Strain the mixture over the cherries. Reheat until the cherries come floating to the top of the sauce. Remove cherries to a plate.

- Carve the ducks and arrange them on a serving platter. Garnish with the cherries.

- Meanwhile, using a baster, separate the lean gravy from the fat. Add the gravy to the Port sauce and reduce over high heat until the mixture glazes the back of a spoon lightly. Correct the seasoning and spoon over the ducks.

NOTE
You may vary this dish and serve with quartered peeled apples, poached in cider, and with cranberry compote.

BOILED TURKEY ROAST
(Dinde Roulée au Pot)

■ Easy
6 servings
Affordable
1 hour and 35 minutes

2 leeks
1 celery rib
4 whole cloves
2 onions
6 carrots
salt and pepper
2 turnips
bouquet garni
1 turkey roast, 3½ lbs. (1.75 kg)
3½ lbs. Brussels sprouts (1.75 kg)

• Tie leeks and celery rib together. Stick the cloves into the onions. Put the carrots in 2 quarts (2 L) cold water, and bring to a boil. Add salt and pepper to taste and cook for 10 minutes. Add leeks, celery, onions, turnips and the *bouquet garni*. Simmer over moderate heat.

• When the vegetables are almost done, remove them from the water and set them aside.

• Divide the vegetable broth into halves. In the first half poach the turkey, allowing 20 minutes per pound.

• Blanch the Brussels sprouts in plain water for 5 minutes. Drain.

• Bring the second half of the vegetable broth to a boil and add the drained Brussels sprouts. Bring back to a boil and cook until sprouts are tender.

• Just before the turkey has finished cooking, return all the vegetables to the cooking broth to reheat. Slice the roast and garnish the platter with the vegetables.

• If the broth is still quite abundant, do not hesitate to serve it in small soup bowls. Also serve a jar of good mustard with this dinner.

BRAISED TURKEY ROAST
(Dinde Roulée Braisée)

- Easy
  6 servings
  Affordable
  1½ hours, 55 minutes in pressure cooker

  2 red peppers
  6 tomatoes
  1 small turkey roast, 3½ lbs. (1.75 kg)
  Meat Stock (see Index)
  12 baby onions
  salt and pepper
  bouquet garni
  1 sprig of fresh rosemary
  US ½ cup, UK ⅓ cup, water (1 generous
  dl)

- Peel the peppers, remove the seeds, and cut peppers into thin strips. Cut the tomatoes horizontally into halves and seed them.

- In an oval braising pot, brown the turkey roast in a few tablespoons of meat stock.

- Remove the roast and place the onions and the peppers in the pot. Sauté them for a few minutes. Add the tomatoes, and toss until they are heated through.

- Put the roast in the center of the pot. Add salt and pepper to taste, the *bouquet garni,* rosemary sprig and water. Cover and simmer for 1½ hours, turning the roast once during the cooking. The roast is done when a skewer inserted at its center comes out clean.

QUAIL WITH GRAPES
(Cailles aux Raisins)

■ Easy
  6 servings
  Expensive
  1 hour

  12 quails
  1 carrot, sliced
  1 onion, sliced
  1 oz. Armagnac or Cognac (1 TB)
  salt and pepper
  1 large bunch of seedless white grapes
  US 1⅓ cups, UK 1¼ cups, Meat Stock
  (see Index) (3 to 4 dl)
  6 brine-packed grape leaves

● Preheat oven to 400°F., 200°C. or 6 Regulo.

● Clean and truss the quails. Put carrot, onion, the chosen spirit, and salt and pepper to taste in a large pot; toss. Add the quails, leaving the pot uncovered, and brown in the oven for 10 minutes.

● Meanwhile, squeeze enough grapes to obtain about 1 deciliter or US ½ cup, UK ⅓ cup, juice. Add the juice to the quail pot with the meat stock. Cover and simmer on top of the stove for 15 minutes if you like the quails medium rare, or for 40 to 45 minutes if you like them well done.

● Meanwhile, remove the grape leaves from their brine and blanch them for 1 minute. Remove the cooked quails from the pot and set two of them on each leaf on a large serving platter.

● Put 48 grapes in a large sauteuse pan. Strain the cooking juices of the quails over the grapes and reduce quickly over high heat. The grapes will poach as the sauce reduces. Spoon sauce and grapes over the quails.

THE HUNTER'S RABBIT
(Lapin Chasseur)

- Easy
  6 servings
  Affordable
  1 hour

2 boxes (2¼ lbs. each, or 1 kg each) frozen rabbit parts, or 2 young rabbits
2 onions, finely chopped
3 garlic cloves, finely chopped
4 shallots, finely chopped
Meat Stock (see Index)
US 1½ cups, UK 1¼ cups, dry white wine (generous 3.5 dl)
US 1½ cups, UK 1¼ cups, water (generous 3.5 dl)
bouquet garni
salt and pepper
US 1 TB, UK ½ TB, tomato paste (½ TB)
nutmeg
3½ lbs. mushrooms (1.75 kg)
chopped parsley

- If rabbit is frozen, defrost it.
- If you are using a whole rabbit, cut it into pieces. In a nonstick pan, brown the onions, garlic and shallots in a bit of meat stock. Remove to a plate.
- In the same pot, brown the pieces of rabbit. Add the white wine, an equal amount of water, the *bouquet garni*, salt and pepper to taste, the tomato paste and some freshly grated nutmeg. Bring to a boil, turn down to a simmer, and cover.
- Clean and quarter the mushrooms. Add them to the pot after 30 minutes of cooking. Leave the pot cover off and simmer for another 15 minutes.
- Serve the rabbit in the pot, and sprinkle with chopped parsley.

JELLIED RABBIT
(Lapin en Gelée)

■ **A bit difficult**
6 servings
Medium expensive
2 hours, plus 5 hours for marinating

2 boxes (2¼ lbs. each) frozen rabbit parts
    (1 kg each), or 2 small rabbits
1 pig's foot
6 white onions
1 bunch of parsley
thyme
6 slices of prosciutto, trimmed
salt and pepper
⅔ bottle of dry white wine

- If rabbit is frozen defrost it. Either way, bone the rabbit completely.

- Boil the pig's foot in 2 cups water (.5 L) until tender. Cool it, bone it, and chop it finely. Reserve the cooking water.

- Chop the onions and the parsley finely. Mix with a bit of thyme.

- Line the bottom of an earthenware terrine dish with 3 slices of prosciutto. Place a layer of rabbit meat and pig's foot meat on top of the ham; season with salt and pepper, and half of the chopped onions and herbs. Continue the process; top with the rest of the prosciutto. Add the wine and the broth from cooking the pig's foot. Let the mixture marinate in the refrigerator for at least 5 hours.

- Preheat oven to 350°F., 170°C. or 4 to 5 Regulo.

- Cover the terrine and put it to bake. Check it after 30 minutes. The cooking juices should not overflow. Cook for 1½ hours, adding a bit more wine if necessary.

- When the terrine has finished cooking, remove the cover and place a weight on the meat. Cool completely and refrigerate overnight. Serve the following day with artichokes cooked in white wine.

RABBIT PACKAGES
(Lapin Paquets)

- Easy
  6 servings
  Medium expensive
  1¼ hours

  **2 boxes (2¼ lbs. each) frozen rabbit parts
  (1 kg each), or 2 small rabbits**
  salt and pepper
  marjoram
  rosemary
  thyme
  12 thin slices of prosciutto
  5 onions
  5 tomatoes

- If rabbit is frozen, defrost it.
- Try to cut the rabbit meat into uniform shapes. Season each piece with salt, pepper, marjoram, rosemary and thyme. Wrap each piece in a slice of prosciutto and tie.
- Finely chop the onions and quarter the tomatoes. Place them in a baking dish and add the rabbit packages.
- Preheat oven to 375°F., 185°C. or 5 Regulo.
- Bake the packages for 35 to 45 minutes, basting with the cooking juices at regular intervals. Serve with celery.

RABBIT WITH PRUNES
(Lapin aux Pruneaux)

- Easy
  6 servings
  Medium expensive
  1 hour

  **2 boxes (2¼ lbs. each) frozen rabbit parts
  (1 kg each), or 2 small rabbits, cut up**
  24 large pitted soft prunes
  **US ⅔ cup, UK ½ cup, dry Sercial Madeira
  (2 scant dl)**
  ¼ lb. ham, in 1 slab (225 g)
  Meat Stock (see Index)
  salt and pepper

- If the rabbit is frozen, defrost it.
- Soak the prunes in the Madeira. Cut the ham into cubes.
- Brown the rabbit pieces in a few tablespoons of meat stock. Add the ham, Madeira and a shot glass of water. Season with salt and pepper.
- Put the prunes to steam on top of the rabbit. Cover the pot and simmer for 45 minutes.
- Serve with unsweetened applesauce or stewed apples.

VEGETABLES

(Les Légumes)

Do not consider yourself limited to the few vegetable preparations described in this chapter. Any of the low-calorie vegetables can be prepared by blanching, or by braising or stir-frying with a little meat or fish stock; then they can be dressed with any of the compound butters. In the chapter of butters and sauces you will note that some butters are recommended for particular vegetables, and even a few sauces are suggested. Try any of these, also experiment with other combinations to give your meals greater variety.

ARTICHOKES IN WHITE WINE
(Artichauts au Vin Blanc)

- Easy
  6 servings
  Affordable
  1¼ hours, 30 minutes in pressure cooker

  36 baby artichokes
  2 carrots, diced
  2 onions, diced
  US 6 TB, UK 3 TB, Meat Stock (see Index)
     (3 TB)
  salt and pepper
  US 3 cups, UK scant 3 cups, white wine
     (.75 L)
  US 3 cups, UK scant 3 cups, bouillon
     (.75 L)
  4 garlic cloves

- Cut the stem end and tips of the leaves of each artichoke and remove as many outer leaves as needed to obtain a 1-inch-wide corklike heart.
- Sauté the carrots and onions in the meat stock. Add the artichokes and salt and pepper to taste. Cook over low heat until the onions start browning.
- Add the white wine, increase the heat, and let the liquid reduce by half.
- Add bouillon and garlic. Cover and simmer for 35 to 40 minutes. The artichokes must be very tender and discolored. Serve in a vegetable dish.

NOTE
If you are serving the artichokes with a fish, you may replace the meat stock by fish stock.

PROVENÇAL-STYLE GREEN BEANS
(Haricots Verts à la Provençale)

■ Easy
  6 servings
  Medium expensive
  45 minutes

  3½ lbs. green beans (1.75 kg)
  3 medium-size onions, sliced
  US ⅓ cup, UK ¼ cup, Meat Stock (see
      Index) (1 scant dl)
  7 tomatoes, peeled, seeded, and coarsely
      chopped
  2 garlic cloves, chopped
  salt and pepper
  chopped parsley

- Wash the beans. Blanch them uncovered in boiling salted water until crisp tender.
- Cook the onions in the meat stock until translucent. Add the tomatoes and garlic, and season with salt and pepper. Cover and simmer.
- Drain the beans well and add to the tomato sauce. Continue cooking for an additional 5 to 6 minutes.
- Turn into a warmed serving dish and sprinkle with chopped parsley.

BRAISED CABBAGE WITH CARAWAY
(Chou Braisé au Karvi)

■ Easy
  6 servings
  Thrift recipe
  1 hour

  2 small heads of Savoy cabbage
  salt
  2 onions, chopped
  US ⅓ cup, UK ¼ cup, Meat Stock (see
      Index) (1 scant dl)
  pepper
  caraway seeds

- Separate the leaves of the cabbage; cut off the ribs. Roll the leaves into large cigars, then cut them across into ⅓-inch strips. Wash well and reserve.
- Meanwhile, bring a pot of water to a boil. Salt it well, add the cabbage, and blanch. Drain well.
- Brown the onions slowly in the meat stock in a braising pot. Add the cabbage, salt and pepper to taste, and caraway seeds to taste.
- Cover and cook until tender. Toss gently once or twice during cooking to insure even doneness all through the pot.

GREEN CABBAGE AND TOMATOES
(Chou Vert à la Tomate)

■ Easy
6 servings
Inexpensive
1 hour

3½ lbs. tomatoes (1.75 kg)
2 large onions, chopped
bouquet garni
salt and pepper
US ¼ cup, UK 2 TB, Meat Stock (see Index) (2 TB)
3 heads of green cabbage
1 egg
chopped parsley

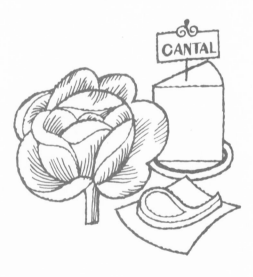

- Peel, seed, and coarsely chop the tomatoes. Simmer them with the onions, the *bouquet garni* and some salt and pepper for 25 minutes. When the tomato pulp is cooked, purée the sauce in a blender. Add the meat stock.

- Cut the cabbages into quarters. Remove the cores and blanch the leaves in boiling salted water. Drain very well.

- Preheat oven to 400°F., 205°C. or 6 Regulo.

- Chop the cabbage leaves coarsely, put them into a baking dish, season, and cover with the tomato sauce. Bake for 20 minutes.

- Meanwhile, hard-boil the egg, cool it under running cold water, and chop it.

- When the cabbage is done, sprinkle the dish with the chopped egg and parsley.

BRAISED RED CABBAGE
(Chou Rouge à l'Étouffée)

■ Easy
6 servings
Inexpensive
1¼ hours, 35 minutes in pressure cooker

1 large red cabbage
US ⅔ cup, UK ½ cup, Meat Stock (see Index) (2 scant dl)
1 onion, chopped
US ⅔ cup, UK ½ cup, red-wine vinegar (2 scant dl)
salt and pepper
6 sweet apples

- Discard the coarse outer leaves of the cabbage. Separate each leaf and remove the rib. Wash leaves, and cut them into ⅓-inch strips.

- Heat the meat stock and add the cabbage, onion and vinegar. Season with salt and pepper. Cover and simmer for 40 minutes.

- Meanwhile, peel the apples and cut into small diamonds, discarding all seeds. Add the apples to the cabbage. Cook for another 20 minutes. Correct the seasoning.

- An excellent table companion to pork.

BRAISED CARROTS
(Carottes Braisées)

■ Easy
6 servings
Inexpensive
35 minutes

2 lbs. baby carrots (1 kg)
4 small onions
5 oz. fat-free smoked ham (150 g)
US ½ cup, UK ⅓ cup, Meat Stock (see Index) (1 generous dl)
salt and pepper

- Peel the carrots. Slice the onions. Cut the ham into ⅓-inch cubes; set ham aside.

- Brown the onions with the help of the meat stock for a few minutes.

- Add the carrots and salt and pepper to taste. Add enough water to barely cover the vegetables.

- Cook uncovered over high heat until most of the water has evaporated. Shake the pan back and forth from time to time to stir the carrots without breaking them. Correct the seasoning.

- Add the diced ham last to allow reheating without hardening.

CAULIFLOWER AND PICKLES
(Chou-Fleur aux Cornichons)

- Easy
  6 servings
  Inexpensive
  45 minutes

1 large head of cauliflower
vinegar water for soaking
2 egg whites
1 small red onion, finely chopped
2 shallots, finely chopped
US 3 TB, UK 1½ TB, finely chopped capers (1½ TB)
US 2 TB, UK 1 TB, finely chopped sour pickles (1 TB)
US 2 TB, UK 1 TB, finely chopped herbs of your choice (1 TB)
1 small tomato, peeled, seeded, and chopped
US 2 TB, UK 1 TB, prepared mustard (1 TB)
1 recipe Hollandaise Sauce (see Index)
salt and pepper

- Break the cauliflower into small flowerets. Peel them. Soak them in the vinegar water for 10 minutes. Drain. Cook in boiling salted water for 3 minutes.

- Meanwhile, prepare the sauce. Poach the egg whites in simmering salted water to hard-boil them. Chop them. Add the chopped whites to the chopped onion and shallots. Mix with capers, pickles, herbs and tomato. Mix those aromatics into the mustard, then into the hollandaise sauce. Correct the seasoning with salt and pepper.

- As soon as the cauliflower is cooked, drain it well, arrange it on a serving platter, and cover it with the sauce.

CELERY HEARTS
(Cœurs de Céleri au Jus)

- Easy
  6 servings
  Inexpensive
  1¼ hours

  6 celery stalks
  2 carrots, sliced
  3 medium-size onions, sliced
  US ⅓ cup, UK ¼ cup, Meat Stock (see Index) (1 scant dl)
  bouillon
  veal roast gravy (optional)
  salt and pepper

- Remove the thick ribs of the celery stalks until you reach the pale yellow heart. Cut the hearts to 4-inch lengths. Blanch them in boiling salted water. Drain them well.

- Cook the carrots and the onions in hot meat stock and place the celery on top of these aromatics. Add enough bouillon to cover. Simmer for 20 to 25 minutes.

- Remove the cover and reduce the sauce over medium-high heat for 5 minutes. Add the veal gravy if you have it, and cook for a few more minutes.

- Season with salt and pepper and serve with beef or veal.

LEEKS WITH FINELY CHOPPED HERBS
(Poireaux aux Fines Herbes)

- Easy
  6 servings
  Medium expensive
  40 minutes

  18 medium-size leeks
  salt
  2 eggs
  US 1 cup, UK 1 scant cup, Meat Stock (see Index) (2.5 dl)
  lemon juice
  finely chopped herbs
  pepper

- Preheat oven to 350°F., 175°C. or 4 Regulo.

- Clean the leeks. Use only the white part; reserve the greens for a meat stock. Blanch the leeks in salted water for 10 minutes.

- Hard-boil the eggs; cool and chop them. Drain the leeks well and transfer them to a baking dish.

- Add the meat stock and bake for 15 to 20 minutes. When leeks are tender, remove them to a serving dish.

- Mix the meat stock left in the baking dish, lemon juice to taste, and the chopped eggs and herbs. Add seasoning to taste and spoon the herb mixture over the leeks.

STUFFED EGGPLANTS
(Aubergines Farcies)

- Easy
  6 servings
  Affordable
  45 minutes

3 eggplants
4 shallots, finely chopped
US 4 TB, UK 2 TB, Meat Stock (see Index)
  (2 TB)
US 6 TB, UK 3 TB, fresh bread crumbs (3
  TB)
3 hard-boiled eggs, chopped
2 garlic cloves, chopped
¼ lb. mushrooms, finely chopped (125 g)
salt and pepper

- Preheat oven to 400°F., 205°C. or 6 Regulo.

- Cut the eggplants lengthwise into halves and cut a crisscross pattern ¼ inch deep into the eggplant pulp. Bake until soft.

- In a nonstick pan, cook the shallots in the meat stock. Add the bread crumbs and cook for 1 or 2 minutes. Mix well with the remaining chopped ingredients, and cook for a few minutes more to make a stuffing.

- Remove the cooked eggplant halves from the oven. Scoop out the center pulp, leaving only ⅓ inch of pulp attached to the shell.

- Mash the removed pulp and mix it into the prepared stuffing. Correct the seasoning. Fill the half shells. Bake again until the top is golden brown.

EGGPLANT GRATIN
(Aubergines au Gratin)

- **Easy**
  6 servings
  Affordable
  1 hour

  3 medium-size eggplants
  2 medium-size onions, finely chopped
  US ⅓ cup, UK ¼ cup, Meat Stock (see
      Index) (1 scant dl)
  1 garlic clove
  US 2 TB, UK 1 TB, chopped parsley (1
      TB)
  4 anchovies, rinsed and finely mashed
  salt and pepper
  3 eggs, separated
  3 oz. Gruyère cheese, grated (90 g)
  US 4 TB, UK 2 TB, dry bread crumbs (2
      TB)

- Preheat oven to 400°F., 205°C. or 6 Regulo.
- Peel the eggplants and cut them into 3 or 4 pieces. Blanch them in boiling salted water for 10 minutes. Drain well and chop.
- Brown the onions in half of the meat stock. Add garlic, parsley and anchovies. Mix with the chopped eggplants and season with salt and pepper.
- Remove from the heat. Add the egg yolks and Gruyère cheese, and stir until homogenous.
- Beat the egg whites until they can carry the weight of a raw egg in its shell. Mix one quarter of the volume of the egg whites into the eggplants and fold in the remainder.
- Brush a baking dish with the remainder of the meat stock and pour in the eggplant mixture. Sprinkle with bread crumbs. Bake for 15 to 20 minutes.

BRAISED ENDIVES
(Endives Braisées)

■ Easy
  6 servings
  Expensive
  45 minutes

  12 endives
  water
  salt
  lemon juice

• Wash the endives well and dry them without cutting them. Remove the root core and the leaf tips.

• Heat ¼ inch of water in a nonstick pan and add the whole endives. Salt lightly, cover, and simmer for 35 minutes.

• Should the endives stick to the pan, add a few more tablespoons of water. Squeeze a few drops of lemon juice over the endives. Correct the seasoning.

• A good side vegetable with all meats.

Endives with Ham: Once the endives are cooked, wrap them in slices of fat-free boiled ham. Place the rolls in a baking dish. Sprinkle with grated Gruyère cheese. Place under the broiler for a few minutes to color the cheese.

FENNEL WITH PARSLEY
(Fenouil au Persil)

■ Easy
  6 servings
  Medium expensive
  45 minutes

  6 fennel bulbs
  US ⅔ cup, UK ½ cup, Meat Stock (see Index) (2 scant dl)
  salt and pepper
  chopped parsley
  2 lemons

• Cut off the fennel greens and discard the rough outer leaves. Wash the fennel hearts, cut them lengthwise into halves, and blanch them in salted water until crisp-tender. Drain.

• Heat the meat stock in a nonstick skillet, sprinkle with salt and pepper, and add the fennel. Cook fennel gently in the stock until it is tender and almost candied. Sprinkle wth chopped parsley.

• Transfer to a warm serving platter and garnish with lemon wedges. Serve with any fish or meat.

JERUSALEM ARTICHOKES IN MUSTARD SAUCE
(Topinambours à la Moutarde)

- Easy
  6 servings
  Medium expensive
  40 minutes

1 lemon
2 lbs. Jerusalem artichokes (1 kg)
salt and pepper
US 1 cup, UK 1 scant cup, Meat Stock
  (see Index) (2.5 dl)
US 1 TB, UK ½ TB, prepared Dijon mustard (½ TB)
US 2 TB, UK 1 TB, chopped parsley (1
  TB)

- Squeeze the juice of the lemon into a mixing bowl.

- Peel the Jerusalem artichokes, cut them into ¼-inch-thick slices, and toss them immediately in the lemon juice.

- Bring a large pot of water to a boil. Add the artichokes and blanch them for 3 minutes. Drain. Salt and pepper artichokes while still wet.

- In a nonstick skillet, heat the meat stock well. Add the artichokes and cook over high heat until the meat stock is reduced by half. Toss gently 2 or 3 times during cooking.

- As soon as the vegetables are tender, remove them to a vegetable dish, using a slotted spoon. Off the heat mix the mustard into the reduced meat stock. Add the parsley, correct the seasoning, and spoon over the vegetables.

BRAISED LETTUCE
(Laitues Braisées au Fromage)

- Easy
  6 servings
  Affordable
  45 minutes to 1 hour

6 heads of soft-leaf lettuce
¼ lb. Gruyère cheese, cut into thin strips
    (120 g)
salt and pepper
US ½ cup, UK ⅓ cup, Meat Stock (see
    Index) (1 generous dl)
bouillon as needed, about 1 US and UK
    cup (2.5 dl)
2 raw egg yolks
US 3 TB, UK 1½ TB, skim milk (1½ TB)
nutmeg

• Wash the lettuce heads well, trim the stem ends, and cut lengthwise into halves. Blanch in boiling, salted water for 2 minutes. Drain on paper towels.

• Once the lettuce has drained completely, place strips of Gruyère cheese, seasoned, between the leaves.

• Heat the stock in a braising pot; add the lettuce halves and enough bouillon to barely cover them. Cover with a parchment paper and the pot lid and cook for 30 minutes.

• Remove the lettuce to a warm serving platter as soon as done (test with a skewer). Reduce the cooking juices to ½ cup or so. Mix the egg yolks with the skim milk. Add a tablespoon or so of the hot braising juices. Then pour the *liaison* back into the bulk of the juices and thicken over low heat.

• Correct the salt and pepper, add nutmeg to taste, and spoon the sauce over the braised lettuce.

BRAISED STUFFED PEPPERS
(Poivrons Farcis Braisés)

■ Easy
6 servings
Affordable
1 hour

½ lb. mushrooms, chopped (250 g)
US ½ cup, UK ⅓ cup, Meat Stock (see
   Index) (1 generous dl)
5½ oz. chopped cooked white meat of
   chicken (165 g)
6 green peppers
2 raw egg yolks
salt and pepper
US 1 TB, UK ½ TB, paprika (½ TB)
5½ oz. trimmed smoked ham (165 g)
6 medium-size tomatoes, peeled, seeded,
   and chopped

- Cook the mushrooms in half of the meat stock.
- Meanwhile, have the chicken meat ready. Remove the stems of the peppers and the seeds. Blanch the peppers in salted boiling water for 2 minutes.
- Mix the mushrooms and the chicken. Bind the mixture with the egg yolks; season with salt, pepper and paprika.
- Drain the peppers very well and fill each pepper with an equal amount of the stuffing.
- Heat the remainder of the meat stock in a sauteuse pan. Add the ham, cut into cubes, and the chopped tomatoes. Place the peppers on the ham-tomato bed. Cover and simmer gently for 30 minutes or so.
- Transfer the peppers to a warm serving platter. Correct the seasoning of the sauce and spoon it over the vegetables.

SPINACH GRATIN
(Épinards au Gratin)

- Easy
  6 servings
  Inexpensive
  45 minutes

  3½ lbs. fresh spinach (1.75 kg)
  US ⅓ cup, UK ¼ cup, Meat Stock (see
    Index) (1 scant dl)
  salt and pepper
  3 eggs
  ¼ lb. Gruyère cheese, grated (125 g)
  US 5 TB, UK 2½ TB, bread crumbs (2½
    TB)

- Wash the spinach and cut it into chiffonade.

- Heat three quarters of the meat stock in a pan and add the spinach and salt and pepper to taste. Cook until all liquid has evaporated.

- Off the heat, add the beaten eggs and mix in quickly.

- Brush a baking dish with the remainder of the meat stock. Pour the gratin mixture into the dish. Sprinkle with grated Gruyère and bread crumbs and brown under the broiler.

- Especially good with fish and veal.

SWISS CHARD AND GRUYÈRE
(Bettes au Gruyère)

- Easy
  6 servings
  Inexpensive
  1 hour

  3½ lbs. Swiss chard ribs (1.75 kg)
  US ½ cup, UK ⅓ cup, Meat Stock (see
    Index) (1 generous dl)
  salt and pepper
  4 oz. Gruyère cheese, grated (120 g)
  leftover gravy of a pork or veal roast (op-
    tional)
  3 raw egg yolks
  US 1 TB, UK ½ TB, vinegar (½ TB)

- Cut the Swiss chard ribs into pieces 2½ inches long (6 cm). Peel off the fibers and blanch ribs in boiling salted water. Drain and dry in a paper towel.

- Add vegetable to the meat stock and season with salt and pepper. Toss with grated Gruyère cheese and any gravy if you have it on hand.

- Beat the egg yolks and vinegar together. Pour mixture over the Swiss chard ribs; shaking the pan back and forth over low heat, let the sauce thicken lightly. Remove from the heat as soon as thickened.

- Immediately turn into a serving dish and correct the seasoning.

NOTE
If after preparing a veal or pork roast you have leftover gravy, store in a small bowl and refrigerate. The next day, lift off the layer of fat, discard it, and reheat the juices to flavor any vegetable with them.

SAUTÉED TOMATOES
(Tomates Sautées)

- Easy
  6 servings
  Medium expensive
  15 minutes

  6 medium-size tomatoes
  salt and pepper
  chopped parsley
  snipped chives
  US ⅓ cup, UK ¼ cup, Meat Stock (see
     Index) (1 scant dl)
  US ¼ cup, UK 2 TB, grated Parmesan
     cheese (2 TB)

- Wash and dry the tomatoes. Cut them into thick slices. In a nonstick skillet, sear the tomato slices for 2 minutes on each side. Sprinkle with salt and pepper and the herbs. Reduce the heat and finish cooking for another 2 minutes.

- Remove the cooked tomatoes to a serving platter. Pour the meat stock into the pan and add the cheese. Heat well together, correct the seasoning, and spoon over the tomatoes.

BROILED TOMATOES
(Tomates Grillées)

- Easy
  6 servings
  Medium expensive
  30 minutes

  6 medium-size tomatoes
  salt and pepper
  US ¾ cup, UK ⅔ cup, fine gluten bread
     crumbs (6 TB)
  3 thin slices of boiled ham, finely
     chopped
  US 2 TB, UK 1 TB, chopped parsley (1
     TB)
  pinch of crumbled dried rosemary
  US ½ cup, UK ⅓ cup, Meat Stock (see
     Index) (1 generous dl)

- Cut the tomatoes into halves. Salt and pepper the cut side.

- Preheat oven to 375°F., 190°C. or 5 Regulo.

- Mix together the bread crumbs, chopped ham, parsley, rosemary, meat stock, salt as needed and some pepper.

- Spread the mixture over each half tomato. Bake in the preheated oven for 8 minutes. Then broil the top for 2 to 3 minutes to brown the crust.

STEWED CHERRY TOMATOES
(Tomates à la Cocotte)

- Easy
  6 servings
  Affordable
  15 to 20 minutes

  18 cherry tomatoes
  salt and pepper
  2 garlic cloves, finely chopped
  US 3 TB, UK 1½ TB, Meat Stock (see Index) (1½ TB)
  chopped parsley

- Preheat oven to 350°F., 175°C. or 4 Regulo.
- Wash the tomatoes and dry well. Sprinkle with salt and pepper and garlic. Bake until skins split open.
- Add the meat stock to the dish and shake back and forth to roll the tomatoes in it. Sprinkle with chopped parsley and serve.

RATATOUILLE
(Ratatouille Niçoise)

- Easy
  6 servings
  Affordable
  1¼ hours

  6 medium-size tomatoes
  3 eggplants
  4 zucchini
  3 peppers
  4 medium-size onions
  US ⅓ cup, UK ¼ cup, Meat Stock (see Index) (1 scant dl)
  3 garlic cloves, chopped
  bouquet garni
  salt and pepper

- Peel and seed the tomatoes and chop them coarsely. Peel the eggplants, and cut them and the zucchini into ½-inch cubes. Seed the peppers and cut them also into cubes. Peel the onions and chop them finely.
- Heat the meat stock in a pan and cook the onions until they start to brown. Add the zucchini, eggplants and peppers; mix well. Add the tomatoes, garlic and the *bouquet garni*. Season with salt and pepper.
- Cover and simmer for 1 hour or more. The eggplant should be very well done. Serve warm or cold.

TURNIPS AND CHIVES
(Navets à la Ciboulette)

- **Easy**
  6 servings
  Thrift recipe
  25 minutes

  2 lbs. white turnips (1 kg)
  salt
  US ⅔ cup, UK ½ cup, Meat Stock (see Index) (2 scant dl)
  freshly chopped chives
  pepper

- Peel the turnips. Cut them into ¼-inch-thick slices, then cut them across into ¼-inch julienne strips. You may, if you prefer, process the vegetable through the julienne blade of a food processor.

- Bring a large pot of water to a boil, salt it, and blanch the turnips for 2 minutes. Drain.

- Heat the meat stock in a nonstick skillet; add the turnips. Turn the heat very high and reduce the stock. Toss several times while reducing. The cooking should be completed by the time the stock has almost completely evaporated. Add chives and seasoning to taste.

NOTE
Carrots, parsnips, rutabagas, kohlrabi and Jerusalem artichokes may be prepared with this same method.

BRAISED ZUCCHINI
(Courgettes à l'Étouffée)

- **Easy**
  6 servings
  Inexpensive
  20 minutes

  8 baby zucchini (marrows or courgettes)
  3 medium-size onions, chopped
  US ⅓ cup, UK ¼ cup, Meat Stock (see Index) (1 scant dl)
  salt and pepper

- Cut the zucchini into ⅓-inch-thick slices. Cook the onions in the meat stock until they begin to color. When they are soft, add the zucchini. Season with salt and pepper, and simmer for 6 to 8 minutes.

- Correct the seasoning and serve in a warmed vegetable dish.

Liliane's Zucchini: Add freshly chopped tarragon to the basic recipe. Excellent with fish and all white meats.

VEGETABLE MEDLEY
(Jardinière de Légumes)

- Easy
  6 servings
  Affordable
  45 minutes

4 zucchini
1 lb. baby carrots (500 g)
1 lettuce heart, cut into chiffonade
12 small artichokes, peeled and trimmed,
    or 6 artichoke bottoms
4 small turnips, cut into cubes
12 baby onions
5½ oz. trimmed smoked ham, cut into ⅓-
    inch cubes (165 g)
US ⅓ cup, UK ¼ cup, Meat Stock (see
    Index) (1 scant dl)
salt and pepper
bottled meat extract
US 2 cups, UK 2 scant cups, water (.5 L)

- Prepare and wash all vegetables. Drain well.

- In a nonstick skillet, cook the onions and the ham in the meat stock over fairly high heat. Add the other vegetables and season with salt and pepper.

- Dissolve a pea-size nugget of meat extract in the water, add to the pan, cover, and bring to a boil. Reduce and simmer for 20 to 25 minutes.

- Serve in a heated vegetable dish. Best with chicken, meat or variety meats.

DESSERTS

(Les Desserts)

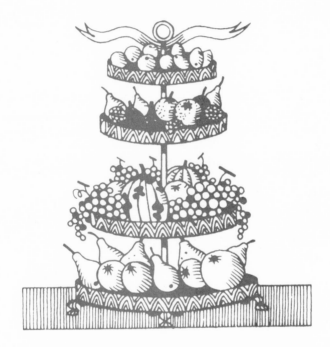

BAKED FRUITS
(Fruits au Four)

■ Easy
6 servings
Inexpensive
40 minutes

6 apples or pears
1 small bunch of grapes, blended and
    strained
sugar substitute (optional)

- Preheat oven to 375°F., 185°C. or 5 Regulo.
- Peel the fruits and remove the cores. Place fruits in a baking dish and bake until a skewer offers no resistance when inserted. Remove from the oven.
- Pour the grape juice into the baking dish and mix with the caramelized fruit juices. (If you prefer not to use the grape juice, use a sugar substitute mixed with water.)
- Serve each fruit with some of the juices spooned over.

CHILLED FRUITS
(Fruits Rafraîchis)

■ Easy
6 servings
Medium expensive
20 minutes

2 oranges
2 pears
2 apples
½ lb. strawberries (250 g)
1 pineapple
lemon juice
1 oz. Grand Marnier (1 TB)

- Peel the oranges to the blood. Slice them crosswise. Peel the pears and the apples and cut into ¼-inch strips. Clean the strawberries.
- Peel and slice the pineapple and cut the meat into small diamonds. Arrange all fruits except strawberries on a platter and squeeze lemon juice over them. Chill.
- When ready to serve, garnish the platter with the fresh strawberries, whole or sliced.
- Heat the Grand Marnier and pour it flaming over the fruits.

STEWED APPLES
(Compote de Pommes)

■ **Easy**
  6 servings
  Inexpensive
  45 minutes

  6 apples
  **1 small bunch of very sweet grapes,
      puréed**
  rind of 1 lemon

- Wash the apples. Peel them and cut them into ⅛-inch slices.

- Keep the skins, seeds and cores. Cook these for 20 minutes in half water, half juice from the puréed grapes, and flavor with a strip of lemon rind. Strain.

- Put the apple slices in a pan and add the strained syrup. Cover, bring to a boil, and simmer for 10 minutes. Turn off the heat. Cool the apples, covered.

- Carefully remove apple slices to a compote dish, pour the syrup over them, and serve chilled.

ROASTED APPLES WITH ORANGE
(Pommes Rôties à l'Orange)

■ **Easy**
  6 servings
  Inexpensive
  1 hour

  6 apples
  3 oranges

- Leave the apples whole, but cut a ¼-inch-deep slash all around each fruit, one third of the way from the top.

- Do not peel the oranges; cut 6 thick slices from them.

- Preheat oven to 375°F., 185°C. or 5 Regulo.

- Place the orange slices in a baking dish; set an apple on each slice. Put to bake in the preheated oven.

- Squeeze the juice from the leftover oranges. As soon as the cut in the apples starts bulging open, pour the orange juice over the apples.

- Continue baking until a skewer meets no resistance when inserted to the core of the apples.

APPLE GRATIN
(Gratin de Pommes)

- Easy
  6 servings
  Affordable
  1 hour

  8 baking apples
  1 tsp. butter
  US ⅓ cup, UK 3 TB, dark raisins (3 TB)
  US 2 TB, UK 1 TB, Calvados or applejack
     (1 TB)
  ground cinnamon
  grated rind of 1 lemon
  US 2 cups, UK 2 scant cups, natural un-
     sweetened cider (.5 L), approximately

- Preheat oven to 350°F., 170°C. or 4 Regulo.
- Peel the apples; cut them into halves, then into quarters. Smooth the inside of each quarter so it can sit on the bottom of a baking dish without bobbling.
- Spread the butter on the bottom of a 1-quart (1 L) baking dish. Add the raisins.
- Toss the apples with the liqueur, cinnamon to taste, and lemon rind, and arrange them, core side down, in the baking dish.
- Add just enough cider to barely cover apples and bake until tender, adding more cider as needed. Serve lukewarm.
- No sugar substitute should be necessary. The dish should be sweet-tart and very pleasant.

MELON SURPRISE

- Easy
  6 servings
  Expensive
  10 minutes

1 pint strawberries
½ pint raspberries
½ lb. cherries (250 g)
1 large melon
½ oz. Kirschwasser (½ TB)
sugar substitute (optional)

- Wash the fruits well. Empty the melon and cube the pulp.
- Drain the melon shell upside down on paper towels. Pit the cherries and mix them with the other fruits.
- Place the mixture in the melon shell. Add some Kirsch, and if you wish, sweeten with sugar substitute. Refrigerate and serve chilled.

ORANGE SALAD
(Salade d'Oranges)

- Easy
  6 servings
  Inexpensive
  10 minutes

8 oranges
1 small bunch of red grapes, peeled
US 1 oz., UK 1 TB, Cognac (1 TB)

- Peel the oranges to the blood and slice them. Save all the juices escaping from the fruit. Peel the grapes; cut them lengthwise into halves.
- Arrange the orange slices as a border on a platter. Put the grapes in the center. Pour the reserved orange juice over the fruit and chill.
- Just before serving, heat the Cognac, ignite it, and pour it flaming over the fruit.

STUFFED ORANGES WITH MERINGUE
(Oranges Meringuées)

■ Easy
  6 servings
  Medium expensive
  1 hour

  6 oranges
  4 apples
  2 pears
  ¼ cup raspberries (2 TB)
  2 egg whites
  US ⅓ cup, UK 3 TB, oatmeal flakes (3 TB)
  grated rind of ½ lemon
  sugar substitute

- Cut the tops off the oranges and scoop out the insides without piercing the skins. Cut the orange sections into small pieces. Peel the apples and the pears and cut them into small pieces also.

- Mix all the fruits and use to fill the orange shells. Let stand for 2 hours.

- Beat the egg whites until they are very stiff; fold in the oatmeal, lemon rind and sugar substitute to taste.

- Place a topping of oatmeal crisp on each orange.

- Preheat oven to 500°F., 300°C. or 9 Regulo for 15 minutes, then turn off the oven. Place the oranges in the oven for about 25 minutes. The topping will cook without coloring.

FLAMBÉED PEACHES
(Pêches Flambées)

■ Easy
   6 servings
   Affordable
   15 minutes

6 peaches
US ⅔ cup, UK ½ cup, dry Marsala (2
   scant dl)
US 3 TB, UK 1½ TB, Curaçao (1½ TB)

● Preheat oven to 425°F., 220°C. or 6
   Regulo.

● Peel the peaches and cut them into
   halves. Remove the pits. Place the
   halves in a decorative baking dish,
   pit side down. Pour the Marsala
   over.

● Bake in the oven for 8 to 10 minutes.
   The Marsala will evaporate a little,
   reduce, and mix with the peach
   juices.

● Heat the Curaçao in a small saucepan, ignite it, and pour it flaming
   over the peaches.

NOTE
This may also be made with pears and
Grand Marnier; apples and cider and Cal-
vados; bananas and rum; or apricots with
Cognac.

FRUIT-FILLED PINEAPPLE
(Ananas Fourré aux Fruits)

■ Easy
   6 servings
   Medium expensive
   20 minutes

2 pineapples
1½ lbs. assorted fruits (oranges, pears,
   raspberries, blackberries, strawberries)
   (750 g)
1 lemon
1 small bunch of very sweet grapes

● Remove the tops from the pineapples. Scoop out the pulp and chop
   it into cubes. Discard the center
   core.

● Slice the oranges and the pears.
   Squeeze some lemon juice over the
   peeled pears to prevent discoloration. Clean the berries. Mix fruits
   and pineapple chunks. Chill.

● Purée the grapes in a blender. Strain
   the juice into a pitcher.

● When ready to serve, fill the pineapple shell with the fruits and pass the
   very sweet grape juice in its pitcher
   as a natural sweetener.

PEARS IN PORT
(Poires Sautées au Porto)

- Easy
  6 servings
  Affordable
  30 minutes, plus 4 hours to chill

  6 ripe Bartlett pears
  US 1 cup, UK 1 scant cup, white Port (2.5 dl)
  dash of cloves

- Peel the pears. Cut them into quarters.

- Put a few drops of Port in a nonstick skillet. Add the pears and cook over high heat until caramelized. Turn the heat down and cook until pears are tender. Remove to a deep dish.

- Heat the rest of the Port with a dash of cloves and simmer for 5 minutes. Pour the Port over the pears and refrigerate for 4 hours.

PEARS IN RED WINE
(Poires au Vin Rouge)

- Easy
  6 servings
  Affordable
  45 minutes

  6 ripe pears
  US ⅓ cup, UK ¼ cup, red wine (1 scant dl)
  sugar substitute

- Wash, peel, and core the pears. Leave them whole and place them in a pan. Add just enough water to cover one third of the pears, then add the wine.

- Cover and simmer for 30 minutes. Let the pears cool in the pan. Add some sugar substitute to the cooking liquid and pour over the fruit.

COTTAGE CHEESE AND RASPBERRIES
(Fromage Blanc aux Framboises)

- Easy
  6 servings
  Medium expensive
  10 minutes

  US 1 cup, UK 1 scant cup, evaporated
    skim milk (2.5 dl)
  ¾ lb. 99% fat-free cottage cheese or
    skim-milk ricotta (375 g)
  1 pint fresh raspberries

- Pour two thirds of the skim milk into a small bowl. Place in the freezer so it starts freezing at the edges, while you clean the berries.

- Process the cheese of your choice in a blender or food processor. Empty into a bowl.

- Clean the raspberries.

- Beat the deep-chilled milk with an electric mixer until it foams very heavily. Fold the foamy milk into the cheese and spoon into 6 dessert dishes.

- Decorate the top of the cheese mousse with the raspberries.

NOTE
This dessert must be served and enjoyed as soon as finished, otherwise the foam will liquefy again.

STRAWBERRY SURPRISE
(Fraises Surprise)

- Easy
  6 servings
  Expensive
  15 minutes

  1½ quarts strawberries
  ½ quart raspberries
  2 peaches, white if possible and very ripe
  1 small bunch of sweet grapes, or sugar
    substitute to your taste

- Carefully wash and clean all fruits. Mix raspberries with strawberries.

- Purée the peaches and grapes in a blender to make a sweet sauce, or, if you prefer, do not use the grapes, but only peach purée sweetened to your taste with sugar substitute. Strain to discard the skins.

- Toss the berries with the purée.

RUSSIAN-STYLE FRUIT SALAD
(Salades de Fruits à la Russe)

■ Easy
 6 servings
 Medium expensive
 30 minutes, plus 2 hours for chilling

 ½ pineapple, sliced
 3 peaches, pitted
 pulp of ½ melon
 1 pint raspberries
 US 1 cup, UK 1 scant cup, dry white wine
     (2.5 dl)
 1 cinnamon stick
 grated rind of 1 lemon
 sugar substitute
 1 pint strawberries

● Peel and slice pineapple and peaches; cut the slices into diamonds. Wedge the melon; cut the wedges into diamonds also. Mix these fruits with the raspberries and chill.

● In a small saucepan, heat the wine and infuse the cinnamon stick for 10 minutes. Add the lemon rind and mix well. Bring to a boil for 1 minute. Let cool and add sugar substitute to your taste.

● Purée the strawberries and add sugar substitute to your taste. Strain the wine-cinnamon mixture into the strawberry purée. Mix well and pour over the fruits. Chill for 2 hours.

BERRIES AND YOGURT MEDLEY
(Fruits Rouges au Yaourt)

- Easy
  6 servings
  Affordable
  10 minutes

  ½ lb. natural unsweetened yogurt (250 g)
  1 pint ripe strawberries
  ½ pint ripe raspberries

- Empty the yogurt into a bowl.
- Wash and slice the strawberries. Mix them into the yogurt. Turn the mixture into a deep dish and chill for 1 hour.
- When ready to serve, top the yogurt with the raspberries.

ENGLISH CUSTARD
(Crème Anglaise)

- Easy
  6 servings
  Affordable
  15 minutes

  US 4 cups skim milk (1 L)
  1½ tsps. vanilla extract
  pinch of salt
  16 egg yolks
  sugar substitute of your choice

- Scald the milk, vanilla and salt.
- Beat the egg yolks and gradually add the hot milk. Put the mixture over low heat, stirring constantly with a wooden spoon. The custard is cooked when it coats the spoon.
- Add sugar substitute to your taste. Strain and chill the custard.

NOTE
English custard is used as a sauce on many puddings and fresh berries, and as a base for ice cream.

VANILLA FLAN
(Flan à la Vanille)

■ Easy
6 servings
Inexpensive
1 hour and 10 minutes

6 cups skim milk (1.5 L)
¼ tsp. salt
2 tsps. vanilla extract
12 eggs
sugar substitute of your choice
1 tsp. butter

- Scald the milk; add the salt and vanilla. Remove from the heat.
- Beat the eggs, add them to the milk, and mix them well. Add sugar substitute to your taste, bearing in mind that once chilled the custard will be less sweet than it appears at this stage.
- Preheat oven to 300°F., 150°C. or 2 Regulo.
- Butter an 8-cup charlotte mold very evenly and very lightly with the butter. Strain the flan into it.
- Set the mold in a baking dish; put the dish on the oven rack. Pour boiling water to reach two thirds of the way to the rim of the mold. Bake until a knife blade inserted at the center comes out clean. Neither custard nor water should boil during cooking.
- Remove dish from the oven and let the mold cool in the water bath. Deep chill.
- When ready to serve, run a knife blade around the edge of the mold and turn the flan onto a serving platter.

KIWI FLAN
(Flan aux Groseilles de Chine)

■ Easy
6 servings
Expensive
4 hours, chilling included

6½ oz. evaporated skim milk (195 g)
1½ tsps. unflavored gelatin
3 egg yolks
US ⅔ cup, UK ½ cup, skim milk (2 scant dl)
pinch of salt
sugar substitute
4 kiwis
US 2 TB, UK 1 TB, Grand Marnier (1 TB)

● Chill the evaporated skim milk in the freezer until the edges freeze.

● Melt the gelatin in a small bowl with 1 tablespoon or so of water. Keep warm and liquid over hot water.

● Mix egg yolks and skim milk in a small heavy pot and thicken over medium-low heat. As soon as thickened, add the gelatin and a pinch of salt. Cool and sweeten to your taste. Let cool until very thick.

● Meanwhile, peel the kiwis and cut into ⅙-inch slices. Marinate them in the Grand Marnier. Set six of the best slices aside.

● Now beat the evaporated skim milk to a heavy foam, sweeten to your taste, and mix one third of it into the custard. Fold in the remainder.

● Spoon one third of the custard into 6 dessert cups. Add half of the kiwis. Top with a second third of the custard. Add the remaining kiwis. Cover with the rest of the custard. Decorate the top of each custard cup with 1 slice of the kiwis you set aside. Chill and serve.

EXPRESS COFFEE MOUSSE
(Mousse au Café Express)

■ Easy
  6 to 8 servings
  Affordable
  24 hours, due to dripping of cheese and
    chilling of mousse

  1 lb. skim-milk ricotta cheese (500 g)
  US 2 TB, UK 1 TB, instant coffee crystals
    with or without caffein (1 TB)
  1 can (13 oz.) evaporated skim milk (400
    g)
  sugar substitute
  ½ tsp. aniseeds
  cocoa powder

• Put the ricotta in a stainless-steel strainer lined with a layer of cheesecloth. Let it drip overnight over a bowl.

• Dissolve the instant coffee in about one third of the skim milk. Mix into the remainder of the milk and store in the freezer for 1 hour or until crystals of ice start forming around the bowl.

• Beat the ice-cold milk and coffee mixture until it foams heavily like heavy cream. Sweeten to your taste.

• Beat the ricotta, sweeten to taste, and add the aniseeds. Mix in one quarter of the coffee mousse, fold in the remainder, and turn into a dessert mold or cups. Sprinkle with a dash of unsweetened cocoa powder and keep deep chilled until ready to serve.

• Should the dessert have to wait several hours, freeze it or it will separate. Allow enough time for it to defrost before serving.

MOCHA ICE CREAM
(Glace au Café)

- Easy
  6 to 8 servings
  Affordable
  15 minutes, plus 45 minutes for freezing

  1 envelope unflavored gelatin
  US ¾ cup, UK ⅔ cup, double-strength
    coffee (2 dl)
  US 3 cups, UK 3 scant cups, skim milk
    (.75 L)
  US 1 cup, UK 1 scant cup, nonfat dry-
    milk solids (2.5 dl)
  2 tsps. vanilla extract
  ¼ tsp. salt
  1½ oz. unsweetened chocolate (45 g)
  4 raw egg yolks
  sugar substitute

- Soften the gelatin in the coffee and melt together.

- Mix skim milk, milk solids, vanilla and gelatin. Stir over medium heat until the gelatin has dissolved. Add salt.

- Melt the chocolate in the top part of a double boiler over hot water. Add it to the milk mixture, using a whisk. Homogenize well.

- Mix with the egg yolks and thicken over medium-low heat. Cool completely. Chill. Sweeten with sugar substitute to your taste.

- Freeze in an ice-cream machine for 30 to 45 minutes. Store in freezer to ripen.

NOTE
It is essential to wait until the batter of an ice cream is very cold to sweeten it with sugar substitute, for the colder a dessert is the more sweetener it will need.

STRAWBERRY ICE MILK
(Glace aux Fraises)

■ Easy
6 to 8 servings
Affordable
1 hour, plus 30 to 45 minutes for freezing

1 can (13 oz.) evaporated skim milk (400 g)
1 envelope unflavored gelatin
2 quarts strawberries
juice of 1 lemon
sugar substitute
pinch of salt

- Empty the milk into a small saucepan. Add the gelatin, sprinkling it over the surface of the milk, then heat gently until the gelatin has completely dissolved. Chill the milk in the freezer until almost solid.

- Divide the berries into 2 parts. One part should be the best berries and represent one third of the total volume. Thinly slice these and macerate them in the lemon juice. Keep refrigerated.

- Purée the remainder of the berries and deep-chill while the milk sets.

- When the milk is almost set, empty it into a mixer bowl and whip it until it foams heavily. Add the fruit purée to this foam, proceeding very gradually so as to obtain a very homogenous mixture.

- Fold in the sliced berries and sweeten with enough artificial sweetener to suit your taste. Add a pinch of salt. Immediately put to freeze in an ice-cream maker.

- When set, ripen in the freezer for 24 hours.

NOTE

An ice cream made without cream or egg yolk must mellow in the refrigerator for 30 minutes before being served.

MENUS FOR LIGHT CUISINE

When planning menus, you can use all of the recipes in the first part of this book, and use them without worry, since most of the fat and most of the carbohydrate have been removed from them. Mix and match, enjoy yourself building menus that you personally find attractive; if you respect the portions indicated in the previous pages, there is absolutely no possibility for you not to lose weight. To get you started, here are some suggested weight-control dinner menus in light cuisine style.

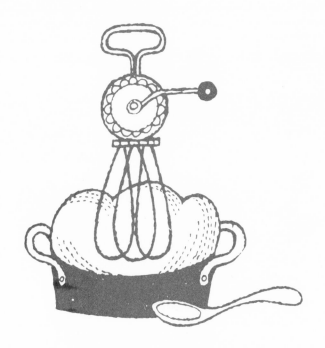

Provençal Fish Soup
Rib Steak Bordelaise
Braised Endives
Chilled Fruits

Curried Carrot Salad
Sauté of Veal and Artichokes
Braised Zucchini
Melon Surprise

Eggs Stuffed with Shrimps
Paprika Rib Steak
Braised Cabbage with Caraway
Express Coffee Mousse

Poached Eggs Royal Printemps
Anchovy Steaks
Leeks with Finely Chopped Herbs
Flambéed Peaches

Scrambled Eggs with Asparagus
Red Snapper and Fennel
Jerusalem Artichokes in Mustard Sauce
Kiwi Flan

Garlic and Basil Soup
Broiled Lamb Steaks
Ratatouille
Pears in Red Wine

Belgian Endive Salad
Poached Chicken for Dieters
Swiss Chard and Gruyère
Fruit-Filled Pineapple

Mussel Salad
Veal Cutlets with Provençal Herbs
Eggplant Gratin
Strawberry Surprise

Country-Style Soup
Burgundy-Style Ham
Celery Hearts
Cottage Cheese and Raspberries

Artichoke Bottoms Vinaigrette
Salmon Steaks in Anchovy Sauce
Fennel with Parsley
Orange Salad

Duck Salad with Orange Slices
Baked Smelts
Provençal-Style Green Beans
Pears in Port

Island Chicken Salad
Shellfish Medley in Lemon Sauce
Sautéed Tomatoes
Strawberry Ice Milk

Recipes for all the dishes in these menus can be found in Part I. Consult the Index for pages.

PART II

CELEBRATION MEALS

ABOUT CUISINE NOUVELLE:

You will immediately notice the chief difference between the superlight cuisine of the diet recipes and those used in the celebration meals: eggs, butter, creams and oils are used; if not present in very large quantity, they are at least noticeably there. At no time is there any intention of omitting them.

The recipes are all based on ideas used in the main provinces of France. The countrywomen of the French provinces were often too poor to buy much flour; as a result, flour was always kept to make bread and simple pastries. Therefore, to thicken their gravies, these women reduced them and then transformed them into sauces by adding a good pat of their homemade butter, as well as herbs and/or spices. It is only in *bourgeois* households, where means were more affluent, that the house cook would consider thickening her sauces with a *roux*, thus preparing a cuisine which, while still using the local ingredients, put them in a more expensive context, similar to the classic cuisine in techniques and presentation.

The menus presented in this chapter use the countrywomen's method, which has been adopted by the sauce makers of the *nouvelle cuisine*. The most typical example of this method is the *beurre blanc* of the Maine, Anjou and Touraine; over low heat butter is fluffed into an acid base of reduced vinegar and shallots. Fernand Point was probably the first of all French chefs of the twentieth century to render homage to the cuisine of his mother. If one looks through the book that has been put together to present some of his ideas, one soon realizes that he made a number of his sauces by reducing stock or wine and finally adding butter to them in fine emulsions.

I have chosen here to remain in the French provinces, to stay in character with the very French collection of recipes of the authors. I could just as well have looked toward the Far East, the Middle East or even the diverse ethnic cuisines of Europe to build a completely different collection of menus, still in *cuisine nouvelle*, but with very different ingredients in many different styles. After all, *cuisine nouvelle* reflects our varied and now wide-open world, accessible in all its parts by air travel and other rapid transportation; it reflects also our care for staying relatively slim always; it reflects the cuisines of the countries we visit on vacation or business; and it has even brought back many of the culinary con-coctions and spices of the Middle Ages, for a few chefs have taken to perusing ancient texts for forgotten ideas, which now appear new to an unknowing public.

FRENCH BREAD

This is a plain lean loaf which will do minimum damage to the waistline if consumed in small amounts, preferably with cheese only.

■ **Easy**
   Inexpensive
   24 to 36 hours

3 cups flour (12 oz. or 375 g)
1 envelope active dry yeast (7 g)
lukewarm water
1½ tsps. salt (7.5 g)
US 1 TB, UK ½ TB, olive oil (½ TB)
cornmeal
1 egg white

● The day before your dinner, in the morning, mix one third of the flour with the yeast and enough lukewarm water (110°F. or 37°C.) to make a batter. Let stand overnight, covered loosely with a plate. This makes a leaven.

● The next morning, make a well in the remainder of the flour. Add the leaven as prepared in the first step, add the salt and enough lukewarm water to make a good bread dough. Knead for 10 minutes, or until smooth as silk. (Some say as smooth as a baby's bottom.)

● Pour 1 tablespoon olive oil into a mixing bowl. Add the dough and roll it into the oil. Let stand in a draft-free place until the dough is double in bulk.

● Punch the dough down and shape it into 2 French loaves 17 inches x 1 inch. Barely brush an unbendable cookie sheet with a bit of oil and sprinkle with cornmeal. Set the loaves 1 inch away from each long edge of the baking sheet.

● Slash slanted cuts ⅓ inch deep into each loaf. Let loaves rise until double in bulk. The bread will rise at a speed proportional to the temperature of the day; the warmer the faster.

● Preheat oven to 425°F., 220°C. or 7 Regulo.

● Place the loaves on the top shelf of the oven to bake. Immediately spray the loaves with a fine spray of water. Close the oven. Bake for 6 minutes and spray again. Bake for 6 more minutes and finally brush with the egg white lightly mixed with 3 tablespoons of water.

● Finish baking until the bread has taken on a deep golden color and sounds hollow when tapped. Cool on a rack.

NOTE
Please use dry yeast; the bread has a better flavor.

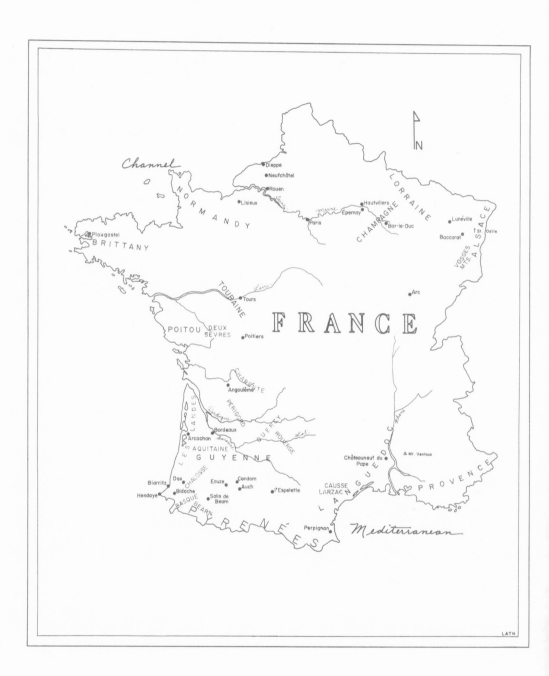

SO, YOU HAVE LOST
FIVE POUNDS . . .

Provence
Languedoc

DINNER IN PROVENCE AND LANGUEDOC

Now let us celebrate with two meridional menus to enjoy yourself while you get acquainted with some of the food ideas of Provence and Languedoc.

Shellfish is, of course, abundant in the Mediterranean. Lamb in these regions is especially delicious; in Provence some of the best is raised on the slopes of Mont Ventoux and bears the name of *broutard* while the best of the Languedoc comes from the Plateau du Larzac, a *causse*; the *causses* are the chalky and cavernous plateaux which separate Southern Auvergne from Languedoc.

The vegetables, you will notice, are mostly those of the Mediterranean climate—succulent peppers and zucchini. But one area of Languedoc produces the best turnips, so I have used them, just to show how delicious turnips can be. Notice the herbs used, they grow in the natural *garrigues*, or dry rocky soils, of both provinces and they are mostly the turpentine-heavy thyme, rosemary and savory. The favorite aromatic is garlic; it is used generously but never abused.

The cheeses are made with the milk of those favorite milk producers of the Mediterranean basin: the goat and the ewe. Try to find a fresh Banon wrapped in its brandy-soaked chestnut leaves. In the late winter it will be made with ewes' milk and in the summer with goats' milk; it can be found also nicely sprinkled with savory leaves. Roquefort is well known enough so that no comments need be added, with the exception maybe that tastes in Roquefort vary with the geography. Where Paris likes its Roquefort white or still almost sweet, it is not so in the southern provinces where some like it extremely strong. The city of Perpignan is said to have a taste for only the strongest and sharpest Roquefort in the nation.

As wine, choose a good old strong and full-bodied Châteauneuf-du-Pape for the leg of lamb and maybe a Cahors for the rabbit of the Languedoc. Cahors is relatively inexpensive and always well rounded and smooth.

MENU I—PROVENCE

SOUPE de MOULES au PASTIS
GIGOT d'AGNEAU à la PERSILLADE
JULIENNE AVIGNONNAISE
BANON
PÊCHES POCHÉES à la CRÈME d'ORANGE

SOUPE DE MOULES AU PASTIS
(Mussel Soup with Pastis)

■ Easy
6 servings
Medium expensive
1 hour

3 quarts mussels (3 L)
½ bottle Cassis white wine
2 onions, finely chopped
2 shallots, finely chopped
1 garlic clove, crushed
coarsely chopped parsley stems
pepper from the mill
2 cups Fish Stock (see Index) (.5 L)

LIAISON
1 egg yolk
1½ tsps. lemon juice
2 garlic cloves, mashed
⅓ cup finely chopped parsley
¼ cup fruity olive oil (2 TB)
US 1 cup, UK 1 scant cup, light cream
   (2.5 L)
US ¼ cup, UK 2 TB, Pastis or Pernod (2
   TB)
salt and pepper
chopped parsley

- Scrub the mussels and place them in a large kettle. Add the wine, onions, shallots, crushed garlic clove, parsley stems and some pepper from the mill. Cover the pot. Holding it by both handles toss to mix mussels and vegetables. Place over medium high heat and steam mussels open, tossing twice more during the steaming process.

- Drain the mussels into a colander placed over a large mixing bowl. Strain the cooking juices through a cheesecloth and mix them with the fish stock. Reduce by half.

- Meanwhile, shell the mussels and keep them in a bowl covered with plastic wrap.

- As soon as the mussels are shelled, prepare the *liaison*. Mix the egg yolk, lemon juice and mashed garlic in a small bowl; add the chopped parsley and gradually whisk in the olive oil. The result will be a very thick small sauce resembling a very tight mayonnaise.

- As soon as the cooking broth has reduced enough, add the mussels to it. Also slowly dissolve the *liaison* with the light cream.
- To this mixture, add 1 cup of the very hot reduced mussel broth, then pour the mixture into the mussel pot. Reheat very well, but *positively do not boil.*

- Heat the Pastis or Pernod in a small pot and pour it flaming into the soup. Correct the seasoning with salt and pepper, add chopped parsley, and serve immediately.
- If you like, you can have 1 or 2 slices of your French bread, lightly toasted.

GIGOT D'AGNEAU À LA PERSILLADE
(Leg of Lamb with Parsleyed Jus)

- Easy
  6 servings
  Expensive
  1½ hours

  1 small leg of lamb, no heavier than 5 lbs.
      (2.5 kg)
  1 garlic clove
  olive oil
  rosemary
  thyme
  savory
  2 cups Meat Stock (see Index) (.5 L)
  1 garlic clove, finely chopped
  US 3 TB, UK 1½ TB, chopped parsley
      (½ TB)
  unsalted butter
  salt and pepper

- Remove the leg of lamb from the refrigerator 24 hours ahead of time and let it stand at room temperature if the weather is cool, or hang it in a cool cellar if the weather is warm. The leg of lamb will have a much better flavor.
- Trim all the fat and gristle from the surface of the meat. Remove the thigh bone, tuck it under, and tie the leg so that the sirloin hides the head of the femur. Insert a garlic clove between the muscles of the top of the leg. If you desire, remove the eye of the Pope (see Note).

- Preheat oven to 400°F., 200°C. or 6 Regulo.
- Rub the leg of lamb with the olive oil. Crush rosemary, thyme and savory together. Sprinkle the leg of lamb well on top and bottom with the mixture of herbs. Place the meat on a rack. Roast for 1 hour and 15 minutes.
- Meanwhile, reduce the meat stock to 1¼ cups (3 generous dl), and set it aside to wait until the lamb is cooked.
- When the meat is done, remove it to a platter and let it stand for 5 minutes. Remove most of the fat from the roasting pan and deglaze it well with the reduced meat stock. Add the chopped garlic and parsley and 1 ounce of butter (1 TB).

- Salt and pepper the outside of the leg of lamb well. After you slice the meat, sprinkle a bit more salt and pepper over each slice. Serve on piping hot plates.

NOTE

A leg of lamb must be well aged to be good, otherwise it will feel crunchy when tasted. Do not hesitate to keep the leg on a rack on the bottom shelf of the refrigerator for a good week to mellow the meat. The last day at room temperature finishes the aging process well.

The "eye of the Pope" is considered a delicacy by some but a disaster by others; I am on the disaster side and always remove it for the reason that it contains a lymph node. It is easy to locate just above the shank. Slide a finger between the small muscles at the end of the rounds and you will find a lump of fat; work your finger in until you have identified the lump very well with your finger. Slip a knife blade into the opening and excise the lump. If you cut it open, you can see the node inside; most of the time it is healthy, but it has been known to show traces of infection.

JULIENNE AVIGNONNAISE
(Vegetables Julienne Avignon Style)

- Easy
  6 servings
  Inexpensive
  30 minutes

  4 baby zucchini (marrows or courgettes)
  4 red peppers
  4 green peppers
  1 TB olive oil (½ TB)
  1 TB butter (½ TB)
  salt and pepper

- Cut the zucchini on the slant into ¼-inch slices. Then cut those slices into ¼-inch-wide julienne strips. Set aside.

- Peel the red and green peppers; this is easily done with a potato peeler and does not take that much time; this peeling is only optional but makes a great deal of difference in the final taste and digestibility of the dish. Cut peppers also into ¼-inch julienne.

- Heat the olive oil in a frying pan and add all the zucchini. Toss until well heated through; remove to a plate. In the same pan, add the butter and all the pepper strips and toss over high heat until peppers are very hot but still crunchy.

- Return zucchini to the pan; salt and pepper them well. Serve immediately, all the vegetables very hot and still crunchy.

PÊCHES POCHÉES À LA CRÈME D'ORANGE
(Poached Peaches with Orange Cream)

- Easy
  6 servings
  Medium expensive
  1 hour

  6 peaches, nice and ripe
  2 cups red Côtes du Rhône wine (.5 L)
  2 cups sugar (500 g)
  6 cloves
  orange liqueur of your choice
  US 1 cup, UK 1 scant cup, heavy cream,
  **   whipped (.25 L)**

- Bring a pot of water to a boil and blanch the peaches. Peel them.

- Pour the wine into a saucepan, add the sugar and cloves, and bring to a boil to obtain a good syrup.

- Add the peaches and poach them whole in this syrup. Transfer the cooked peaches to a crystal dish.

- Reduce the syrup to approximately 1½ cups (3 generous dl). Add orange liqueur to your taste and refrigerate until very cold.

- Whip the cream to the light Chantilly stage and flavor it with as much orange liqueur as you like.

- To serve, put 1 peach in a dessert dish; top with the cream and as much syrup as you like.

NOTE
The syrup can be extended with more plain wine and reused to poach more peaches or pears.

ADVANCE PREPARATION:

EARLY MARKETING:
Approximately 1 week before dinner purchase the following ingredients:
    A. Wines: To drink: choose a Cassis for the mussels and a full-bodied, preferably old Châteauneuf-du-Pape to drink, and let it stand at room temperature.
    To cook the peaches: A bottle of good Côtes du Rhône which should not cost a fortune.
    B. The leg of lamb: The better aged a leg of lamb is, the more tender it will be and the more flavorful. Purchase it at least a week ahead. Unwrap it and let it stand on a cake rack on the bottom shelf of your refrigerator until the day before your celebration dinner.
    C. Is there any meat or fish stock in the house, in the refrigerator or the freezer? If not, think about it now; prepare it and store it properly.

The day before your dinner:

A. Order the mussels from the fish store. Choose if at all possible mussels cultivated in environment-controlled areas. They are much more expensive but also larger and juicier, and they render a lovely semisalty juice which is untainted by petroleum offtastes. Please be aware of the problem nowadays; it can spoil the taste of the best shellfish. The offtaste can have been acquired by the shellfish in not too clean waters or in diesel-powered trucks. Every country in the world has its share of shellfish men who cultivate healthy mussels, clams and oysters.

B. Reduce the meat stock while you cook that day's dinner, and keep it covered and refrigerated.

C. Peel and poach the peaches. Keep them immersed in their fragrant syrup so they acquire a delicious taste during an overnight to 24-hour stay in the refrigerator.

The day of your dinner:

A. 9 A.M. Remove the leg of lamb from the refrigerator.

B. 9 A.M. Reduce the peach syrup by two thirds and add the liqueur. It is most probable that some of it will be left over after you enjoy the dessert. Keep it in a small sealed jar and use it, 2 tablespoons at a time, to sweeten fresh fruit salads. A bit of that heavy syrup goes a long way.

C. 9:30 A.M. Scrub the mussels. Steam and shell them. With their juices, prepare the base of the soup as described in the recipe. Prepare the "aïoli" *liaison*. Keep everything covered with plastic wrap and refrigerated.

D. 10:30 A.M. Prepare the leg of lamb. Trim it, season it with herbs and aromatics, and oil it with a bit of olive oil. Arrange it on its roasting pan. Cover it loosely with a linen tea towel or cheesecloth and let it stand at room temperature until ready to roast it.

E. 11:15 A.M. Julienne the zucchini. Peel peppers with a potato peeler, and julienne peppers. Mix well and set aside in a bowl. Empty whipping cream into a large bowl, preferably metal. Keep it covered with plastic wrap on the coldest shelf of the refrigerator.

F. 11:30 A.M. Rest, stop, relax, and have fun if you can.

One hour before dinner:

A. Put leg of lamb to bake.
Halfway through the baking, finish and serve the soup.

At dinnertime:

A. Remove leg from the oven; let stand. Reheat reduced meat stock. Clear soup plates.

B. Meanwhile, quickly stir-fry vegetables and heat dinner plates in the dying oven.

C. Remove cheese from the refrigerator.

D. Deglaze the roasting pan with stock and add *persillade* and butter to the jus.

Serve meat and vegetables.

E. Serve cheese.

F. Whip cream for peaches and serve peaches.

MENU II—LANGUEDOC

CAVILHADA de GAMBAS
SAUPIQUET de LAPIN
NAVETS comme au PARDAILHAN
ROQUEFORT
FIGUES FRAÎCHES aux HERBES de GARRIGUES

CAVILHADA DE GAMBAS
(Shrimps with Garlic Purée)

- **Easy**
  6 servings
  Expensive
  1 hour

  2½ lbs. medium-size shrimps or prawns in shells (1 kg and 150 g)
  olive oil
  2 heads of garlic (30 cloves)
  1½ cups Fish Stock (see Index) (3 generous dl)
  salt and pepper
  chopped parsley

- Sort the shrimps and discard all foreign material.

- Heat the frying pan with 2 tablespoons olive oil (1 TB). Add the shrimps, approximately 12 at a time, and sauté over high heat until shells just turn red. Repeat operation with the remainder of the shellfish. Remove shrimps to a plate; do not wash the frying pan.

- Bring a pot of water to a boil. Add the garlic cloves and blanch them. Peel the garlic. Once it is peeled, heat a bit more olive oil in the frying pan, add the garlic cloves, and cook them until they turn light golden, but do not let them take on too much color or they will taste bitter.

- When the cloves are cooked, add the fish stock and let reduce by half. Empty the mixture into a blender container and purée. Empty the purée into the frying pan again.

- While the garlic cooks, shell the shrimps. As soon as the purée of garlic is in the pan, toss the shrimps into it and salt and pepper well. Reheat gently together, and add plenty of freshly chopped parsley.

- Serve hot with a slice or so of the French bread.

SAUPIQUET DE LAPIN
(Rabbit Saupiquet)

- **Easy to medium difficult**
  6 servings
  Medium expensive
  2 hours, plus 48 to 72 hours for marinating

2 small rabbits, each cut into 8 pieces (see Note)
rabbit livers
1½ bottles Cahors or Corbières wine, an older vintage if possible
1 carrot, thickly sliced
3 onions, thickly sliced
2 garlic cloves, mashed
12 juniper berries, crushed
6 each black and white peppercorns
US ¼ cup, UK 2 TB, red-wine vinegar (2 TB)
1 tsp. dried thyme
1 bay leaf, crumbled
6 cloves
¼ tsp. grated nutmeg
6 oz. dry Madeira (6 TB)
2 oz. Armagnac or Cognac (2 TB)
olive oil
Meat Stock (see Index)
5 oz. pancetta (150 g) (see Note)
3 dozen baby onions
parsley

- Put the rabbit pieces into 2 flat baking dishes (not aluminum). Keep the livers, well covered, in a separate dish.

- Empty the wine into a saucepan. Bring to a boil and add all the aromatics from the carrot to the grated nutmeg. Simmer for 20 minutes and turn the heat off. Let stand until completely cold.

- When cold, add the Madeira and 1 ounce (2 TB) of Armagnac or Cognac. Mix well and pour over the rabbits in both dishes. (Keep livers separate still.)

- Let rabbits marinate from 48 to 72 hours, depending on how much you like a gamey taste; turn the pieces of rabbit several times during marinating.

- To cook the rabbits, remove them from the marinade and dry each piece very carefully with a paper towel. Separate vegetables from the liquid of the marinade and reserve both. Heat some olive oil in a large sauteuse and brown the rabbit pieces, with the exception of the livers, which you will keep for the finishing of the sauce.

- Remove the browned pieces of rabbit to a plate, replace them in the sauteuse by the vegetables of the marinade, and cook until these are dry and starting to brown well. Return the rabbit pieces to the pot and arrange them on the vegetables of the marinade.

- Bring the marinade to a boil in a smaller pot and cook it for a few minutes. Strain the marinade over the meat, using a *chinois* to discard all the solids of the marinade (see Note). Add enough meat stock to barely cover the rabbit pieces. Cover the meat with a large piece of foil, dull side up, and fit it snugly over the meat so as to form an inverted lid. Cover with a pot lid and cook for 45 minutes or so, or until tender.

- Meanwhile, cut the *pancetta* into ⅓-inch cubes and render it gently until light golden outside but still soft inside (see Note). As soon as the *pancetta* is done, remove it to a plate and replace it in the pan by the baby onions. Sauté them until golden brown adding, if you desire, a very light pinch of sugar to accelerate the caramelization. Remove to the same plate as the *pancetta* and set aside.

- When the rabbit is done, remove the pieces to a dish. Taste the sauce and be glad if it tastes good enough. If not, do not hesitate to reduce it until it does. Strain it well into a clean saucepan, add the *pancetta*, baby onions and rabbit pieces, and reheat well together.

- Meanwhile, cut the livers (see Note) into small pieces and put them into a blender container. Blend to a purée; as soon as puréed coarsely, gradually add a good cup of the warm sauce, then more and more sauce until the mixture is well homogenized. Strain the liver binding back into the pot and mix well, shaking the pan back and forth on the burner. Reheat well without ever boiling.

- Finally heat the second ounce of Armagnac or Cognac and pour it flaming into the finished sauce. Correct salt and pepper carefully. Serve rabbit sprinkled with chopped parsley.

NOTES

This dish is not a true *saupiquet* but an imitation only since the sauce of a true *saupiquet* is bound with the blood of the rabbit or hare used. The liver replaces the blood here. If these livers are huge, *use only one of them*. The sauce should have a lovely rose color and never a tinge of green. *Remember that liver should poach only, never boil.*

The reason for reheating the marinade is to coagulate the blood in suspension in it. As the blood coagulates it agglutinates with the tannic acid in the wine and the marinade turns clear. This way, the final sauce is not muddy.

Also, please note that crunchy pork garnishes are not in the French Provincial taste and crisp bacon pieces are not liked by the Southern French.

NAVETS COMME AU PARDAILHAN
(Turnips as in Pardailhan)

- Easy
  6 servings
  Inexpensive
  30 minutes

20 oz. fresh white turnips (560 g)
US 2 TB, UK 1 TB, butter (1 oz.)
1 tsp. sugar
½ cup Meat Stock (see Index) approxi-
      mately (1 generous dl)
salt and pepper
chopped parsley

- Peel the turnips and cut them into ½-inch sticks. With a paring knife round off the angles of the sticks to obtain pieces that will roll easily in the glaze. Blanch the turnips until crunchy.
- Heat the butter in a skillet; add the sugar and approximately ½ cup meat stock (1 generous dl). Bring to a boil and add the turnips. Continue cooking until the glaze coats the turnips. Season with salt and pepper and serve sprinkled with parsley.

FIGUES AUX HERBES
(Figs with Herbs)

- Easy
  6 servings
  Expensive
  1 hour

24 green-skinned Kadota honey figs
US 1 TB, UK ½ oz., butter (15 g)
sugar
½ cup dry white wine (1 generous dl)
thyme
orégano
US 1 cup, UK 1 scant cup, light cream
      (2.5 dl)

- Preheat oven to 350°F., 165°C. or 5 Regulo.
- Cut off the stem of each fig; wash each fruit well.
- Butter a baking dish with the tablespoon of butter. Arrange the figs in the baking dish, stem side down.
- Sprinkle the figs with as much sugar as you like, and add the white wine to the baking dish. Bake in the preheated oven until golden and until the juices are forming a caramel at the bottom of the dish.
- Crumble thyme and orégano into the cream and pour the cold cream over the figs. The cream will dissolve the caramel. Mix well by twisting the dish back and forth.
- Let stand at room temperature until all the caramelized juices of the figs have melted and are mixed into the cream; then, refrigerate and serve chilled.

ADVANCE PREPARATION:

EARLY MARKETING:
Four days before your dinner, purchase the following ingredients:

A. The rabbits. Preferably use fresh rabbits which can always be located in Italian neighborhoods. Choose the rabbits very young. If you cannot find fresh rabbits, 2 boxes (2¼ lbs. each) of frozen California rabbits will be an adequate if not perfect replacement.

B. The *pancetta*. Pick it up while you are in the Italian market; it is the closest replacement for the *ventreche* of the Languedoc and Occitania.

C. Pick up fresh and fragrant garlic heads with fleshy cloves wrapped in pink skins.

D. Purchase semiripe figs and finish ripening them in a paper bag.

E. Purchase a bottle of Cassis for the shrimps, 2 bottles of good Corbières to marinate the rabbit, and the same or a Cahors or Châteauneuf-du-Pape wine for dinner. For the figs use a Banyuls or Frontignan.

F. Prepare the rabbit marinade as indicated in the recipe; let it cool completely and stand at room temperature overnight.

Three days before your dinner:

A. Marinate the rabbit for 48 to 72 hours. Turn several times during marinating and keep covered with plastic wrap. The longer the marination, the more like a wild rabbit the meat will taste.

The day before your dinner:

A. Purchase shrimps, and fish bones to make fish stock if you have none prepared.

B. Prepare and refrigerate fish stock if necessary.

C. Purchase Roquefort cheese.

The day of your dinner:

A. 9:30 A.M. Stir-fry shrimps and prepare garlic purée. Chop parsley for shrimps and turnips.

B. 10:30 A.M. Bake the figs and dilute their juices with the cream. Refrigerate.

C. 11:00 A.M. Cook the rabbit.

D. 11:30 A.M. While the rabbit stews, peel, shape, and blanch turnips.

E. 12:00 Noon Finish the *pancetta*-onion garnish for the rabbit. Strain the sauce and reduce it if necessary. Clean livers and cut into tiny pieces.

In the evening:

A. Let the wine breathe from 1 hour to ½ hour before dinner depending on your choice.

At dinnertime:

A. Remove Roquefort from refrigerator.

B. Reheat shrimps in garlic purée, season, and serve.

C. While shrimps are being enjoyed, reheat rabbit well and heat turnips in stock.

D. Remove shrimp plates.

E. Finish liver *liaison* of rabbit. Finish glazing turnips. Serve turnips and rabbit together.

F. Serve figs.

TEN POUNDS LOST

Basque Country, Béarn
Guyenne and Gascogne

DINNER IN THE BASQUE COUNTRY, THE BÉARN

The Béarn blends very suddenly into the Basque country at a small town called Bidache. The road going from Salis de Béarn to Bidache is dotted with farms, and here ducks are raised for the production of *foie gras* and *magrets*, the thick meaty breast of duck served as medium rare as a steak with a number of excellent garnishes.

From Bidache, all the way to the Spanish border the hills get higher and steeper, and huge flocks of sheep travel up and down slopes topped with the neatest and happiest Basque homes. A Basque town has the freshest and the most refreshing look especially when in the summer the town decks its windowsills with multiple flowers; in the winter it appears somewhat more austere.

This is corn country ever since corn was brought back from America. Corn is used in many dishes and in a solid bread called the *meture*. The woods are full of ferns which the artists of the ancient manufactures of faïence at l'Espelette reproduced on the edges of the plates; many modern versions of these designs exist.

The sheep produce several excellent cheeses. The best known in the United States is the Fromage des Pyrénées, but in the Basque country one prefers the Ardigazna, a fresh sweet goat cheese served in the afternoon with a heavy cup of chocolate or on delicious corn pancakes with homemade jams.

The Basque country ends at the rocks which make up the coast from Hendaye to Biarritz. One of the favorite fish dishes is the *Ttoro*; you will find here one of the multiple versions. Notice the favorite herb: thyme.

Izarra is a Basque mountain liqueur which you can replace by yellow Chartreuse or even Galliano if it proves difficult to locate; although there is some resemblance, the Basque liqueurs remain distinctively different.

MENU I—PAYS BASQUE

TTORO de FRUITS de MER
MAGRETS de CANARD MADAME DUTRONC
SALADE TIÈDE de POIVRONS et d'ARTHOUA
FROMAGE des PYRÉNÉES
COCA à l'IZARRA
WINES: CHÂTEAU CARBONNIEUX
MADIRAN or HAUT-MÉDOC

TTORO DE FRUITS DE MER
(Basque Shellfish Soup)

- **Easy**
  6 servings
  Expensive
  2 hours

  butter, corn oil or lard
  2 leeks, finely chopped
  6 garlic cloves, finely chopped
  2 onions, finely chopped
  2 red peppers, peeled and diced
  salt and pepper
  thyme
  1 bay leaf
  US 2 cups, UK 1¾ cups, dry white wine
      (4.5 to 5 dl)
  1 quart mussels, scrubbed (1 L)
  US 3 cups, UK 2⅔ cups, Fish Stock (see
      Index) (7.5 dl)
  US ½ cup, UK ½ scant cup, tomato purée
      (1 generous dl)
  6 squids, cleaned and chopped
  ½ lb. shrimps in shells (250 g)
  ½ lb. sea scallops, diced (250 g)
  6 slices of French bread
  1 garlic clove, whole and peeled
  chopped parsley

- Heat 2 to 3 tablespoons (1 to 1½ TB) of the fat of your choice in a large sauteuse and add all the vegetables. Salt and pepper them, cover them, and let them cook until translucent.

- Now, remove the pot lid and raise the heat, tossing the vegetables in the hot fat until they lose their moisture and start browning.

- Add thyme, bay leaf, white wine and the mussels. Steam the mussels opened.

- Remove the mussels to a plate, shell them, and put them in a bowl. Strain the broth carefully into a clean pot.

- To the pot of mussel broth, add the fish stock and tomato purée. Add the squids and bring to a boil. Simmer for 40 minutes, or until tender.

- Meanwhile, sauté the shrimps in a bit of oil or butter in a skillet, and shell them. Put the shelled shrimps in the same bowl as the mussels.
- When the squids are done, raise the heat and bring the soup to a boil. Add the scallops, the mussels and the shrimps. Reheat to the boiling point. Correct seasoning.

- While the soup reheats, toast the bread slices and rub them with the whole garlic clove.
- Serve in large soup bowls, well sprinkled with chopped parsley. There is little broth and a lot of shellfish.

MAGRETS DE CANARD DE MADAME DUTRONC
(Duck Fillets as Prepared by a Frenchwoman)

- **Medium difficult**
  6 servings
  Medium expensive
  1 hour, over 2 days

  6 breasts of duck (fillets)
  1½ to 2 oz. Armagnac (1½ to 2 TB)
  quatre-épices (see Glossary)
  US 4 TB, UK 2 TB, butter (60 g)
  1 lb. button mushrooms (500 g)
  salt and pepper
  2 garlic cloves, finely chopped
  US 2 TB, UK 1 TB, chopped parsley
  (1 TB)
  US 1 cup, UK 1 scant cup, Meat Stock
  (see Index) (2.5 dl)

- To lift the fillets of the ducks, first remove the legs. Then, pull the skin covering backward, thus exposing the 2 fillets or *magrets* (see Introduction).
- With a sharp knife, separate the *magret* from the breast bone and remove the clearly visible tendon that attached it to the wingjoint. No skin should be left attached to the *magrets*.

- Put the *magrets* in a baking dish. Sprinkle them with Armagnac and a little bit of *quatre-épices*. Cover the dish with a plastic wrap and refrigerate overnight.
- The next day, approximately 1 hour before dinner, heat a tablespoon or so of butter (15 g) in a large sauteuse. Add the mushrooms; season with salt and pepper. Cover and cook until the moisture has exuded. Uncover the pan, let the juices evaporate, and sauté until the mushrooms start browning. At this point add the garlic and parsley and toss well together. Remove to a bowl. *Do not wash the skillet.*
- Just before serving the *magrets*, pan-fry them in butter, so they remain rare. Remove them to a plate; keep them warm.
- Deglaze the pan with 1 ounce of Armagnac (1 TB). Add the meat stock and reduce the stock by one third.

- Add the mushrooms and the remainder of the butter, keeping the sauce at a rolling boil until the butter has been completely emulsified.
- Roll the *magrets* into the sauce and serve promptly with the lukewarm pepper salad.

NOTES
To know what to do with duck legs and skin see Périgord dinner.

I have enjoyed this presentation of duck *magrets* at "l'Auberge de Beuste" in Salis de Béarn, a tiny, lovely inn of which Madame Dutronc and her children are the owners. I have added the mushrooms.

SALADE TIÈDE DE POIVRONS ET D'ARTHOUA
(Lukewarm Pepper and Corn Salad in the Basque Style)

- Easy
  6 servings
  Very affordable
  40 minutes

  3 green peppers
  3 red peppers
  US 2 cups, UK 1¾ cups, yellow corn kernels (.5 L)

  DRESSING
  1 small red onion
  1 garlic clove
  1 tsp. tomato paste
  chopped parsley
  US 2 TB, UK 1 TB, cider vinegar (1 TB)
  US ½ cup, UK ⅓ cup, corn oil (1 generous dl)
  salt and pepper
  3 large lettuce leaves

- Cut all the peppers, red and green, into quarters. Peel them, using a potato peeler, and cut them into ¼-inch-wide julienne strips. Keep red and green peppers separated on 2 different plates.
- Blanch the corn. Keep it warm in its blanching water.
- *Prepare the dressing:* Chop the red onion and mash the garlic clove.

Mix with tomato paste, US 2 tablespoons, UK 1 tablespoon, chopped parsley (1 TB). Add vinegar, oil, salt and pepper to taste, and mix very well. Let stand for about 1 hour to blend flavors. The dressing will separate.

- After the dressing has been ripening for 1 hour, spoon US 2 tablespoons, UK 1 tablespoon, oil (1 TB) directly from its surface into a skillet. Heat well. Add the green pepper strips and sauté for a few minutes, then add the red pepper strips and toss well together until heated through but still crunchy.
- Drain the corn, pat dry, and toss into the peppers. Mix well and add the dressing. Correct seasoning.
- Line a vegetable dish with lettuce leaves and empty the salad into the dish. Serve with the *magrets*.

NOTE
Arthoua is the Basque word for maize (in French, *maïs*); corn is well liked in the Basque provinces.

COCA À L'IZARRA
(Baked Custard Flavored with Basque Liqueur)

- Easy
  6 servings
  Inexpensive
  1¼ hours

  US ¾ cup, UK ⅔ cup, sugar (190 g)
  butter
  6 large eggs
  US 2½ cups, UK 2¼ cups, milk (6 dl)
  1-inch-long piece of vanilla bean
  US ½ cup, UK ⅓ cup, Izarra or Galliano
    (1 generous dl)
  US ¾ cup, UK ⅔ cup, whipping cream
    (2 generous dl)

- Place one third of the sugar in a saucepan with a few tablespoons of water and cook it to the deep caramel stage. Pour it into a 1½-quart charlotte mold. Twist the mold in all directions to coat it well with the hot caramel. Finally, turn it upside down over a plate. Let cool.

- When the mold is cold, butter every little bit of the inside surface that is not coated with caramel.

- Break the eggs into a bowl. Place the remainder of the sugar in the saucepan in which the caramel cooked. Add the milk and bring to the scalding point. Cut the piece of vanilla bean open and scrape the seeds into the hot milk. Stir well to mix the vanilla and dissolve the sugar.

- Beat the eggs; gradually beat in the flavored milk. Add half of the liqueur. Strain the mixture into the prepared charlotte mold.

- Preheat oven to 325°F., 165°C. or 5 Regulo.

- Set the charlotte mold in a baking dish. Bring a large kettle of water to a full boil. Put the baking dish on the middle shelf of the preheated oven. Pour the boiling water into the baking dish to form a water bath, and cover the charlotte mold with a large lid.

- Bake for 35 to 40 minutes, or until a skewer inserted two thirds of the way to the center of the custard comes out clean and dry.

- Remove the baking dish from the oven and let everything cool together; the custard will finish cooking in the cooling water bath. When cold, remove from the water bath, wrap in clear plastic, and refrigerate overnight.

- To serve, unmold onto a platter with a raised edge. Beat the cream very lightly until barely foamy. Add the remaining liqueur and pour over the custard.

ADVANCE PREPARATION:

EARLY MARKETING:
One week before your dinner, purchase the following:
    A. Wines to drink:

        Château Carbonnieux

        Madiran

    B. Wines to cook:

        1 bottle of ordinary white Graves

        Armagnac for your duck sauce. If Armagnac proves difficult to find, buy a small flask of Cognac or even brandy of local origin. Since there is quite a bit of cider consumption in Basque countries, applejack distilled from apple cider could also do very well. Check your shelves before buying something new.

        1 bottle Izarra or replacement (see Introduction)

The day before your dinner:
    A. Order and pick up mussels, shrimps, scallops and squids as well as fish bones to make fish stock.

    B. Prepare fish stock (see Index).

    C. Make sure that you have meat stock (see Index). If you do not, purchase some meaty bones and prepare some.

    D. Purchase the bell peppers, peel and julienne them, store them in plastic bags.

    E. Purchase 3 ducks and a box of Kosher salt.

    F. Bone the ducks to obtain 6 clean *magrets* and marinate them in Armagnac.

    G. Salt the legs and wing tips of the ducks to prepare them for a *confit* (see Périgord dinner), and render the duck fat.

    H. Purchase the mushrooms for the *magrets* dish and store them in the refrigerator.

    I. Prepare and bake the Coca dessert. Keep it refrigerated until ready to use.

The day of your dinner:

A. 4 P.M. Beat the cream with the Izarra for the dessert and store in the refrigerator ready to use.

B. 5 P.M. Start cooking the Ttoro. Prepare all the shellfish and set them on separate plates or dishes. Steam the mussels and cook the squids. Stir-fry and shell the shrimps; dice the scallops.

C. 5:30 P.M. Cook the mushrooms Remove the *magrets* and the meat stock from the refrigerator so they reach room temperature before you cook them.

D. 6 P.M. Blanch the corn for the salad. Prepare the dressing.

At dinnertime:

A. Bring Pyrénées cheese to room temperature.

B. Finish the Ttoro and serve it.

C. Finish preparing the ingredients for the salad; keep them in separate containers up to the last minute: peppers in skillet, corn hot in a colander over its blanching water.

D. Start cooking the *magrets*. While they cook, put the salad together.

E. Finish the sauce for the *magrets*. Put the dish together.

F. Serve *magrets* and warm salad.

G. Serve cheese.

H. Serve custard.

DINNER IN GUYENNE AND GASCOGNE

Your dinner will transport you somewhere in the Landes between Dax and Bordeaux. A long busy road cuts like a huge knife blade through one of the most majestic pine forests still existing in western Europe. Toward the west are huge beaches constantly battered by the gigantic waves of the Atlantic. The dunes extend for close to 150 miles, interrupted only by the huge basin of Arcachon, a chic resort in the summer and a quiet very sleepy town in the winter. In Arcachon, the main source of income besides tourism is ostreiculture. The people of Bordeaux eat the small Arcachon oysters with hot little sausages, a custom that probably only a Bordelais can find attractive.

In all the local dishes, much use is made of the huge mushrooms that grow at the foot of pine trees, that are known in the area as the "Bolet de Bordeaux," a local name for the *Boletus* known elsewhere as *Boletus edulis*. Some of these *Boleti* weight as much as a pound each; a few years back a farmer picked one weighing over three pounds.

Toward the west beyond the Chalosse country of peace and fattened ducks and geese, lies the birth ground of that brandy of all brandies, the golden Armagnac which is distilled in a triangle of countryside limited by the cities of Auch, Condom and Eauze. Every Thursday Eauze offers an Armagnac market, which is immensely interesting. Armagnac, always 104 proof, gives the food of these regions its strength and great character.

The favorite pastry, of which I give you here a flat version in the Feuilleté Landais, is a "Serpent," close relative to the strudel and left as an inheritance by the Saracens as they retreated toward the depth of the central mountains of the Auvergne after being beaten at Poitiers by Charles Martel in 732 A.D.

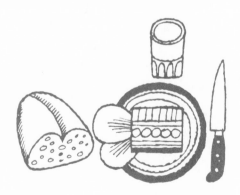

MENU II—GUYENNE AND GASCOGNE

ANGUILLES aux POIREAUX
STEAKS de VEAU aux CÈPES
HARICOTS VERTS à la LANDAISE
AMON or SAINT PAULIN
FEUILLETÉ LANDAIS
WINE: AN EXCELLENT PAUILLAC ALL THROUGH THE MEAL

ANGUILLES AUX POIREAUX
(Eels with Leeks)

- **Easy**
  6 servings
  Medium expensive
  1 hour

  2 large or 3 medium-size eels
  6 sole heads
  1 large onion, sliced
  6 medium-size leeks
  6 medium-size carrots, thickly sliced
  chopped parsley stems
  1 bay leaf
  ½ tsp. dried thyme
  **1 bottle of good oldish Pauillac of your
      choice**
  6 shallots
  **3 slices of white bread, crusts removed,
      cut into 2 triangles each**
  US ¾ cup, UK 6 oz., butter (180 g)
  salt
  chopped parsley
  meat extract as needed
  coarsely cracked pepper

- Preferably have the fish store kill the eels for it is not an easy task. The eels will be delivered to you skinned and dressed. Demand the heads please; you need them.

- First, make a good red-wine stock using the eel heads and 5 or 6 sole heads. Place the sliced onion, the green part of the leeks, the sliced carrots, chopped parsley stems, bay leaf and a large pinch of thyme in a large saucepan. Add the fish heads and the bottle of wine. Bring to a boil. Turn down to a simmer and cook for 40 minutes. As the stock cooks, break the fish heads down to a pulp to release a maximum of flavor. Cool completely. Strain through a *chinois*.

- Cut the eels into 2½-inch-long pieces. Chop the shallots extremely finely. Set aside.

- Toast the triangular croutons and fry them in US 2 tablespoons, UK 1 tablespoon, butter (1 TB).

- Cut the white part of the leeks into ½-inch-wide pieces. Do not blanch them, but heat US 2 tablespoons, UK 1 tablespoon, butter (1 TB), and sauté the leeks in it. Salt and pepper the leeks and étuvé them until they are soft. Add the shallots; mix well.

- Strain the fish stock over leeks and shallots. Bring to a rapid boil, add the pieces of eel, and bring back to a boil. Remove from the heat, and let stand covered for 5 minutes.

- Remove the eels and leeks to a deep dish; keep warm.

- Bring the cooking juices of the eel to a violent boil. Reduce to US ⅔ cup, UK ½ cup (2 dl) and whisk in the remaining butter. Add parsley, meat extract, salt if needed, and a lot of coarsely cracked pepper.

- Return eel and leeks to the sauce. Heat well together and serve promptly. Decorate with the fried croutons. Each portion should be spooned onto a crouton. Note that the sauce is *not strained*. The shallots should remain in it. Sprinkle each serving with freshly chopped parsley.

NOTE

Eels are not always easy to find. You can replace them by striped bass slices or bluefish steaks or any fish usually cooked with a red-wine sauce in your area.

The sediment of the wine can also be used in this sauce; the wine need not be decanted for cooking.

STEAKS DE VEAU AUX CÈPES
(Veal Steaks with Cèpes)

- Medium difficult
  6 servings
  Very expensive
  1 hour

  1 side (half) of a loin of veal
  2 small onions
  1 small carrot
  3 shallots
  3 large Boleti eduli, or 1 oz. dried Boleti eduli presoaked in a little lukewarm water plus ½ lb. medium-size fresh mushrooms (250 g)
  ¼ lb. unsalted butter (125 g)
  salt and pepper
  US 2 TB, UK 1 TB, Armagnac (1 oz.)
  US ⅔ cup, UK ½ cup, Meat Stock (see Index) (2 scant dl)
  chopped parsley

- Bone the side of the veal loin completely to obtain a whole sirloin strip of meat and a tenderloin also. Remove all traces of fat from the surface of the meat.

- Tie the sirloin strip at ¾-inch intervals so as to block it into a round shape. Cut between the ties to obtain ¾-inch-thick veal steaks. You should have 2 steaks per person.

- Now prepare the *brunoise*. Chop onions, carrot and shallots into ⅛-inch *brunoise*. Set aside.

- If you are using fresh *Boleti*, remove the stems, clean them, and slice them. Remove the foam (tubes) from under the caps and slice the caps into ⅛-inch-thick slices. Set aside. If you use dried cèpes, soak them in very little lukewarm water. Slice the fresh mushrooms thinly; set aside.

- First cook the fresh cèpes or the revived dried cèpes/mushroom combination. Heat US 2 tablespoons, UK 1 tablespoon butter (1 TB) in a large skillet; add the prepared *brunoise* and étuvé nicely together. When onions and shallots are soft, add the cèpes or the combination of revived cèpes with their soaking water and mushrooms. Salt and pepper the mixture and cover to extract more moisture. When all the moisture has exuded, pour it off into a small cup and continue cooking the

vegetables until they brown. Add a bit more butter if necessary. Remove the mushrooms or cèpes to a plate.

- Do not clean the pan. Add a bit more butter and cook the steaks in the butter, keeping them pink inside, *this is essential*. Salt and pepper the steaks well.

- Remove steaks to a plate. Deglaze the pan with the Armagnac. Add the reserved mushroom juices and the meat stock, and return the mushrooms to the skillet. Reduce together to about US ⅓ cup, UK ¼ cup (1 scant dl) liquid, and add US 6 tablespoons, UK 3 tablespoons, butter (3 TB), softened. Keep boiling very hard until the butter has melted.

- Add chopped fresh parsley. Correct final seasoning. Serve steaks topped with mushroom ragout.

HARICOTS VERTS À LA LANDAISE
(Green Beans as Prepared in Dax)

- **Easy**
  6 servings
  Expensive
  25 minutes

  1 lb. fine green beans (500 g)
  6 shallots
  US 4 TB, UK 2 TB, butter (2 TB)
  salt and pepper
  2 oz. prosciutto, in 1 thick slice ¼ inch
  thick, diced (60 g)
  chopped parsley

- Blanch beans in boiling water for 7 to 8 minutes. Drain well and rinse under cold water. Pat dry.

- Slice the shallots very thinly. While the beans are cooking, sauté shallots in half of the butter until tender. Proceed very gently so as not to burn them.

- Add remaining butter to the pan and toss the beans in it. Pepper them well and add the diced prosciutto. Add a sprinkling of chopped parsley. Correct seasoning and serve.

FEUILLETÉ LANDAIS
(Specialty Cake of the Landes)

■ **Difficult**
6 servings
Medium expensive
1½ hours

US **2 cups, UK 1¾ cups, sifted flour**
   (225 g)
½ tsp. salt
US **2 TB, UK 1 TB, oil of your choice**
   (1 TB)
US **½ cup, UK ½ scant cup, lukewarm to**
   warmish water (1 generous dl)
½ lb. butter, melted and cooled (250 g)
US **¾ cup, UK ⅔ cup, granulated sugar**
   (190 g)
US **½ cup, UK ⅓ cup, Armagnac (1 gen-**
   erous dl)
1 tsp. orange-flower water

- Make a well in the flour; add the salt, the oil and the lukewarm water. Work into a dough.

- Knead the dough for a full 20 minutes, or until no more air bubbles show in the dough when it is cut into halves.

- Divide dough into 12 equal pieces. Shape each piece into a 1½-inch disk, flattened. Let them rest, loosely covered with a tea towel, for 30 minutes.

- With a rolling pin, flatten each disk as flat as it can be. Brush with butter.

- Butter a large pizza pan well. Stretch the dough paper-thin over the whole width of the pan. Brush with butter, and sprinkle with US 1 tablespoon, UK ½ tablespoon, granulated sugar (½ TB). Mix Armagnac with orange-flower water. Using your finger, sprinkle some of the Armagnac mixture over the dough.

- Repeat this operation with all 12 pieces of dough, ending with a sprinkling of sugar and a sprinkling of Armagnac and orange-flower water.

- Preheat oven to 350°F., 180°C. or 5 to 6 Regulo.

- Refrigerate the cake for 30 minutes. Cut the excess dough flush with the edge of the pizza pan. Bake in the preheated oven until golden and very crisp.

- Remove the cake to a cake rack. As soon as it is cool, cut into wedges.

- Finish the dinner with a snifter of Armagnac.

ADVANCE PREPARATION:

EARLY MARKETING:
One week before your dinner, purchase the following ingredients:

A. Several bottles of quite good older Pauillac. I propose no name since all stores offer a wide choice at diverse prices. The older the wine, the better. Let the bottles stand at room temperature to allow sediment to settle at the bottom of the bottle.

B. Order the loin of veal.

C. Look for fresh *Boleti* if your area offers them; if not, remember that dried *Boleti* are not always easy to find, but an Italian neighborhood is sure to have them in 1-ounce packages. Their Italian name is *porcini*.

The day before your party:

A. Purchase eels, fish bones and leeks.

B. Purchase the loin of veal; bone it. If you have no meat stock, use all the bones and belly flaps to prepare some stock.

C. Purchase and refrigerate the fresh mushrooms if you are using them. Also the green beans.

D. Purchase the cheese. The Amon mentioned here is not easy to find in cheese stores, but can be replaced by Saint-Paulin. If you are in an Italian neighborhood, try to locate fresh ricotta or semiripened Roman ricotta imported from Italy.

E. Purchase all aromatics needed for both first and main course.

The day of your party:

A. 11 A.M. Soak the dry *Boleti* in lukewarm water for 2 to 3 hours.

B. 2:15 P.M. Prepare the first part of the fish sauce—the stock using the eels and sole heads. Strain and set aside.

C. 2:30 P.M. While stock cooks, prepare the shallots, leeks, etc., for sautéing; chop parsley for the whole meal.

D. 3 P.M. If you use regular fresh mushrooms, slice them, étuvé them, keep them covered with plastic wrap. See recipe for details.

E. 3:30 P.M. Cook the shallots for the beans, and blanch the beans.

F. 4 P.M. Tie and cut the veal as directed in the recipe. Set slices on a plate. Cover with plastic wrap and leave outside of the refrigerator in a cool place; the meat will cook faster and better. Keep refrigerated only if the weather is very hot.

G. 4:30 P.M. Prepare the *feuilleté*. You may want the help of a family member or friend to help you stretch the dough better. Bake the *feuilleté*. It keeps for several days quite deliciously since it is very rich.

H. 5:30 P.M. Try to rest and set your table if you have no help.

At dinnertime:

A. While you are toasting your friends and your success at already losing so much weight, poach the eels and put the sauce to reduce (use your timer to call you back to the kitchen!).

B. Bring the cheese to room temperature.

C. Finish the fish dish and serve it.

D. Meanwhile, reheat the mushrooms over very low heat. Reheat the meat stock also in a small pot over low heat. Cook the veal.

E. While the veal cooks, reheat the shallots for the bean dish, and toss the beans into it to reheat them.

F. Finish the veal sauce. Present the veal steaks arranged around the edge of a round platter; pile the beans in the center.

G. Serve the cheese.

H. Serve the *feuilleté*.

FIFTEEN POUNDS LOST

Périgord, Rouergue, Quercy
Bretagne

DINNER IN PÉRIGORD, ROUERGUE AND QUERCY

Welcome to the lands of truffles and *confits*, great flocks of geese raised for *foie gras*, and even more, land ancestrally graced by human emotions; the caves of Cromagnon man can be seen, with their startling wall paintings of animals.

Much later in history, this part of France was part of the inheritance of Eleanor of Aquitaine and passed from French into English hands when she married Henri of Anjou or Plantagenet, Henry II of England. A whole series of cities survive along the Dordogne which were fortified by Eleanor and were called *bastides*. The French armies, south of the Dordogne, held a corresponding line of fortified *bastides* along the valley of the Lot and the Garonne rivers.

Life in those *bastides* was enriched with beautiful fare. The truffles of course are famed; who does not know about the truffle-digging pigs? but the truffle is becoming rarer and rarer in Périgord. The food lore remains rich in fruits, walnuts and barnyard animals producing some of the most delightful dishes ever to be enjoyed. Soups remain favorites, made with all the vegetables grown behind one's house on a small plot where one cultivates fresh greens and roots. The Saracens left the herb saffron in an ancient version of their *chorba*, prepared exclusively for funeral dinners, found from Périgord through Quercy and Rouergue. I am giving you a recipe for it. Rabbits, ducks, chickens and pigeons reign supreme among the foods of the women of these regions. The *confit*, or meat preserved by salting and cooking in its own fat to preserve it through the winter, is not an exclusive monopoly of the Périgord, but it is done there with such perfection and dedication that it is a joy to behold a larder full of earthen-ware jars filled to the brim and covered with the neatest covers of frilled white paper. *Confits* are always made with those animals which fatten so much that their body weight is almost 50 percent fat: duck, geese, pork, even fat hens.

Local fruits are plentiful, and every fruit grows to the most delicious and colorful maturity. The dessert I am giving you here was a favorite in my cousins' house where it was made in the hearth, in a frying pan embedded in hot coals, then cooked on top with a salamander.

MENU I—PÉRIGORD, ROUERGUE AND QUERCY

MOURTAYROL
CONFIT de CANARD
JULIENNE de CÉLERI aux NOIX
ECHOURGNAC
FLAUGNARDE aux REINES-CLAUDE
WINES: PÉCHARMANT or CAHORS with the CONFITS
MONBAZILLAC with or after the FLAUGNARDE

MOURTAYROL
(A Saffron Vegetable Soup)

■ Easy
6 servings
Affordable
20 minutes for preparation, plus 4 hours
    for cooking

12 chicken wings
12 chicken necks
2 lbs. chicken gizzards (1 kg)
1½-lb. piece of pork rind (250 g)
3 large older carrots, cut up
2 onions, stuck with 2 cloves
3 shallots
1 head of garlic, cloves crushed but left in
    their skin
3 larger leeks, cut into ⅓-inch slices
2 small white turnips, cut up
2 small sprigs of celery
½ tsp. quatre-épices (see Glossary)
salt

GARNISH
1 garlic clove
US 3 TB, UK 1½ TB, chopped parsley
    (1½ TB)
2 baby zucchini (marrows or courgettes)
1 large carrot
US 6 TB, UK 3 TB, butter (90 g)
salt and pepper

1 small envelope whole saffron, .045 oz.
    (1.5 g)
6 slices of French bread

- Place the chicken wings, necks and gizzards and the pork rind, cut into 1-inch cubes, in a pot. Cover with cold water, and bring to a boil slowly. Discard the water as soon as it boils.

- Replace the blanching water by 3 quarts cold water (3 L). Bring to a boil again; add all the vegetables and aromatics, then 2 teaspoons salt. Cook steadily until reduced to 1½ quarts. Strain and defatten.

- *Prepare the garnish:* Chop both garlic and parsley. Cut zucchini and carrot lengthwise into halves. With a melon baller, remove the core of each vegetable so as to obtain vegetable "boats." Set the boats, rounded side up, on a slicing board and cut into ⅛-inch half-moons.

• Heat US 3 tablespoons, UK 1½ tablespoons, butter (1½ TB) in a skillet. Add the carrots, season with salt and pepper, and sauté for 2 to 3 minutes. Add the zucchini, chopped garlic and parsley, and the envelope of saffron. Ladle 1 full ladle of hot broth over this garnish and let steep for 10 minutes.

• To serve, toast the bread slices, brush them lightly with melted butter, and sprinkle with salt. Break the slices into irregular cubes. Present the cubes in a bowl with a large serving spoon.

• To finish the soup, bring the bulk of the broth to a boil. Add the vegetable and saffron garnish. Correct salt and pepper one last time and serve.

NOTE
Do not hesitate to replace chicken giblets by goose, turkey or duck giblets.

The vegetable garnish gives the soup a "modern" look; in the old days it was made with a *farci*, or cabbage leaves filled with lightly seasoned forcemeat.

CONFIT DE CANARD
(Duck Cooked in its own Fat)

■ **Easy**
6 servings
Affordable
24 hours for salting, 2½ hours for cooking

6 duck legs (see Basque dinner)
6 duck wings (see Basque dinner)
coarse salt
fat and skin of the duck
water
thyme
1 bay leaf
3 garlic cloves
US ⅓ cup, UK ¼ cup, Meat Stock (see Index) (1 scant dl)

• Place the duck legs in a large baking dish, place the wings in a smaller one. Sprinkle both dishes generously with coarse salt. Turn the joints over and sprinkle again. Cover with plastic wrap and either refrigerate or keep in a cool place. Keep in salt for a full 24 hours.

• Cut the duck skins and fat pads into ¾-inch cubes. Place them in a large pot and cover them with water. Slowly bring to a boil. Let cook gently. The water will evaporate and the fat will melt and render to a clear liquid. The fat will be ready to use when the cracklings of skin are nice and golden. Strain the fat. Cool it.

• Remove the duck joints from the salt about 3 hours before dinner. Wipe off excess salt and place joints in a single layer in a flat baking dish. Sprinkle them with thyme; add a bay leaf to the dish and the garlic cloves. Spoon large spoonfuls of duck fat on top of the duck.

• Preheat oven to 325°F., 165°C. or 5 Regulo.

- Bake the duck until a skewer inserted at the thickest part of the leg comes out easily.

- To serve, remove the duck pieces from the fat. Pat very dry with a paper towel. Pour the duck fat carefully into a bowl, leaving only those very brown bits of juice at the bottom of the dish. Dissolve the brown bits with the meat stock. Set this aside for your celery.

- Arrange the pieces of *confit* on a heated rustic serving platter; in the center place the celery and walnut dish described in the next recipe.

NOTES

A book could be written about the uses of those cracklings. Try them on a slice of rye bread rubbed with a clove of garlic! or in a salad.

Any leftover *confit* can be potted in its own fat. Keep the fat stored; if you have no time to render duck fat on another occasion, you will have it ready to use. Stored in the refrigerator, fat keeps for 1 full year or more.

JULIENNE DE CÉLERI AUX NOIX
(Sautéed Celery and Walnuts)

- Easy
  6 servings
  Inexpensive
  20 minutes

  1 celery stalk
  salt
  US ¼ cup, UK 2 TB, butter (60 g)
  pepper
  US ½ cup, UK ⅓ cup, chopped walnuts
     (50 g)
  US 3 TB, UK 1½ TB, chopped parsley
     (1½ TB)

- Remove the thick ribs of the celery from the root. Keep the yellow heart for making soup or stock. Peel each celery rib carefully, removing all the strings and fibers on the vegetable. Cut each rib across into paper-thin half-moons.

- Bring a large pot of water to a boil. Add 1½ teaspoons salt per quart of water. Put the sliced celery in a large conical strainer and blanch for 1 minute, no more. Pat dry in a tea towel.

- Heat the butter well in a very large skillet. Add the celery and toss in the butter over very high heat just until heated through. Season with salt and pepper; toss in the walnuts and the parsley.

- Serve with the *confit* of duck.

FLAUGNARDE AUX REINES-CLAUDE
(Greengage Custard Pie)

- Easy
  6 servings
  Medium expensive
  1 hour

  12 ripe greengage plums
  1 oz. Armagnac or Cognac (1 TB)
  US ½ cup, UK ⅓ cup, flour (60 g)
  US 3 TB, UK 1½ TB, sugar (1½ TB)
  ½ tsp. salt
  2 large eggs
  US 2 TB, UK 1 TB, sour cream (15 to 20 g)
  US ⅔ cup, UK ½ cup, milk (2 scant dl)
  grated rind of 1 lemon
  butter
  confectioners' sugar

- Preheat oven to 375°F., 190°C. or 6 Regulo.

- Cut up the plums to remove the pits. Put plums and Armagnac in a mixing bowl. Let stand while you prepare the flan batter.

- In a mixer bowl, put the flour, sugar, salt, eggs and sour cream. Mix until smooth. Dilute with milk, add lemon rind, and homogenize on high speed.

- Butter a 9-inch porcelain pie or quiche plate. Strain one third of the batter into the dish. Bake until set. Arrange the fruit on top. Pour the maceration juices of the fruit into the remaining batter and pour this over the fruit.

- Bake for 35 to 40 minutes. Serve cool, sprinkled with confectioners' sugar.

ADVANCE PREPARATION:

Remember that the duck can be made as much ahead of time as you wish; it can be stored in a container completely immersed in its own fat and well covered. Refrigerated or stored in a cold pantry or cellar, the duck will keep for as long as 6 months. If you have not prepared the duck ahead of time, here is the complete schedule to follow:

EARLY MARKETING:
One week before your dinner:
    A. Purchase the wines: Try to find red Pécharmant or Cahors, which are local or close-by wines. If unavailable, a good red Côtes du Rhône such as Gigondas or Cornas will do very well with the *confit* and the cheese.
    Find a nice Monbazillac for dessert or after dessert.

B. Purchase the cheese; if Echourgnac is difficult to find, purchase a good chèvre.

The day before your dinner:

A. Purchase the chicken giblets for the soup and prepare the broth of the soup. Prepare the garnish of the soup; do not cook it. *Do not use the saffron* in the garnish until 15 minutes before serving.

B. Purchase the ducks if you have no *confit* ready in your larder already. Salt the duck parts. Render the fat and filter it through several layers of cheese-cloth.

C. Purchase the celery; string it and slice it. Wash it and store it in a plastic bag.

D. Chop the walnuts. Chop the parsley and store it in a cup covered with plastic wrap.

E. Purchase the plums; check that you have either Armagnac or Cognac.

The day of your dinner:

A. 4 P.M. To finish the Mourtayrol, strain the broth, taste it, and correct the seasoning. Have the vegetable garnish and the saffron ready to use later.

B. 4:30 P.M. Wipe the *confit* of its salt; prepare it for baking and put to bake. Count 2½ hours from this point to dinnertime.

C. 5 P.M. Prepare the plums for the *flaugnarde* and prepare the batter. Put the pie together, but do not bake yet.

At dinnertime:

A. Etuvé the vegetable garnish of the soup, add the saffron, let it steep, then add to the bouillon. Correct the seasoning and serve.

B. Remove the cheese from the refrigerator.

C. Before you serve the soup, put the *flaugnarde* to bake.

D. The duck *confit* should be done before you serve the soup; check that it is.

E. Prepare the celery at the last minute.

F. Serve the *confit* and celery.

G. Serve the cheese.

H. Serve the *flaugnarde*.

DINNER IN BRETAGNE

Imagine that you are in Brittany, at the tip of the peninsula where the winds and the ocean batter the land with such unmerciful strength that the land slowly wears away.

Civilization has not been tender to Brittany; the forever larger cities steadily encroach over what is left of the original moors. A few villages and small ports have escaped this onslaught and still nest sleepily in rocky coves. Every morning at dawn the small local fishing fleet brings in the catch of the night, which is swiftly collected by the trucks of shippers or put directly on the Paris train if the little town is large enough to have a train station. The old women of the village are always there to work at the cleanup of the fish and to pick up whatever inferior morsels are at hand for the night's dinner. The baskets of sea crayfish and of huge sea scallops in their shells are impressive. Whatever fish is too small to be marketable goes into the local pots.

Meals in Brittany are rounded with a lot of the glorious vegetables that the peninsula nurtures, thanks to a mild climate brought by the Gulf Stream. Artichokes and cauliflower as well as onions and beans are the all-time favorites. Artichoke heads are often as large as that of a toddler, but the tiny baby artichokes are also widely used in stews and ragouts, as you will see in the *poularde* presented here. The butter in Brittany is mostly salted but delicious; it is sold all over France under the name of "Demi-Sel." This butter spread over a slice of bread topped with crisp radishes is nothing short of a joy.

The favorite fruit is the strawberry; Plougastel is said to be the capital of the strawberry area. It is a rather large fruit that is allowed truly to ripen on the vine. As a result these strawberries are sold dark crimson and explode with flavor when bitten into.

The favorite drink of Brittany is cider, which is drunk hot or cold with huge crêpes called locally *galettes*. But Muscadet is grown and made in Lower Brittany.

Flowers grow in multitudes due to the mild weather conditions. Houses are surrounded by large hedgerows protecting the largest and bluest hydrangeas ever.

MENU II—BRETAGNE

BOUILLON de COQUILLES SAINT-JACQUES à la BRETONNE
POULARDE aux CINQ PRIMEURS DU LEON
RIZ de SAINTE-ANNE
FROMAGE du CURÉ
MOUSSE de FRAISES PLOUGASTEL
WINES: CIDER with the whole meal, or
MUSCADET sur LIE with the scallop soup
YOUNG BEAUJOLAIS with the chicken

BOUILLON DE COQUILLES SAINT-JACQUES À LA BRETONNE
(Sea Scallop Soup with Herbs and Shredded Crêpes)

- Medium difficult
  6 servings
  Expensive
  1 hour

1½ quarts Fish Stock (see Index) (1.35 L)
US ¼ cup, UK 2 TB, flour (2 TB)
1 egg
US 2 TB, UK 1 TB, milk (1 TB)
salt and pepper
freshly grated nutmeg
US and UK ¼ lb. butter (125 g)
3 onions, chopped
6 shallots, chopped
1 garlic clove, mashed
6 leeks, white part only, sliced ⅙-inch
   thick
2 medium-size carrots
bouquet garni
US 2 cups, UK 2 scant cups, clam juice
   (scant .5 L)
US and UK ½ lb. spinach leaves (250 g)
US and UK ¼ lb. sorrel leaves (125 g)
chopped parsley
chopped chervil
chopped tarragon
chopped chives
1 lb. deep sea scallops (500 g)

- Prepare the fish stock, but use twice as many fish bones.

- Prepare the crêpe batter: Put the flour, egg and milk into a small bowl and mix well. Add salt, pepper and nutmeg to taste, and let batter stand until ready to use.

- Prepare the vegetable garnish: Heat US 2 tablespoons, UK 1 tablespoon, butter (1 TB) in a large pot; add the chopped onions and sauté until translucent. Add shallots, garlic clove, white part of leeks, carrots and *bouquet garni*. Etuvé for a few minutes. Add the fish stock and clam juice. Bring to a boil and reduce to a simmer. Cook for 30 minutes.

- Meanwhile, cook 3 crêpes about 6 inches in diameter (10 cm) in 1 teaspoon butter each. Roll the crêpes into cigars and cut them into ⅙-inch-wide strips.

- Chop well the spinach, sorrel and fresh herbs to your taste. Clean and dice the scallops.
- Remove the *bouquet garni* and bring the soup to a violent boil. Add all the greens, bring back to a boil, and add the scallops. Remove immedi-

ately from the heat. The scallops should poach without ever boiling.

- Add the crêpes and correct the seasoning carefully. Serve in chowder bowls or soup plates. Add a large piece of butter to each plate.

POULARDE AUX CINQ PRIMEURS DU LEON
(Braised Chicken with Favorite Brittany Vegetables)

- **Medium difficult**
  6 servings
  Medium expensive
  1½ hours

  2 chickens, 3½ to 4 lbs. each (1.5 to 2 kg each)
  salt and pepper
  chopped tarragon
  US 2 TB, UK 1 TB, butter (25 g)
  1 large onion
  1 small carrot
  US 3 cups, UK 2¾ cups, Meat Stock (see Index) (6.5 dl)
  bouquet garni
  36 baby artichokes
  1 very small head of cauliflower
  ½ lb. very small green beans (250 g)
  36 baby silverskin onions
  36 cherry tomatoes
  4 egg yolks
  US 1 cup, UK 1 scant cup, heavy cream (2.5 dl)
  1 lemon
  chopped parsley
  chopped chives

- Preheat oven to 400°F., 200°C. or 6 Regulo.
- Truss the 2 chickens after seasoning them with salt, pepper and tarragon in the cavity. Brush with melted butter.

- Slice the large onion and small carrot. Sauté them in butter and put the chickens on this bed of vegetables. Sear chickens in the preheated oven for 25 to 30 minutes.
- Add enough meat stock to reach halfway to the top of the birds; add the *bouquet garni*. Cover with a large sheet of aluminum foil arranged dull side up into an inverted lid. Put the pot lid on the pot. Bake in the oven, reduced to 325°F., 165°C. or 4 to 5 Regulo, for another 35 to 40 minutes, basting the birds at regular intervals with the cooking juices.
- While the chickens sear, trim the baby artichokes to ¾-inch corks. Blanch them in boiling water until still crunchy.
- Also peel and trim the cauliflower to very small flowerets, and blanch these.
- String the beans and blanch them.
- Sauté the silverskin onions in a small frying pan until they turn golden.

- Mix all the vegetables in a bowl and keep ready to use.
- Blanch and skin the tiny tomatoes. Keep them ready on yet another plate.
- When the chickens are done, remove them to a country-style deep dish and keep them warm.
- Strain the cooking juices into a sauteuse pan and add all the vegetables of the garnish except the tomatoes.

Reduce together until only US ⅔ cup, UK ½ cup (2 scant dl) of very heavy broth remains in the sauteuse.

- Mix egg yolks and cream, pour into the pan, and thicken by shaking the pan back and forth on the burner. Correct the seasoning with lemon juice and salt and pepper to taste. Add fresh herbs and the small tomatoes. Reheat well *without boiling*, and pour around the chickens.

RIZ DE SAINTE-ANNE
(Rice as in Sainte-Anne-d'Auray)

■ Easy
6 servings
Inexpensive
45 minutes, oven-drying included

US 1½ cups, UK 1⅓ cups, uncooked rice
(275 g)
salt and pepper
US ½ cup, UK 4 oz., unsalted butter
(125 g)
a pinch each of ground bay leaf, ground
cardamom, and finely grated lemon
rind

- Bring a large pot of water to a boil; add the rice and bring back to a boil. Add salt and pepper to taste, reduce heat to a simmer, and cook for 14 minutes.
- Drain the rice in a colander and rinse under warm water until the water runs clear. Let drip very well.
- Butter a large baking dish. Empty the rice into the dish. Salt and pepper it and put it to dry in a slow 275°F., 140°C. or 3 to 4 Regulo oven.
- Melt the butter in a small skillet and add bay leaf, cardamom and lemon rind. Mix well. Gradually mix the aromatic butter into the rice.
- Correct the salt and pepper before serving with the chickens.

MOUSSE DE FRAISES PLOUGASTEL
(Strawberry Mousse)

■ Easy
6 servings
Medium expensive
1 hour

2 quarts very ripe strawberries
US ½ cup, UK ⅓ cup, granulated sugar
   (125 g)
pinch of salt
US 2 TB, UK 1 TB, Kirschwasser (1 TB)
US 1 cup, UK 1 scant cup, heavy whipping cream (2.5 dl)
US 2 TB, UK 1 TB, confectioners' sugar
   (1 TB)

• Put 1 quart strawberries in a pot. Add the granulated sugar and a pinch of salt, and reduce together until thick and like a purée. Homogenize by whirling in a blender for a few seconds. Cool completely.

• Cut 10 more berries into ¼-inch cubes and macerate them in Kirsch for 10 minutes. Mix dice with the purée. Refrigerate for 20 minutes.

• Beat the heavy cream with the confectioners' sugar until it mounds lightly. Fold it into the cold strawberry purée and turn into a pretty crystal dish.

• Decorate the top of the mousse with the remaining berries arranged in a circle around the edge of the glass bowl.

ADVANCE PREPARATION:

EARLY MARKETING:
One week before your dinner purchase the following ingredients:

   A. The cider if you are using it. It should be French or English cider, not sweet, but tart and slightly bubbly.

   B. If you choose wine, look for Muscadet sur Lie and a fruity Beaujolais.

   C. Purchase also the cheese. The fromage du curé should be very nice and ripe, very soft to the touch of the thumb.

The day before your dinner:

    A. Purchase the fish for stock, the scallops, the vegetables for the soup and the chicken dish, the strawberries; let them ripen. Purchase also meaty bones for meat stock.

    B. Purchase the chickens—choose them squat, meaty and round rather than long and bony.

    C. Prepare a good rich Fish Stock and a very rich Meat Stock (see Index for pages).

    D. You can also prepare and store, covered with plastic wrap, the crêpe batter for the soup garnish, the vegetable garnish for the soup; the braising onion and carrot for chicken; the vegetables used as a garnish for the chicken—peel, pare, and blanch them.

    E. Mix egg yolks and cream thoroughly and store in a jar.

    F. Prepare the sweetened strawberry purée base for the mousse so it cools overnight. The mousse will be stiffer and better.

    G. You can even, if you prefer, prepare the whole mousse ahead, but because of the macerated strawberries, you may want to do it only a few hours before dinner for a better final texture.

The day of your dinner:

    A. 3:30 P.M. Prepare the soup, to the point where you are ready to add spinach, sorrel and scallops. This should be done just before serving.

    B. 1½ hours before serving, start braising the chickens.

    C. 4:30 P.M. Finish the strawberry mousse and keep it chilled.

    D. 5:30 P.M. Cook the rice. Keep well buttered and covered with a foil; it keeps for hours.

At dinnertime:

    A. Finish and serve the soup.

    B. While the soup is being enjoyed, have the cooking juices of the chicken reducing over low heat.

    C. Also, bring cheese to room temperature.

    D. Remove soup plates. Finish chicken sauce and garnish; it takes no more than 3 minutes. Serve chicken and rice.

    E. Serve cheese.

    F. Serve mousse.

TWENTY POUNDS LOST

TOURAINE
POITOU

DINNER IN TOURAINE

Welcome to Touraine. East of the Bretagne spreading lazily along the Loire Valley at the very heart of France, lies the essence of loveliness: Touraine. Named after its capitol of Tours, this beautiful and soft province is made of quiet white stone towns reflecting into nonchalant rivers, vineyards, fields of fresh vegetables and flowers, flowers, flowers, more flowers than the mind can encompass. Among them the blue-eyed clinging clematis and the startling Rieger begonias spot the sills of all windows and encircle the frames of all doors with large splashes of vivid colors.

Everyone knows that the French spoken in Touraine is the best spoken in France and that this is the favorite province of French Kings, the province that gave birth to Rabelais and where he chose to have his Gargantua and Pantagruel live. Some of the foods vividly described in both books still exist nowadays; the *fouaces*, or brioche flavored with orange-flower water, the *rillettes*, or fine forcemeat of pork faintly flavored with *quatre-épices* and the *rillons* of pork, reminiscent of the pork *confits* of the Occitania, and the best *andouillettes*.

Some of the best veal in France is produced in Touraine, where it is often accompanied with the multiple mushrooms still to be found in ancient royal forests. When mushrooms are not in season, they are replaced by the most delicious baby carrots. The local wines, the red Chinon and Bourgueil, are extensively used for the cooking and marination of wild rabbits and hares or even deer, of which there are still a few left. Touraine is one of the provinces of France where one still hunts on horseback, a dramatic happening worth seeing at least once in a lifetime.

The white wines of Vouvray and Montlouis are grown on the plateau that dominates the Loire and vinified in the cellars that hide under the vineyards. The doors of these cellars can be seen along the big rivers and their tributaries. Try Vouvray *Mousseux*, which is vinified by the same method as Champagne and is a treat, so well fitted to a celebration.

MENU I—TOURAINE

FILETS d'ALOSE GRILLÉS au BEURRE BLANC
LONGE de VEAU BRAISÉE aux CAROTTES
HARICOTS VERTS FINS à la TOURANGELLE
SAINTE-MAURE
PRUNEAUX de TOURS au VOUVRAY et au COINTREAU
WINES: VOUVRAY, SEC or BRUT MOUSSEUX
CHINON

FILETS D'ALOSE GRILLÉS AU BEURRE BLANC
(Grilled Shad Fillets with White Butter)

■ Medium difficult
  6 servings
  Expensive
  15 minutes

1½ lbs. shad fillets, skin on (750 g)
US ¼ cup, UK 2 TB, melted butter (2 TB)
salt and pepper
US 1 cup, UK 1 scant cup, fresh bread
    crumbs (125 g)
US 1 cup, UK 1 scant cup, dry white wine
    (2.5 dl)
US ⅓ cup, UK ¼ cup, white-wine vinegar
    (1 scant dl)
6 medium-size shallots, very finely
    chopped
US ¾ cup, UK 6 oz., butter (160 g)
chopped parsley

• Have the fillets prepared and boned
by the fish store.

• Prepare fillets for broiling: Brush fillets on the flesh side with melted
butter. Salt and pepper them, then
sprinkle them with bread crumbs
only on the side on which they will
be broiled. Arrange the fillets on a
buttered broiler pan. Set aside.

• Prepare the *beurre blanc.* Mix the
white wine, white-wine vinegar and
chopped shallots in a heavy 1½-
quart saucepan. Add salt and pepper. Reduce slowly until only US ¼
cup, UK 2 tablespoons (2 TB) of
mixed solids and liquids are left in
the saucepan.

• Preheat the broiler and slide in the
broiler pan 4 inches from the source
of heat. Let fillets broil for 4 to 5
minutes; the fish will be done.

• While the fish broils, finish the
beurre blanc. Keeping the reduction
over very low heat, whisk in the butter so as to obtain a smooth, creamy
emulsion. Correct seasoning and
strain into a sauceboat, preheated to
lukewarm with warm water.

• Serve the fillets sprinkled with
chopped parsley and pass the sauce
separately.

LONGE DE VEAU BRAISÉE AUX CAROTTES
(Braised Veal Loin and Carrots)

- **Difficult**
  6 servings
  Very expensive
  2½ to 3 hours

  1 side of veal loin (half of a pic)
  salt and pepper
  1 egg
  US 1 cup, UK 1 scant cup, bread crumbs
    (125 g)
  freshly grated nutmeg
  US ¼ cup, UK 2 TB, heavy cream (50 to
    60 g)
  2 onions, thickly sliced
  1 large carrot, thickly sliced
  US 2 TB, UK 1 TB, butter (1 TB)
  US 3 cups, UK 2¾ cups, Meat Stock (see
    Index) (7.5 dl)
  medium-large bouquet garni
  1½ lbs. fresh baby carrots (750 g)
  snipped fresh chives

- Have the butcher bone the loin of veal for you, but leave it in one large piece of brisket covering with the sirloin strip attached and the tenderloin separated.

- Lay the whole side of meat flat on a board. Remove all traces of fat on the outside brisket covering. Salt and pepper it.

- Put the tenderloin, cut into cubes, the egg, the bread crumbs, salt, pepper and nutmeg to taste, and heavy cream in a food processor, and process until a fine forcemeat is obtained. Remove a teaspoon full of the forcemeat and drop it into salted boiling water to cook it and taste it. Add seasoning as needed.

- Spread the forcemeat in one long strip between the sirloin strip and the brisket. Roll the piece of meat from the sirloin strip out, wrapping the brisket covering around the sirloin. Tie well.

- Preheat oven to 400°F., 200°C. or 6 Regulo.

- Put the piece of meat on a roasting pan, brush it with melted butter, and sear it in the preheated oven for 30 minutes.

- Meanwhile, sauté the sliced onions and sliced large carrot in a bit of butter. As soon as the roast is well seared, arrange it on top of the vegetables. Salt and pepper it, and cover it halfway with excellent meat stock. Add the *bouquet garni*.

- Reduce oven heat to 325°F., 165°C. or 4 to 5 Regulo.

- Arrange a large piece of foil, dull side up, on top of the meat as an inverted lid and cover with the pot lid. Braise in the oven until a skewer inserted at the center of the piece of meat comes out freely.

- While the meat braises, peel and trim the baby carrots. Add them to the braising pot during the last 15 minutes of cooking.

- To serve, remove the meat to a platter, cut and remove the strings, and slice the meat. Arrange the baby carrots around the meat and sprinkle them with snipped fresh chives.

- Strain the gravy, defatten it with a baster (see Glossary), correct the seasoning, and serve the gravy as is in a gravy boat.

NOTE

Ask the butcher to give you the bones; you can use them to prepare meat stock.

HARICOTS VERTS FINS À LA TOURANGELLE
(Fine Green Beans in Cream and Nutmeg Sauce)

- Easy
  6 servings
  Expensive to medium expensive
  25 minutes

  1½ lbs. superfine green beans (750 g), or 2 lbs. regular green beans, knife trimmed (1 kg)
  US 1 cup, UK 1 scant cup, heavy cream (2.5 dl)
  freshly grated nutmeg
  salt and pepper

- String the beans. If they are larger, remove the strings by knife.
- Bring a large pot of water to a boil and blanch the beans for 7 to 8 minutes.
- Drain in a colander and rinse under cold water.
- Meanwhile, reduce the cream by half; add nutmeg, salt and pepper to taste. As soon as the cream has reduced enough, toss the beans into it and reheat very well.

PRUNEAUX DE TOURS AU VOUVRAY ET AU COINTREAU
(Prunes Soaked in Vouvray Wine)

- Easy
  6 servings
  Expensive
  25 minutes, plus 48 hours for macerating

  1 bottle of Vouvray, dry or mellow
  1 tsp. finely grated orange rind
  5 cloves
  pinch of ground cinnamon
  1 lb. prunes (500 g)
  US 2 oz., UK 2 TB, Cointreau (2 TB)
  US ½ cup, UK ⅓ cup, heavy whipping
      cream (1 generous dl)

- Empty the Vouvray into a sauteuse pan; bring to a boil. Add the grated orange rind, the crushed heads of 5 cloves and the cinnamon.

- Place the prunes in a crystal bowl and pour the hot wine over them. Let cool completely.

- Add half of the Cointreau, mix well. Serve only after 48 hours of maceration in a cool place or on the lowest shelf of the refrigerator.

- With the prunes, serve the cream whipped semistiff and flavored with the second half of Cointreau. Do not sweeten the cream as the prune syrup turns very sweet.

ADVANCE PREPARATION:

EARLY MARKETING:
One week before your dinner purchase the wines:
A. Vouvray for drinking and preparing the prune dessert.

B. Chinon or Bourgueil for the veal main course. Purchase also the Cointreau for the preparation of the dessert.

C. Purchase one of the goat cheeses of Touraine, Sainte-Maure or Valençay. Try to buy those prepared on farms rather than in dairy plants.

Two days before your party:
A. Prepare the prune dessert. Cover and let macerate.

The day before your party:
A. Prepare the Meat Stock (see Index), with the bones of the pic.

B. Peel and trim the carrots for the veal dish. Keep them in water in a plastic bag.

C. String or knife-trim the beans. Wash them, bag them. Close the plastic bag hermetically.

D. Reduce the cream to dress the beans; store it covered with a plastic wrap.

The day of your dinner:
A. Prepare the fillets of shad for broiling and the base of the *beurre blanc*.

B. Prepare the loin for braising and the onion and carrot.

C. Two hours before dinner, put the veal to sear, then braise. Add the baby carrots 15 minutes before veal is done.

At dinnertime:
A. Cook the fillets; while they broil, finish the *beurre blanc*.

B. Bring the cheese to room temperature.

C. Finish the gravy of the veal roast and serve.

D. While you prepare the gravy, also reheat the beans in their nutmeg-flavored cream. Serve veal and beans.

E. Serve cheese.

F. Serve prune dessert.

DINNER IN POITOU

Come to dine in Poitou, a somewhat retiring province which unfolds slowly south of Touraine. A most ancient province, it was the inheritance of Eleanor of Aquitaine, who resided a lot in its capital city of Poitiers. The modern province is one of agricultural vocation and produces abundantly a large variety of goat cheeses, excellent butter, beautiful vegetables, all turned into some of the most interesting dishes in France.

The ancestral foods were mostly wild rabbits and birds and the small gray snails, called Lumas in that area, which people starve for many weeks in brick flower pots, well covered with plates. The snails, having to face starvation, window their shell opening with a layer of calcium carbonate and go into hibernation; they are then called *dormeurs* or "sleepers," and are supposed to be choice morsels. Cultivated snails have now replaced the wild ones. The countryside continues producing some of the best rabbits, ducks and chicken in France, for which recipes are as plentiful as varied and original. Meals invariably finish with a great goat cheese such as Chabichou or La Mothe-Saint-Héray. The butter of the neighboring Deux-Sèvres and Charente is the favorite of most great French cooks.

The cultivation of vines for many different country growths, both red and white, was drastically curtailed by the phylloxera epidemic at the end of the 19th century.

South of the Poitou, around Angoulême, starts the production of Cognac. You may want to try the wonderful apéritif wine called Pineau des Charentes which is produced locally by all housewives. A few excellent brands of this are exported all over the world.

MENU II—POITOU

SALADE au BEURRE FONDU
CANARD RÔTI au PAUVRE HOMME
POMMES de TERRE en BRASELIET
FROMAGE de la MOTHE-SAINT-HÉRAY
POMMES CLOCHARD
WINES: CHENIN d'ANJOU
GAMAY or BOURGUEIL

SALADE AU BEURRE FONDU
(Melted Butter Salad)

- **Easy**
  6 servings
  Medium expensive
  45 minutes

  ½ **lb. mushrooms (250 g)**
  3 sun-ripened tomatoes
  1 large or 2 small red onions
  1 very tight head of Boston or other soft-
    leafed lettuce
  US 1 cup, UK 1 scant cup, cooked rice
    (200 g)
  salt and pepper
  US ½ cup, UK 4 oz., butter (125 g)
  2 shallots, very finely chopped
  US 3 TB, UK 1½ TB, wine vinegar
    (1½ TB)
  US ½ cup, UK ⅓ cup, dry white wine
    (1 generous dl)
  1 tsp. tomato paste
  US 2 TB, UK 1 TB, Cognac (1 TB)
  US 2 TB, UK 1 TB, walnut oil (1 TB)
  chopped parsley

- Cut the mushrooms into paper-thin slices. Set aside.

- Peel the tomatoes and cut them into ¼-inch-thick slices.

- Peel the red onion. Cut it into paper-thin slices and soak it in salted water for 30 minutes. Drain and pat dry.

- Remove the dark green leaves of the head of lettuce and cut the tender yellow center into a chiffonade.

- Line a 10-inch porcelain pie plate with the cooked rice. Season it well with salt and pepper. Arrange a ⅓-inch-thick layer of rice in the dish.

- Cook the butter until it browns deeply to become noisette butter.

- *Prepare the dressing:* Sauté the shallots in the hot noisette butter for a few minutes, letting them take on a little bit of color (careful, do not burn!). Add the wine vinegar and wine and reduce by half over high heat. Add tomato paste and Cognac, salt and pepper to taste, and finally the walnut oil. Mix very well and toss a bit of this hot dressing into the rice.

- Now, alternate layers with half of the mushrooms, tomatoes and red onion on top of the rice; salt and pepper layers and baste with some of the dressing.
- Top with the shredded lettuce and baste with some more dressing. Finally, put on another and last layer

of mushrooms, tomatoes and red onion. Sprinkle with salt and pepper and baste with remainder of hot dressing. Sprinkle heavily with parsley and serve immediately.

- The salad will wilt lightly due to the heat of the dressing.

CANARD RÔTI AU PAUVRE HOMME
(Poor Man's Roast Duck)

- **Easy**
  6 servings
  Expensive
  2½ to 3 hours

  2 ducks, 4½ lbs. each (2 kg each)
  salt and pepper
  quatre-épices (see Glossary)
  US ½ cup, UK ⅓ cup, red-wine vinegar (1 generous dl)
  US 1 cup, UK 1 scant cup, excellent red wine (2.5 dl)
  US 1 cup, UK 1 scant cup, Meat Stock (see Index) (2.5 dl)
  5 shallots, chopped
  bouquet garni

  GARNISH
  2 shallots, finely chopped
  1 garlic clove, finely chopped
  chopped parsley
  2 slices of French bread, toasted
  US 2 TB, UK 1 TB, butter (1 TB)

- Preheat oven to 325°F., 165°C. or 4 Regulo.
- Truss the ducks after seasoning them in the cavity with salt and pepper and a good dash of quatre-épices. Put to roast in the preheated oven.

- Mix vinegar and wine with meat stock, chopped shallots and bouquet garni. Reduce by one third.
- Let the ducks roast for 1 hour. Discard the fat in the roasting pan. From now on, baste the ducks with some of the wine-shallot-stock reduction every 20 minutes until all the mixture has been used.
- Tilt the ducks forward to let the natural juices of the ducks escape into the roasting pan every time you add some of the reduction.
- While the ducks bake, chop the shallots and garlic as well as the parsley. Mix well. Crumble the toasted French bread into nuggets ¼-inch wide. Mix into the other chopped ingredients.
- When the ducks are cooked, carve them into 8 serving pieces, and put them on a heated platter.

- Defatten the cooking juices and reduce them to a thick acid glaze. Check the salt of this preparation. Brush some of it on the crisp skin of each piece of duck.

- Sauté the garnish very quickly in the butter and season it with salt and pepper. Sprinkle the garnish on the duck pieces. It will stick to the glaze and taste crunchy and delicious.

POMMES DE TERRE EN BRASELIET
(Baked Potatoes with Hazelnut Butter)

- Easy
  6 servings
  Affordable
  1 hour

  12 small (1½ inches wide) baking potatoes
  US ⅓ cup, UK ¼ cup, whole hazelnuts (90 g)
  US ½ cup, UK 4 oz., butter (120 g)
  salt and pepper
  chopped parsley

- Preheat oven to 400°F., 200°C. or 6 Regulo.

- Wash the potatoes, prick them with a fork, and put to bake in the preheated oven until the skin is almost brittle.

- Meanwhile, toast the hazelnuts (see Glossary), rub them in a tea towel to remove the skins, and put them in the bowl of a food processer to chop them finely. Add salt and pepper to taste and the butter. Process until almost smooth.

- To serve the potatoes, cut them into halves, push the pulp down to make an indentation in it, and add some of the prepared butter. Serve well sprinkled with parsley.

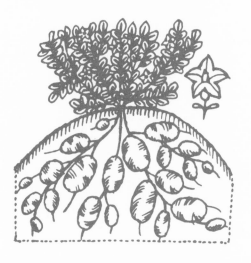

POMMES CLOCHARD
(Pauper's Apples)

■ Easy
6 servings
Inexpensive
30 minutes

4 large green apples
US ¼ cup, UK 2 TB, dark rum (2 TB)
2 eggs
US ½ cup, UK ⅓ cup, milk (1 generous dl)
1 tsp. orange-flower water
pinch of ground cinnamon
pinch of salt
US 2 TB, UK 1 TB, granulated sugar
    (1 TB)
US 6 TB, UK 3 TB, flour (3 TB)
butter or walnut oil

- Peel the apples and cut into ¼-inch-thick slices. Macerate them in rum for 15 minutes.

- Beat the eggs, milk and orange-flower water with cinnamon, salt and sugar. Add two thirds of the flour, mix until smooth, then add whatever rum has not been absorbed by the apples.

- Heat US 4 tablespoons, UK 2 tablespoons, butter or walnut oil in a large skillet.

- Toss the apple slices with the remainder of the flour, then dip into the egg batter.

- Immediately add apple slices to the hot butter in the pan and cook over medium heat, turning over several times until golden and tender.

- Serve heavily sprinkled with more sugar.

ADVANCE PREPARATION:

One week before your dinner:

A. Purchase the wines. Poitou wines are not good travelers and as a consequence can only be enjoyed locally. Any good white Anjou wine and a good Bourgueil will do very well with the ducks.

B. For the cooking of the ducks, you will need a stronger wine, and you may want to invest in one half bottle of good Côtes du Rhône. For the salad, you need dry white wine and Cognac; for the dessert, rum; check your shelves before you buy.

The day before your party:

A. Make sure that you have rice. Purchase the mushrooms, tomatoes, red onions, lettuce and walnut oil.

B. Purchase the ducks. Purchase bones to make meat stock if you do not have any in your larder. Add the ducks' necks and giblets to the bones for the meat stock.

C. Purchase nice fat, fresh shallots that are very juicy.

D. Purchase the cheese. If La Motte-Saint-Héray is not available, try Saint-Saviol which is easier to find.

E. Purchase potatoes, hazelnuts and apples.

The afternoon before your dinner:

A. 3 P.M. Prepare the rice, mushrooms, tomatoes, red onions and lettuce. Keep sealed under plastic wrap.

B. 3:30 P.M. Prepare all the ingredients of the dressing on a small plate.

C. 4 P.M. Truss the ducks. Prepare the vinegar and wine reduction; reduce it as indicated in the recipe.

D. 4:30 P.M. Prepare the duck garnish of shallots, garlic and parsley. Toast and crumble the bread.

E. 5 P.M. Put the ducks to roast. Prepare the hazelnut butter for the potatoes. Scrub the potatoes.

F. 5:30 P.M. Peel and slice the apples, and prepare the egg batter in which to dip them.

G. 6 P.M. Have a glass of wine and sit down.

At dinnertime:

A. Put the potatoes to cook 1 hour before dinner.

B. Bring the cheese to room temperature.

C. Cook the salad dressing and put the salad together. Serve the salad.

D. As soon as the ducks are ready to serve, separate the gravy from the fat with a baster and reduce the gravy quickly.

E. Sauté the garnish of the duck.

F. Serve the duck and the potatoes.

G. Serve the cheese.

H. Prepare apples; they cook in no more than 5 minutes. Serve them as they come out of the pan.

TWENTY-FIVE POUNDS LOST

Lorraine
Alsace

DINNER IN LORRAINE

We are on our way to Lorraine and to the enjoyment of a marvelous meal full of the smells of good bacon and onions.

Lorraine is always wrongly lumped with Alsace because of the sad political events that have linked both their names on the parchments of treaties. There could, however, not be two neighboring provinces more different from each other. Lorraine is a large plateau that slowly goes uphill until it reaches the Vosges, an old massif of mountains full of mushrooms and ancient sanctuaries.

The plateau divides its life between a large industrial and a large agricultural vocation. The natural trees are fruit trees: cherries, plums named Quetsch and Mirabelle grow in large amounts, as do currants. All of them are used to make many a delicious jam, such as Bar-le-Duc currant jam for one example. The purple plums and Mirabelles are distilled into excellent fruit brandies. Beside mushrooms, the forests of the Vosges also yield enormous amounts of tiny huckleberries which in these parts have the pretty name of *bimbrelles*. They are used in cakes, tarts, creams and ice creams to the joy of the whole population, which moves up the slopes in the fruiting season, buckets in hand, to gather the fruit.

A large dairy area, Lorraine produces a number of excellent cheeses, the best being Brie de Lorraine, Carré de l'Est and Géromé, produced in high-altitude farms called *marcaireries*.

The true "quiche Lorraine" is an ancestral bacon and egg pie, prepared with bread dough, eggs, heavy cream and that dusky bacon that fills the mouth with the heaviest of smoky tastes. A far cry from the elaborated quiches full of all kinds of expensive garnishes such as lobster or Roquefort.

Lorraine loves her sauces, and still loves them heavy with flour. Also a favorite are potatoes cooked in bouillon with bacon and bay leaf. A dream of good solid taste, but the quick end of a waistline if one indulges too much. Frogs and crayfish used to be plentiful in the rivers of Lorraine and still are used in fish dishes with regularity, either garnishing a pike or concocted into a marvelously creamy soup.

When in Lorraine, make it a point to visit the birthplace of Joan of Arc, patron Saint of France, the most beloved, trusted, and prayed to of all the Saints in Paradise, and one who has always rallied with all the strength of her spirit to lift the country out of the greatest dangers.

And do not miss the faïences at Lunéville nor the the magnificent crystal at Baccarat.

MENU I—LORRAINE

SOUPE aux GRENOUILLES
CAILLES au VIN GRIS de LORRAINE
KNEPS au SEMSEN
CARRÉ de l'EST
CRÈME aux BIMBRELLES
WINES: RIESLING
VIN GRIS de LORRAINE

SOUPE AUX GRENOUILLES
(Frogs'-Legs Soup)

- Medium difficult
  6 servings
  Quite expensive
  1½ hours

  US ½ cup, UK 4 oz., butter (125 g)
  3 onions, finely chopped
  1 shallot, finely chopped
  US 2 TB, UK 1 TB, chopped parsley stems (1 TB)
  1 large carrot, chopped
  US 1½ quarts, UK 1⅓ quarts, Fish Stock (see Index) (1.5 L)
  36 pairs medium-size frogs' legs
  24 tiny carrots, peeled

3 leeks, white part only, cut into ⅓-inch-thick slices
US 2 TB, UK 1 TB, fresh fines herbes (1 TB), or half that much dried
US ¼ cup, UK 3½ TB, Riesling wine (.5 dl)
US 1 cup, UK 1 scant cup, heavy cream (2.5 dl)
4 egg yolks
chopped parsley
6 slices of French bread, toasted, crusts removed, rubbed with garlic

- Heat the butter very well. In it sauté the onions, shallot, parsley stems and carrot until onions are translucent.

- As soon as the vegetables are ready, add the fish stock, bring to a boil, and simmer together for 30 minutes.

- Add the frogs' legs and let them poach in the stock without boiling until cooked, 5 minutes for large legs, 2 minutes for small ones.

- As soon as they are poached, bone the legs and keep the meat ready to use in a small bowl. Strain the broth.

- Drop the tiny carrots and leeks into the broth. Season well with salt and pepper and cook until crunchy tender. Add *fines herbes* to your taste.

- Prepare the *liaison* with the Riesling, heavy cream and egg yolks.

- Enrich the soup with the *liaison*. Add more chopped parsley, the frog meat and all the garlic croutons.

NOTE
Remember, the *fines herbes* are parsley, chervil, tarragon and chives.

CAILLES AU VIN GRIS DE LORRAINE
(Quails in Rosé Wine from Lorraine)

- Easy
  6 servings
  Medium expensive
  1½ hours

  1 bottle Vin Gris de Lorraine or other dry
     Rosé
  2 onions, chopped
  3 shallots, chopped
  1 garlic clove, mashed
  2 leeks, white part only
  salt and pepper
  12 quails
  1 large onion, cut into thick slices
  1 small carrot, cut into thick slices
  US 6 TB, UK 3 oz., butter (3 TB)
  US ½ cup, UK ⅓ cup, Emperor grape
     juice (1 generous dl)
  US 1 cup, UK 1 scant cup, heavy, double-
     strength Meat Stock (see Index)
     (2.5 dl)
  1 strip of lemon rind
  US 3 oz., UK 3 oz., slab bacon (100 g)
  1 bunch of Emperor grapes
  chopped parsley

- Empty the bottle of wine into a pot. Add the chopped onions, shallots, garlic and leeks and reduce by two thirds.

- Preheat oven to 400°F., 200°C. or 6 Regulo.

- Season the quails in the cavity with salt and pepper, truss them, and brown them in the preheated oven. While they brown, sauté the large onion and carrot in US 2 tablespoons, UK 1 tablespoon, butter (1 TB) in a braising pot large enough to hold the quails in one layer.

- Prepare the grape juice with a blender; strain.

- Transfer the browned quails to the braising pot. Add the reduced wine, the heavy stock, the grape juice and the strip of lemon rind. Braise from 1 to 1¼ hours.
- Chop the bacon finely and render it until golden.
- Blanch the grapes and peel them. Set them aside.
- When the quails are ready, remove them to a country-style serving dish.

- Reduce the cooking juices to a good glaze, and in them emulsify the remainder of the butter by adding it on high heat and at a rolling boil. Correct the seasoning.
- Strain the sauce into a clean pot, add grapes and parsley, and spoon over the quails. Sprinkle the bacon bits on top.

KNEPS AU SEMSEN
(Homemade Noodles with Poppy Seeds)

- **Easy**
  6 servings
  Inexpensive
  30 minutes

  US 2 cups, UK 8 oz., flour (225 to 250 g)
  6 eggs
  US ⅔ cup, UK ½ cup, milk (2 scant dl)
  salt and pepper
  pinch of ground cinnamon
  US ½ cup, UK 4 oz., butter (125 g)
  US 2 TB, UK 1 TB, poppy seeds (1 TB)
  large pinch of grated lemon rind
  1 tiny garlic clove, mashed

- Mix flour, eggs, milk, salt and pepper to taste and cinnamon in a bowl and stir until smooth. Let stand for 10 minutes.
- Bring a large pot of water to a boil. Salt it. Reduce it to a bare simmer.

- Heat the butter; add the poppy seeds and lemon rind as well as the mashed garlic, and toss well together. Turn the heat off and let steep. Pour butter mixture into a baking dish.
- Pour the batter onto a small chopping board and shave ¼-inch-wide bands of it into the barely simmering water. The *kneps* are done just as soon as they come floating to the top of the water.
- With a slotted spoon, lift the *kneps*, drain them for a minute on paper towels, then toss them well into the poppy-seed butter. Correct the seasoning and serve with the quails.

CRÈME AUX BIMBRELLES
(Blueberry Bavarian Cream)

- ■ **Difficult**
  6 servings
  Medium expensive
  2 hours, plus time for cooling and chilling

  US 2 cups, UK 2 scant cups, heavy cream
  (500 g)
  1½ lbs. blueberries or huckleberries
  (750 g)
  US ¾ cup, UK ⅔ cup, sugar (175 g)
  juice of 1 lemon
  US 1 envelope, UK ¼ oz., unflavored gelatin (7 g)
  US 1 cup, UK 1 scant cup, fresh blueberries (200 g)
  US 2 TB, UK 1 TB, Cognac (1 TB)

- Whip half of the heavy cream till barely mounding. Refrigerate.

- Empty 1½ pounds sorted wild blueberries or huckleberries into a pot and reduce to 1 cup or so of very thick purée. Strain to discard all the seeds. Add the sugar; stir well to dissolve. Add the lemon juice.

- Melt the gelatin in a tablespoon or so of water in the top part of a double boiler over simmering water.

- Add gelatin to berry purée and add the remaining berries. Put the bowl over ice and as soon as the gelatin shows signs of setting, fold in the whipped heavy cream.

- Turn into an oiled 1½-quart mold and refrigerate for at least 4 hours.

- Serve with the remainder of the cream, very lightly whipped, sweetened and flavored with the Cognac.

ADVANCE PREPARATION:

EARLY MARKETING:
One week before your dinner, purchase the following ingredients:

　　A. Choose a good Alsatian Riesling for the soup.

　　B. Try to find Vin Gris de Lorraine. Since it does not travel very well, replace it by any very dry Rosé with great freshness (that means a pinch of acidity).

　　C. Check your shelves for Cognac for the dessert.

　　D. Purchase a Carré de l'Est and ripen it to full cream.

At least 4 days before your dinner:

A. Order frogs' legs and quails. They are specialty items not to be found so easily.

The day before your dinner:

A. Purchase fish bones and prepare a very rich fish stock.

B. Purchase Emperor grapes for juice and quail garnish.

C. Purchase meat for stock and prepare a double-strength meat stock.

D. Purchase fresh blueberries or huckleberries. Prepare and store the Bavarian cream. It keeps very well overnight covered with clear plastic.

The day of your dinner:

A. 3 P.M. Prepare the soup up to the addition of the *liaison*.

B. 4 P.M. Prepare the quails for braising.

C. 5 P.M. Prepare the grapes, the parsley and the bacon bits. Prepare grape juice. Braise the quails; they can reheat very well. Prepare and cook the kneps. They keep well covered with foil in a slow oven if very well buttered.

At dinnertime:

A. Bring the cheese to room temperature.

B. Finish and serve the frogs'-legs soup.

C. While the soup is being enjoyed, reduce the cooking juices of the quails.

D. Clear the soup service. Finish the quail sauce and the whole dish. Serve it, with the kneps.

E. Serve the cheese.

F. Serve the Bavarian cream.

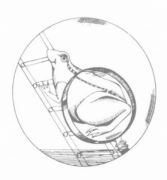

DINNER IN ALSACE

The road from Alsace goes over the Vosges Mountains, crossing the beautiful dark forests and passing such lovely villages as Schirmeck or imposing monasteries such as the one at Sainte-Odile. Odile is the patron saint of Alsace. From the terrace in front of her shrine, one can see the plain of Alsace unfold all the way to the Ill and the Rhine. On clear days, the line of the Black Forest is clearly visible on the other side of the rivers.

The well-husbanded forests of Alsace have kept a large amount of wild life compared to other hunting areas in France. One can still shoot a deer or wild rabbit and hare as well as juniper-flavored pheasant. The pork, the sausage made from its meat, glorious smoked hams, cabbage, sauerkraut and potatoes make up the staple of the diet. These are turned by Alsatian housewives into some of the most beautiful dishes ever invented. Asparagus grows easily in the loess of Northern Alsace and is used extensively all through April.

The small torrents coming down from the Vosges used to offer plenty of trout, which unfortunately have disappeared, but a large hatchery industry has taken over and the Alsatians do not hesitate to purchase the fresh trout at a hatchery, then cure them in the small brooks passing behind their houses. Salmon, which used to run almost of legendary large size in the Rhine, remains one of the choice dishes for celebration meals.

There are two styles of cuisine in Alsace—the Christian, and the Jewish style which follows all the rules of Kosher cuisine and mixes cream only with fish.

Desserts are plentiful. There are some of the most heavenly fruit pies and tarts, and a cream made with Alsatian wine, called *Weinschaum* or "wine foam," which is a local version of a Sabayon, which I have introduced here in your dessert.

MENU II—ALSACE

SALADE d'ASPERGES et de JAMBON FUMÉ
SAUMON POCHÉ à la JUIVE
CONCOMBRES GLACÉS à l'ANETH
MUNSTER
RAISINS POCHÉS à la MOUSSE DE GEÜRZTRAMINER
WINES: SYLVANER
RIESLING
GEWÜRZTRAMINER

SALADE D'ASPERGES ET DE JAMBON FUMÉ
(Asparagus and Ham Salad)

- Easy
  6 servings
  Medium expensive
  1 hour

36 slender asparagus stalks
½-lb. slab of smoked ham (250 g)
1 egg yolk
1 tsp. prepared Dijon mustard
salt and pepper
1 tsp. ground coriander seeds
US ⅔ cup, UK ½ cup, corn oil (2 scant
   dl)
1 lemon
chopped parsley
snipped chives
1 shallot, chopped
3 eggs
1 small head of Boston lettuce

- Wash and peel the asparagus and blanch them in salted water, taking care to keep the stalks a bit crunchy. Cut them into 1½-inch pieces. Be sure to keep the blanching water.

- Cut the ham into sticks as long and as wide as the asparagus pieces.

- With the egg yolk, mustard, salt and pepper to taste, ground coriander and oil, prepare a mayonnaiselike sauce, lightening it to a rather thin texture with lemon juice to your taste and some of the reserved blanching water from the asparagus. Flavor with chopped parsley and chives. Press the shallot in the corner of a towel to get rid of some of the strong juices. Add shallot to the sauce.

- Hard-boil the eggs, rinse them under cold water, shell them, and refrigerate them. When well chilled, slice them.

• *To serve the salad:* Arrange the Boston lettuce leaves on a round platter. Separate 12 asparagus tips. Mix the remaining asparagus pieces with the ham strips, and toss with the mayonnaise. Arrange the ham mixture at the center of the leaves. Surround the salad with the asparagus tips separated by slices of hard-boiled egg. Sprinkle the top of the salad with chopped parsley.

SAUMON POCHÉ À LA JUIVE
(Poached Salmon as Prepared in Alsatian Jewish Style)

■ **Easy**
6 servings
Expensive
1½ hours

COURT-BOUILLON
4 quarts water (4 L)
US 2 cups, UK 2 scant cups, dry white wine (.5 L)
US 1 cup, UK 1 scant cup, wine vinegar (2.5 dl)
3 large onions, chopped
1 large carrot, chopped
large bouquet garni
US 1 TB, UK ½ TB, coriander seeds (½ TB)
US ¼ cup, UK 2 TB, salt (2 TB)
2 dozen peppercorns
FISH AND SAUCE
1 large side of salmon, off the bone (1 whole fillet)
US 4 TB, UK 2 TB, butter (2 TB)
US 2 cups, UK 2 scant cups, Fish Stock (see Index) (.5 L)
US 1 TB, UK ½ TB, tomato paste (½ TB)
US 2 TB, UK 1 TB, chopped parsley stems (1 TB)
US ⅔ cup, UK ½ cup, heavy cream (2 scant dl)
US 3 TB, UK 1½ TB, sour cream (1½ TB)
US ¼ cup, UK 2 TB, dried currants (2 TB)
US 1 to 2 TB, UK ½ to 1 TB, heated Riesling wine (½ to 1 TB)
parsley bouquets
lemon slices
Dilled Cucumbers (following recipe)

• In a large oblong fish poacher, prepare the *court-bouillon:* Bring the water to a boil, add the wine, vinegar, 2 onions, the carrot, *bouquet garni*, coriander seeds, salt and peppercorns. Simmer for 30 to 40 minutes.

• Cut the salmon fillet into 6 portions crosswise. Lightly butter the rack of the poacher with US 1 tablespoon, UK ½ tablespoon, of the butter (½ TB), and put the pieces of salmon on it. Set aside.

• While the *court-bouillon* cooks, prepare the sauce. Mix the fish stock, tomato paste, remaining onion and the parsley stems, and reduce to US ½ cup, UK ⅓ cup (1 generous dl). Reduce the heavy cream by half, and measure the sour cream into a small dish.

• Soak the currants in the heated Riesling until the fish is cooked.

• When the reduction for the sauce is finished, blend it with the reduced heavy cream. Add the sour cream and strain into a clean saucepan.

- Add the currants, bring to a simmer, and whisk in the remainder of the butter, shaking the pan back and forth until butter has melted and sauce is homogenized. Correct the seasoning.
- Bring the *court-bouillon* to a hard boil. Immerse the salmon in it, bring to a second boil, cover, and immediately remove the poacher from the heat. Let stand, covered, for 6 to 7 minutes.

- To serve, drain the salmon pieces; arrange them on a pretty platter. Coat them with the sauce, and arrange parsley bouquets and lemon slices at the end of the dish. On each side, arrange the cucumbers.

NOTE
Keep the *court-bouillon*; it freezes well and can be reused.

CONCOMBRES GLACÉS À L'ANETH
(Dilled Cucumbers)

- Easy
  6 servings
  Inexpensive
  30 minutes

  6 cucumbers, nice and firm
  US 3 TB, UK 1½ TB, butter (45 g)
  US 1 TB, UK ½ TB, of the salmon sauce
       (½ TB) (see preceding recipe)
  chopped fresh dill
  salt and pepper

- Peel the cucumbers; cut lengthwise into halves; remove the seeds with a melon baller, and slice across into ⅛-inch-thick half-moons.
- Heat the butter in a large skillet. Sauté the cucumbers, keeping them crunchy.
- Add the salmon sauce and a large amount of freshly chopped dill. Season to taste and serve with the salmon.

RAISINS POCHÉS À LA MOUSSE DE GEWÜRZTRAMINER
(Poached Grapes in Mousse of Gewürztraminer Wine)

- Easy
  6 servings
  Medium expensive
  1 hour

  1 large bunch of the best white grapes
      possible (see Note)
  US ½ cup, UK ⅓ cup, Gewürztraminer
      wine (120 g)
  US 2 cups, UK 2 scant cups, granulated
      sugar (250 g)
  2 oz. Cognac (2 TB)
  4 egg yolks
  pinch of salt
  US ⅓ cup, UK ¼ cup, heavy cream,
      whipped (75 g)

- Wash the grapes; stem them.

- Bring the wine and sugar to a boil. Add the grapes and poach until grapes come floating to the surface of the syrup. Spoon the grapes into a crystal dish. Add US ⅓ cup, UK ¼ cup, of the syrup (1 scant dl) and 1 ounce of the Cognac (1 TB). Refrigerate overnight, covered with a plastic wrap.

- Twenty minutes before serving, ribbon the egg yolks with US ½ cup, UK ⅓ cup, of the cold syrup (1 generous dl) and a pinch of salt, and cook over low heat, whisking heavily until the mixture thickens. As soon as this happens, add the whipped cream and remaining Cognac. This takes only a few minutes.

- Serve the ice-cold grapes topped with the lukewarm cream.

NOTE
If your area does not have any Gewürztraminer grapes, use any white table grapes available.

ADVANCE PREPARATION:

One week before your dinner, purchase the wines:
A. The Sylvaner, Riesling and Gewürztraminer you need.

B. Check if you need dry white wine for the *court-bouillon* and Cognac for the dessert.

The day before your dinner:
A. Purchase the asparagus and the ham. Prepare all the ingredients of the dish from vegetables to sauce and set in a cold refrigerator, well covered with plastic wrap.

B. Purchase fish bones and salmon. Prepare the fish stock if you have none ready. Also prepare the *court-bouillon*, which is best when done way ahead of time. Keep it in a cool place, a pantry; it will not spoil as long as no fish has been cooked in it.

C. Purchase cucumbers and dill for vegetable dish.

D. Purchase the grapes, poach them, and steep them in their Cognac-flavored syrup overnight.

E. Purchase a very *unripe*, almost white Munster cheese so you can eat it with Gewürztraminer as is done in Alsace.

The day of your dinner:
A. 5 P.M. Prepare the cucumbers.

B. 5:30 P.M. Reheat the *court-bouillon* and prepare the sauce for the salmon.

C. 6 P.M. Let the ingredients of the salad "unchill" a bit at room temperature. Do the same with the salmon.

At dinnertime:
A. Take the cheese out of the refrigerator.

B. Put the salad together and serve.

C. Put the salmon to cook while you remove the salad plates.

D. Finish the sauce for the salmon by adding the currants and butter. Sauté the cucumbers, which will be done in minutes, and serve salmon and cucumbers.

E. Serve cheese.

F. Prepare Gewürztraminer mousse and serve dessert.

THIRTY POUNDS LOST

Normandie
Champagne

DINNER IN NORMANDIE

Normandie, kingdom of butter, cream and the most creamy of cheeses, should really be the place to go and celebrate, with all these delicious ingredients, the new waistline and the figure you have regained.

Everyone has read and heard a lot about Normandie for it was for a season in 1944 the focus of interest of the whole world. Where cannons rumbled once, peace and silence have returned, and again the Channel unfurls its serene or angry moods onto the long sandy beaches.

The countryside that rolls beyond those beaches should be seen in April when apple trees blossom and when, with the settling in of spring, the milk cows with their funny "spectacles" of fur around the eyes push out of barns, mooing with content in the balminess of the marine air.

It seems almost a shame to have to reduce Normandie to a four-course meal for the combinations of seafoods are unending and delicious and the meats, especially veal, tender and white beyond belief. The cream of Normandie is not replaceable; it is something thick, smooth, ivory-colored, silky as it "goes down," a pinch sour, a lot nutty; what it does to a dish is simply indescribable. If in the area you live in, you have cream of this kind, that has been allowed to mature, you will not need to reduce it as indicated in the shrimp recipe, for cream like that is thick by itself; as it melts, it coats foods with that shiny lacquer of exquisite goodness.

Cider, cider, cider and always cider. It has flowed out of the Normandie soil with the regularity of a spring every autumn for centuries, as the ugly little apples are pressed into juice and left to ferment in large barrels. There are all different types of cider, all with lovely characteristics. Caux cider around Rouen and Dieppe is not Bray cider around Neufchâtel, nor is it Auge cider around Lisieux. Each and every one is different, and so is the double-distilled fiery Calvados that is prepared from it and that lends such a lovely flavor to all dishes. The Normands do not hesitate to use it from soups to nuts.

MENU I—NORMANDIE

CREVETTES aux PRIMEURS et à la CIBOULETTE
RIS de VEAU aux CHAMPIGNONS
TOPINAMBOURS et HARICOTS VERTS
CAMEMBERT
CRÊPES au BEURRE de CIDRE
WINES: Normandie cider for the shrimps and sweetbreads
A good BURGUNDY, if you prefer, with the Camembert,
unless you want to continue drinking cider
as is done in Normandie.

CREVETTES AUX PRIMEURS ET À LA CIBOULETTE
(Shrimps with Spring Vegetables and Chives)

- Easy
  6 servings
  Expensive
  1½ hours

  US ¾ cup, UK 6 oz., butter (180 g)
  1½ lbs. small shrimps in shells (if shrimps
      have heads on, use 2 lbs.) (750 g or
      1 kg)
  ½ lb. baby carrots (250 g)
  ½ head of cauliflower
  1 large stem of broccoli
  1 large zucchini
  12 strands of fresh chives
  US 1¼ cups, UK 1 very generous cup,
      heavy cream (275 g)
  US 3 TB, UK 1½ TB, sour cream (50 g)
  fish stock as needed
  1 oz. Calvados (1 TB)

- Heat US 2 tablespoons, UK 1 tablespoon, butter (1 TB) in a large skillet.
  As soon as it is dark brown, add the
  shrimps and stir-fry over high heat
  until the shells turn red.

- Shell the shrimps. Set them aside in
  a bowl and cover with plastic wrap.

- Put the shells of the shrimps in the
  bowl of a food processor. Add US
  ½ cup, UK 4 oz., butter (125 g) and
  process until well blended together.
  Put in a small pot, melt slowly, and
  let steep while you prepare the vegetables.

- Peel and pare carrots; trim cauliflower and broccoli into flowerets.
  Blanch carrots, cauliflower and
  broccoli. Cut the zucchini into small
  olive shapes; stir-fry in a bit of butter
  and blend with carrots, cauliflower
  and broccoli.

- Snip the chives. Reduce the heavy
  cream by one third.

- Toss the shrimps and the vegetables in the cream, then add sour cream and finally strain the shrimp butter into the sauce. If the sauce tends to separate, add fish stock until it becomes homogenous again. Reheat well without boiling.

- Heat the Calvados in a small pot, ignite it, and pour it flaming into the pan. Mix well, correct the seasoning, and add the chives. Serve on heated plates.

RIS DE VEAU AUX CHAMPIGNONS
(Sweetbreads and Mushrooms)

- **Medium difficult**
  6 servings
  Expensive
  1½ hours

  6 large veal sweetbreads (throat and heart sweetbreads)
  1 lb. mushrooms (500 g)
  US ¾ cup, UK 6 oz., butter (180 g)
  salt and pepper
  US 1 cup, UK 1 scant cup, Meat Stock (see Index) (2.5 dl)
  1 lemon
  chopped parsley

- Soak the sweetbreads in running cold water for several hours.

- Put sweetbreads in a large pot, cover with cold water, and bring to a boil. Barely simmer for 5 to 6 minutes. Drain and cool under cold water.

- When the sweetbreads are cold, remove all sinews and cartilage and cut them into ¾-inch-thick escalopes.

- Clean and slice the mushrooms. Heat US 1 to 2 tablespoons, UK ½ to 1 tablespoon, butter (½ to 1 TB), and sauté the mushrooms in it; add salt and pepper. Cover and reduce the heat to extract the liquid from the mushrooms. As soon as this has happened, pour the juices off into a small bowl. Add another pat of butter to the pan and brown the mushrooms well. Set aside as soon as done.

- In the same skillet in which you cooked the mushrooms, melt and heat US 3 tablespoons, UK 1½ tablespoons, more butter (1½ TB), and gently sauté the escalopes of sweetbreads until they take on some color. As they cook, add half of the stock to the pan to build some glaze around them. When the escalopes are nice and brown, remove to a serving platter.

- Dissolve the juices in the skillet with the remainder of the meat stock and the reserved mushroom juices. Add a good dash of lemon juice, salt and pepper to taste, and the remainder of the butter. Add the mushrooms and reheat the mixtures; add chopped parsley. Spoon mushrooms over the escalopes and serve without delay.

TOPINAMBOURS ET HARICOTS VERTS
(Jerusalem Artichokes and Green Beans)

- Easy
  6 servings
  Medium expensive
  45 minutes

1 lb. Jerusalem artichokes (500 g)
lemon juice
½ lb. green beans (250 g)
US 4 TB, UK 2 TB, butter (2 TB)
pinch of ground coriander
pinch of grated nutmeg
pinch of ground cinnamon
salt and pepper

- Peel the Jerusalem artichokes and cut them into a julienne as wide as the green beans. Keep them in lemon water while you work on the beans.

- String the beans, using a knife if the beans are large, and blanch them in salted boiling water for 7 minutes. Rinse under cold water. Roll into a tea towel to dry completely.

- Heat half of the butter in a skillet. When it turns hazelnut brown, add the Jerusalem artichokes and toss them in the hot butter until crisp tender.

- Mix in the beans and the remainder of the butter. Reheat well together. Season with a mixture of the coriander, nutmeg and cinnamon, each in a tiny amount, and toss well. Season with salt and pepper and serve around the sweetbreads.

CRÊPES AU BEURRE DE CIDRE
(Crêpes with Cider Butter)

- ■ **Medium difficult**
  6 servings
  Inexpensive
  **2 hours to reduce the cider, 1 hour for
  the crêpes**

  1 gallon natural cider, not too sweet (4 L)
  US 2 TB, UK 1 TB, butter (30 g)
  **US 1 cup, UK 1 scant cup, sifted flour
  (115 to 120 g)**
  3 eggs
  US ¾ cup, UK ⅔ cup, milk (2 dl)
  US 2 TB, UK 1 TB, heavy cream (1 TB)
  US 2 TB, UK 1 TB, Calvados (1 TB)
  **US 2 TB, UK 1 TB, confectioners' sugar (1
  TB)**
  pinch of salt

- Reduce the cider to about US 1½ cups, UK 1¼ cups (3.5 dl). While still boiling, emulsify the butter in it.
- Cool, stirring at regular intervals, and store in a crystal jam jar.
- *To prepare the crêpes:* Make a well in the flour, add the eggs, milk, cream, Calvados, sugar and salt, and stir until you have a smooth batter. Strain into a bowl or large measuring cup with a spout, and let stand for 30 minutes.
- Bake the crêpes in a very hot crêpe pan. Brush each of them with some cider butter before serving.

ADVANCE PREPARATION:

EARLY MARKETING:
One week before your dinner purchase the following ingredients:
    A. At least 1 case of Normandy cider. If Normandy cider is not available, English or Canadian cider can be an adequate replacement.
    B. The Camembert and a good Burgundy to go with it. Ripen the cheese carefully.
    C. Calvados for the shrimp dish and dessert.

The day before your party:
    A. Purchase the shrimps and all the vegetables needed for all dishes. Purchase fresh chives.
    B. Prepare all the vegetables for the shrimp dish; keep them bagged separately in plastic bags.
    C. Check if you need fish stock; if so purchase bones and heads to make the stock.

D. Purchase the sweetbreads, blanch them, and keep them in plastic bags.

E. Etuvé the mushrooms; store them in a plastic-covered bowl and their juices in a sealed jar.

F. Purchase meaty bones to make stock if you have no stock in your freezer or refrigerator.

G. String or knife-trim the beans. Blanch them. Keep them sealed in a plastic bag, and refrigerate.

H. Prepare the crêpe batter and keep it sealed in a jar.

I. Prepare the cider butter.

The day of your dinner:

A. 4 P.M. Stir-fry the shrimps and prepare the shrimp butter.

B. 4:30 P.M. Brown the mushrooms. Julienne the Jerusalem artichokes and keep them in acidulated water.

At dinnertime:

A. Remove the Camembert from the refrigerator. Finish the shrimp dish.

B. Before serving it, start sautéing the sweetbreads over medium-low heat so they can brown slowly while you enjoy the shrimps. Turn the sweetbreads over and finish the browning while you remove the shrimp plates.

C. Finish the sweetbread dish. While the sauce reduces, heat the beans, stir-fry the Jerusalem artichokes, and blend and season them well. Serve both dishes.

D. Serve the cheese.

E. Service of the crêpes: Crêpes are not too good when prepared ahead and stacked on a plate. They become limp and acquire a steamed flavor. To prevent this, you can either prepare them at the table on a small tabletop convenience burner, or have your guests help you make them in the kitchen with you and enjoy flipping them over; it is fun. This way everyone enjoys them fresh and can spread as much cider butter as desired on each crêpe.

DINNER IN CHAMPAGNE

The best view of the vineyards of Champagne one can have is from the Abbey at Hautvillers above Épernay in the valley of the Marne. There the large majestic vineyards roll down the slopes toward the river and over it back up the hills dominating the southern bank.

Below the vineyards, down many feet into the ground, the cellars where the wine sleeps and matures crisscross the whole area with miles after miles of dark streets where, in millions of bottles, the wine elaborates itself.

Champagne is rich only in great wines and has only a few specialties to offer the gastronome and those are so earthy that Champagne draws her foods from all over France and robes them with glorious sauces, silky with butter and full of the bouquet and aroma of its beautiful wines.

If you can at all afford it, treat yourself to true bubbly Champagne, the one and only, the one made in France, the only one that rightfully is entitled to the glorious name of Champagne. You deserve it today, more than any other celebration day.

MENU II—CHAMPAGNE

MOUSSE de TRUITE au BEURRE de CHAMPAGNE
POULETTES FARCIES à la CHAMPENOISE
ASPERGES RAFRAÎCHISSANTES
CHÈVRE CENDRÉ des RICEYS
SORBET au CHAMPAGNE et aux FRUITS FRAIS
WINES: COTEAUX DE CHAMPAGNE NATURE
BOUZY ROUGE or CHAMPAGNE BRUT all through the meal

MOUSSE DE TRUITE AU BEURRE DE CHAMPAGNE
(Trout Mousse in Champagne Butter)

- Difficult
  6 servings
  Very expensive
  2 hours over 2 days

  MOUSSE
  1⅓ lbs. trout fillets (675 g)
  1 whole egg
  1 egg white
  US 4 TB, UK 2 TB, butter (60 g)
  US 1½ tsps., UK 1⅓ tsps., salt (7.5 g)
  35 turns of the pepper mill
  US 2¼ cups, UK 2⅛ cups, heavy cream
    (250 to 275 g)

  SAUCE
  US 2 cups, UK 2 scant cups, Champagne
    (5 dl)
  6 shallots, finely chopped
  salt and pepper
  US ¼ cup, UK scant ¼ cup, heavy sweet
    cream (2 TB)
  pinch of cayenne pepper
  1 tsp. imported Hungarian mild paprika
  US ⅓ lb., UK 5.5 oz., butter (170 g)
  chopped parsley

DAY ONE:

- Clean the trout fillets of all brown tissues, skins and bones to obtain 1 pound (500 g) of clean trout meat ready to process.

- Put the trout in the bowl of a food processor with the whole egg and the egg white, and process until very smooth. Press 1 tablespoon (½ TB) at a time through a fine-meshed strainer. Gather the trout purée into a bowl, cover with plastic wrap, and store in the coldest part of your refrigerator. *Do not freeze.*

DAY TWO:

- Place the butter in the mixer bowl; cream it. Add the salt and pepper. Still on "creaming" speed, gradually add in the trout meat.

- As soon as the mixture is homogenous, turn the speed down to "slow" and add the cream very slowly in a steady fine stream.
- Preheat oven to 325°F., 165°C. or 4 to 5 Regulo.
- *To cook the mousse:* Butter six 3-ounce fireproof cups, and fill them with the mousse. Cover each cup with a buttered parchment paper. Bake in a water bath in the preheated oven for 16 to 20 minutes. The mousses are done when a skewer inserted at the center of one of them comes out clean and feeling very hot to the top of the hand.
- *Prepare the sauce:* Put the Champagne and shallots with a pinch each of salt and pepper to reduce over medium heat. When the mixture looks as if there is only a mass of very wet shallots left at the bottom of the pot, add heavy sweet cream, salt and pepper to taste, a pinch of cayenne and the teaspoon of paprika.
- Over low heat whisk in the butter as you would for a white butter, whisking very fast and heavily to foam up the sauce nicely. Strain the sauce into a lukewarm saucepan and add chopped parsley.
- *To serve the dish:* Unmold the mousses onto individual plates and top each with an equal amount of the sauce.

POULETTES FARCIES À LA CHAMPENOISE
(Stuffed Half Baby Chickens)

- Medium difficult
  6 servings
  Affordable
  1½ hours

  3 Cornish game hens, 1¼ lbs. each (500 g each)
  salt and pepper
  12 oz. sausage meat (375 g)
  2 slices of white bread, crusts removed and crumbled
  1 egg
  quatre-épices (see Glossary)
  1 shallot, chopped
  1 garlic clove, chopped
  US 3 TB, UK 1½ TB, chopped parsley (1½ TB)
  US ⅓ cup, UK ¼ cup, Champagne nature (1 scant dl)
  US ½ cup, UK ⅓ cup, Meat Stock (see Index) (1 generous dl)
  US 2 TB, UK 1 TB, butter (30 g)
  dash of lemon juice
  dash of Cognac

- Split each small bird into halves. Salt and pepper the cavity side well.
- *Prepare the forcemeat:* Put sausage meat, bread crumbs, egg, salt and pepper to taste, *quatre-épices* to taste, the chopped shallot, garlic and parsley in a bowl; mix until well homogenized.
- Divide the forcemeat into 6 equal portions and stuff 1 portion into the cavity side of each half bird.

- Preheat oven to 350°F., 180°C. or 5 Regulo.

- Roast birds in the preheated oven until nice and golden on both sides. Start roasting skin side down first, then turn skin side up and brush the skin side with some of the fat from the roasting pan and finish cooking.

- When the birds are done, deglaze the roasting pan with the Champagne nature and strain the deglazing into a measuring cup. Separate the lean from the fat, using a baster, and transfer the lean gravy to a small saucepan.

- Reduce gravy by half. Add meat stock and butter, and correct the flavoring with a dash each of lemon juice and Cognac. Serve as a sauce over the chickens.

ASPERGES RAFRAÎCHISSANTES
(Refreshing Asparagus)

- Easy
  6 servings
  Expensive
  40 minutes

  48 medium-size asparagus stalks
  US ½ cup, UK 4 oz., butter (125 g)
  1 garlic clove, mashed
  US 2 TB, UK 1 TB, chopped fresh mint (1 TB)
  salt and pepper

- Peel and trim the asparagus, and blanch for 7 to 8 minutes.

- Melt the butter in a saucepan. Add the garlic, mint, and salt and pepper to taste, and let steep while the asparagus cooks.

- Place the asparagus on a long serving platter. Keep hot.

- Increase the heat under the butter and let it turn hazelnut brown. Strain it into a warmed sauceboat, using a tea strainer to discard all traces of garlic and mint.

- Serve asparagus and butter together.

SORBET AU CHAMPAGNE ET AUX FRUITS FRAIS
(Champagne Sherbet with Fresh Fruits)

- ▪ **Medium difficult**
  6 servings
  Expensive
  1 hour plus 4 hours ripening in freezer

  SHERBET
  US 2 cups, UK 2 scant cups, water (.5 L)
  US 1½ cups, UK 1⅓ cups, sugar (375 g)
  US 2 cups, UK 2 scant cups, Champagne
      Rosé (5 dl)
  juice of 1 lemon
  pinch of salt
  FRUITS
  2 oranges
  18 strawberries
  18 raspberries

- ● *Prepare the sherbet:* Mix water and sugar; bring to a boil to dissolve the sugar in the water. Cool completely.

- ● Mix syrup, Champagne Rosé, lemon juice and pinch of salt. Pour into the container of an ice-cream maker and freeze. Store in the freezer to ripen for 4 hours.

- ● Serve within 24 hours.

- ● *To present the dessert:* Peel the oranges to the blood; cut them into slices, then half slices. Arrange the sherbet on pre-frozen plates. Surround each serving with sliced oranges and strawberries, and top with raspberries.

ADVANCE PREPARATION:

EARLY MARKETING:
One week before your dinner, purchase the following ingredients:

A. The wine. You have your choice of expensive naturally sparkling Brut Champagne (white) and Bouzy (red). For the sherbet, you must use a French Champagne Rosé. If it is expensive for you, replace it by two thirds Coteaux de Champagne nature mixed with one third Bouzy Rouge.

B. Check to see if you have Cognac.

C. Purchase the Cendré. The Riceys may be difficult to find. If so purchase a Montrachet Cendré, which is more common.

The day before your dinner:

A. Purchase the trout. Make the trout purée and store it.

B. Purchase the chickens and the ingredients of the forcemeat. Prepare the forcemeat.

C. Purchase meaty bones and make stock if you need it.

D. You may also purchase the asparagus, and peel and pare it. Store the stalks in a plastic bag. Chop the aromatics for the butter and store them, covered, in a bowl.

E. Prepare the syrup for the sherbet, cook it, and store it.

F. Purchase oranges, strawberries and raspberries for the dessert.

The day of your dinner:

A. 9 A.M. Blend the sherbet mixture and churn it. Prepare the fruits.

B. 9:30 A.M. Finish and mold the trout mousse. Keep it refrigerated.

C. 10:30 A.M. Stuff the chickens; keep them refrigerated.

D. 11 A.M. Prepare the base of the Champagne sauce for the fish and reduce it; set it aside, covered. Prepare the butter for the asparagus.

At dinnertime:

A. Bring the cheese to room temperature. Have a large pot of boiling salted water ready.

B. Put the chickens to roast so they can keep warm while you reduce the oven temperature to cook the mousse.

C. While the mousse cooks, finish the sauce for the fish; it will be finished in minutes.

D. Serve the trout mousse.

E. Finish the gravy of the chicken. At the same time, blanch the asparagus. Reheat the mint butter.

F. Drain asparagus. Serve asparagus and chickens together on the same platter with chicken gravy and asparagus butter in 2 different sauceboats.

G. Serve the cheese.

H. Arrange the fruits on the plates and at the last minute scoop some sherbet in the center of each plate.

GLOSSARY

Aluminum foil: Use the strongest possible aluminum foil. When you cook in it, the dull side should be on the outside. When you want to protect food from further browning, the shiny side should be on the outside.

Anchovies: For light cookery, preferably use anchovy fillets preserved in salt. Rinse them many times under running cold water. Since they remain quite salty, watch the final seasoning of your dish.

Anglaise: In light cookery, an *anglaise* is a mixture of a whole egg or even 1 egg white beaten with a tablespoon or so of water, salt and pepper, until completely liquefied. The mixture is brushed on very lightly floured items which are then rolled in gluten bread crumbs. Food prepared this way lacks zest in light cuisine. It is better replaced by other ways of cooking, for an *anglaise* is good only when nicely browned in butter or oil.

Armagnac: A French spirit prepared in the southwestern part of France south of the Garonne river. Its bouquet and aroma make it the perfect companion to all fowl, game birds and venison. It must be reduced or ignited for flambéing. See FLAMBAGE.

Aromatics: All the ingredients that contribute to enhance and develop both the flavor and the aroma of culinary preparations. Herbs, a *bouquet garni*, certain vegetables, garlic and *persillade* are considered aromatics.

The chief aromatic vegetables are onions, carrots, celery cut into the following sizes: ⅛-inch cubes (*brunoise*); ¼-inch cubes (*mirepoix*); ⅓-inch cubes (*salpicon*); ¼-inch strips (*julienne*); ⅛-inch strips (*paysanne*).

Bain-Marie: see WATER BATH.

Baster and gravy separator: The well-known large kitchen syringe used to baste meats with their gravy or other liquids. A baster is also the best lean and fat gravy separator. Pour any gravy into a glass measuring cup. Squeeze the bulb of the baster tightly, insert the syringe into the lean gravy beneath the fat, release the bulb, and draw up all the lean portion. Pour it off into a saucepan or sauceboat. See also GRAVY.

Binder: In light cookery, a mixture of evaporated skim milk and egg yolk or hard-boiled egg yolks, used to thicken a gravy or sauce without the help of a starch or flour.

Blanching: For young fresh vegetables: cooking in boiling, salted water. For pungent old vegetables (e.g., cauliflower, leeks): parboiling in boiling water to lessen their pungency. The blanching water is discarded. For meats: some salted meats such as bacon may also be blanched, but in this case, the blanching starts in cold water.

Blender: A food processing machine that grinds, purées and liquefies. Almost a must in any modern kitchen.

Boiling vegetables: In French cuisine, boiled or "blanched" vegetables are always cooked in plenty of water, salted with 1½ teaspoons (7.5 g) of salt per quart and kept at a rolling boil all through the cooking time. The pot should never be covered or the vegetables will discolor, especially the green ones. Baking soda should never be added to the water in which the vegetables will cook or they will become mushy on the outside.

Bouillon: see MEAT STOCK.

Bouquet garni: A small or large bundle of parsley stems (for more flavor), a sprig of dried thyme and a bay leaf (a piece of leaf or a whole leaf depending on the amount of liquid to be flavored). The three aromatics are tied together and must be left to float freely in whatever sauce or stock they will flavor, so as to release a maximum amount of taste. Wrapping the *bouquet garni* in cheesecloth or attaching it at the pot handle by a string is often advocated by authors who do not strain sauces. The first method is preferred.

Braiser, braising pot: *Braiser* means to cook in a tightly covered pot with just enough liquid barely to cover the meat in the case of a stew, or to reach halfway to the top of the meat, in the case of a whole piece of meat. The word comes from the French *braise*, which means glowing coal or charcoal. Formerly, when cooking on the hearth, one cooked with charcoal under the pot. More charcoal was put inside of an upside-down lid that was made hollow for that purpose, and the bottom of the lid rested directly on the meat. The meat cooked within two layers of charcoal. Nowadays, braising is done in the oven to reproduce the same enclosed atmosphere as in the old hollow-lid braising pots. Put a large layer of foil on the meat and arrange it flush on the top of the meat so it makes an upside-down lid that will catch any condensation and allow the sauce to concentrate by reduction instead of being constantly rewatered. The meat then "braises" instead of boiling. The best way to convince yourself of the utility of this method is to do a braise once without the upside-down foil and the next time with it. The difference in the texture of the meat and the taste of the sauce will be strikingly in favor of the foil.

Braising pots should always be heavy iron or enameled cast iron. In France women braise in a *cocotte*, a round or oval pot made of cast iron or enameled cast iron.

Bread crumbs: In light cuisine they should be made exclusively from toasted gluten bread or low-calorie cracker meal. Bread crumbs can be flavored with herbs and/or garlic.

Brunoise: see AROMATICS.

Butter replacements: In light cuisine, see Fish Stock and Meat Stock in the introductory chapter.

Calories: According to Webster, the unit of measurement of energy-producing value in food when oxidized in the body. Calories can be, but need not be, the nightmare of a light eater; familiarize yourself with the lists in the first chapter and otherwise forget the word.

Calvados: In Normandy the brandy distilled from cider is called Calvados. It is aged in oak casks and acquires its color from the wood. If you have no Calvados, you can replace it by applejack, an American apple brandy. It must be reduced or ignited for flambéing. See FLAMBAGE.

Chopping board, chopping: Make sure that you own a chopping board of wood or plastic that is washable. Do not cross-contaminate your cooked foods by cutting them on a board which you have used previously to cut and trim raw meat or vegetables. The scrubbing and washing of a chopping board is a serious matter for the health of your family.

To chop, grab hold of the knife handle with your working hand. Block the tip of the blade with your other hand, fingers well extended, and chop from front to back of the board in one straight line. Do not "fan out" and do not hold the tip of the blade between your fingertips. It is dangerous.

Cocotte: The name used in France for a round or oval iron or enameled cast-iron pot used to braise stews and birds.

Cognac: The name of a brandy distilled from wine in the area surrounding the city of Cognac in western France. Cognac is aged in oak casks which give the brandy its color. There are several different types. The best of all Cognacs, called Grande Fine Champagne, should be used for desserts and special dishes only after you have become a crackerjack in the kitchen. Otherwise, three-star Cognac or V.S.O.P. (very superior old pale) Cognac will be adequate. Cognac finishes a sauce beautifully for chicken, veal, beef, game or venison. It must be reduced or ignited for flambéing. See FLAMBAGE.

Condiments: These include any spicy sauce or relish eaten with meats or vegetables to perk up their natural taste, such as mustards, relishes, ketchup, steak sauces and horse-radish.

Conical strainer: A small wire strainer with a plastic handle and wire mesh approximately ⅛-inch square is a must for careful cooks who want a sauce free of unwanted flour lumps and overcooked aromatics. The best investment is a strainer made of stainless steel, which will last almost 25 years.

Court-bouillon: This is the name given to a large water bath flavored with varied aromatics but mostly carrots, onions, a *bouquet garni*, and white-wine vinegar or lemon juice, in which whole fish or fish steaks are poached. To be flavorful enough, the aromatics must be simmered in the water before the fish is added for at least 20 minutes. Adding enough salt to the *court-bouillon* is important to balance the acid of the vinegar.

Lamb's or calf's brains are also poached in a wine vinegar *court-bouillon*. Often some of the *court-bouillon* is reduced (see REDUCE) and butter is whipped into it to make a sauce for the fish or brains.

Court-bouillon freezes well and can be reused and "rejuvenated" by adding more wine and aromatics. The more a *court-bouillon* cooks, the better it tastes.

Cream: Since cream is not used in light cuisine, it can simply be eliminated, or it can be replaced by a few teaspoons of evaporated skim milk. This replacement is usually used in conjunction with egg yolk to obtain a starch-free thickener or binder.

Deglazing: The present participle of "to deglaze" is turned substantive to express the action of dissolving the concentrated and caramelized cooking juices of a meat or a gravy. You can deglaze with water, wine, plain broth or excellent stock. It is always better to discard any fat in a pan before deglazing, especially if you decide to deglaze with wines or spirits that contain alcohol.

Deglazing is also done for roasts of all meats. You can add herbs or mustard to a deglazing to change the taste of the basic gravy.

Deciliter: A deciliter is one tenth of a liter and it measures between ⅓ and ½ cup liquid in the American AVP system and ⅓ cup in the BSI system.

Doneness: There are several ways to check the doneness of a meat:

Chickens are done when the juice runs clear from the cavity or from a hole left in the meat by a skewer inserted at the thickest part of the leg.

Ducks are done when the juices run clear from the cavity.

Braised red meats are done when a skewer inserted into the meat comes out without difficulty.

Panfried steaks and chops are rare when a finger can be pushed ¼ inch into the meat; medium rare when a finger can be pushed ⅛ inch into the meat; well done when a finger meets resistance and does not dent the meat.

Roasted joints are rare when a skewer inserted at the center, then pulled out, feels barely lukewarm when applied to the top of the hand; medium rare when the skewer feels warm; well done when the skewer feels very warm.

Cakes and breads are fully baked when a skewer inserted at the center comes out dry and feels too hot to be bearable to the top of the hand.

Baked custards are done when a skewer inserted two thirds of the way to the center of the custard comes out clean and hot. Cool the custard in its water bath.

Poached fruits are done when a darning needle pierces them and comes out freely.

Eggs: Large eggs are used in all recipes, although jumbo eggs give plumper omelets. A large egg weighs 2 ounces or approximately 60 grams. The best grade is AA fresh fancy quality.

The freshness of an egg can be readily seen from the size of its air pocket. If the air pocket is the size of a dime, then the egg is 3 to 8 days old; if it is the size of a penny, then the egg is 1 to 3 weeks old.

Eggs have the potential to coagulate and to foam, and both of these capacities are used in cooking and baking.

Flambage, flamber: This refers to the action of igniting and burning the alcohol in wines and spirits. Besides being attractive to look at, the *flambage* of an alcohol or wine is necessary so that the alcohol burns off and does not act aggressively on the palate. To *flamber*, heat the alcohol in a small pan, ignite it with a match, and pour it flaming over a dessert or into a sauce.

Flours: In light cuisine flours are not used in sauces and are very rarely used in other dishes.

Folding: This refers to the action of introducing an egg-white foam into an egg-yolk foam or a flour batter, without deflating the egg-white foam so it retains its leavening power. To fold, always start by mixing one quarter of the total volume of the whites into the receiving batter, then empty the remaining bulk of the whites over the lightened batter. Using a large rubber spatula, cut down to the bottom of the batter at its dead center. Bring the batter on top of the whites by turning your wrist toward the center of the bowl. Do not turn the spatula handle, but twist your wrist so that it ends up facing away from you. As you do so, turn the bowl regularly from left to right with your left hand. The faster the folding the better.

For cakes and mousses, fold until the batter is homogenous. For soufflés, overfold a little; it will not hurt.

Food processor: This is the best friend of the modern housewife. Many models are made in the United States. The best remains the Cuisinart, originally designed in France. A food processor does everything from chopping to puréeing, cutting vegetables, and grinding cheese and nuts.

Garlic: *To peel* garlic cloves for chopping, crush them with the flat side of a knife blade. The skin will come off easily. *To chop* garlic, sprinkle a pinch of salt over the pulp and garlic will not stick to the blade. *To mash* garlic, flatten already chopped garlic with the tip of the knife blade until the garlic is reduced to a purée.

Glaze: When applied to meats, this refers to the reduction of an excellent broth which becomes very thick by cooking down or reducing. It also refers to the deglazing of a cooked meat which is reduced further so that it becomes syrupy and thick.

Gram: The basic metric weight measure is the gram. There are 100 grams in a hectogram, 500 grams in a European pound, and 2 pounds or 1000 grams in a kilogram.

The American avoirdupois ounce is just a little over 28 grams and can be rounded off in recipes as weighing 30 grams. An American pound is 454 grams.

Gratin, gratiner: A gratin is any dish allowed to bake in the oven or brown under the broiler to develop a crispy, delicious top. The verb *gratiner* expresses the action of browning and developing that brown top. The brown top can be made with butter and crumbs, with cheese, or with plain heavy cream.

Gravy: A gravy is not a sauce, although the words are used interchangeably. A gravy is made of the cooking juices of a meat which are deglazed and defattened. To make a good gravy, pour the cooking juices into a glass cup. Let fat and lean separate. Extract the lean part with a baster.

In the case of a roast, you may think that there is no gravy because the meat juices are all hardened (caramelized) on the bottom of the roasting pan. Dissolve these hardened juices with hot water or meat stock.

Hazelnuts: These are known in French as *avelines* when they come from wild trees or as *filberts*. Buy them already shelled. *To peel* them, put them on a jelly-roll pan in a medium oven. As soon as you see the skin begin to crack and shred, remove nuts to a tea towel and rub them firmly. The skin will come off easily.

Herbs: The leaves and stems of aromatic plants are used to flavor foods, as well as medicinal teas and compounds. The best herbs are always fresh and come in "taste families" such as mint-basil, anise-fennel-tarragon, and rosemary-savory-marjoram-thyme. When no fresh herbs are available, you can use dried herbs in lesser amounts but you must revive them in a small amount of hot water first.

Julienne: This is a style of cutting vegetables. See AROMATICS.

Knives: A good home cook needs only two knives: a paring knife and a chef's knife. The size of the chef's knife will depend on the size of your hand. An 8-inch blade is a good average. There are many brands and styles to choose from. Whichever you choose, consider that it will be an expensive investment but that it will last a lifetime. See SHARPENER.

Liaison: In light cuisine, the customary mixture of egg yolk and cream called *liaison* in Classic Cuisine is replaced by evaporated skim milk mixed with egg yolk(s).

Lettuce, salad greens: Greens require a great deal of care. First wash the head of lettuce under cold, running water to dislodge gravel from between the leaves. Remove each leaf separately and wash it again. Remove the lettuce ribs and tear each leaf into 3 or 4 bite-size pieces. Put the lettuce on tea towels and roll each towel loosely. Store in the refrigerator until you are ready to use.

Macerate: Another word for marinate, but one that is applied especially to fruits soaking in a liqueur or spirit.

Marinate, marinade: A mixture of wine, or wines, or wine and vinegar, flavored with aromatics in which meats are steeped and allowed to soak for hours or days before being cooked so as to give additional flavor to the meat. Marinades flavor meats, they do not tenderize them for their effect is too superficial. Marinades may be cooked or uncooked. To obtain a cooked marinade, simmer the aromatics in the chosen wine for 20 minutes, but let this cool completely before pouring the liquid over the meat. Large pieces of meat must be turned in their marinade at regular intervals.

Meat extract: This is a semisolid commercial product sold in glass jars to replace homemade meat glaze. Add it in very small amounts to a finished sauce to correct the final taste, or to stews cooked exclusively in wine mixed with some water to supply the lacking meat taste. Be aware that meat extract is very salty, very pungent, and can ruin a good dish. Therefore, add it little by little until you reach the desired meat flavor. Several brands of meat extract exist, so you should choose your favorite brand only after you have tried them all.

Meat stock: A good heavy bouillon; in light cuisine a small amount of this stock is used in a nonstick skillet or sauteuse pan to start the cooking of vegetables and the browning of meat. (See Index for recipe.)

Melon baller: This is the down-to-earth name of the French potato cutter known as *cuillère parisienne*. It is used in France to cut potatoes as well as melon balls. A sturdy French one will last a lifetime and has two sizes of cutters; one is ¾ inch wide; the other is ½ inch wide.

Milk: In light cuisine, this food can only consist of skim milk for drinking and finishing soup; evaporated skim milk for *liaison* and binding; see these words.

Minceur or cuisine minceur: The name given to this light cuisine by the French chef Michel Guérard. The terminology made a great impression on the general public, but the trend of light cuisine itself has been very strong in France since the early sixties; many books on the subject were published and are still being published in France. Some of the nutritionist authors are Simone Martin Vieille Ville and Martine Deloge. The present book is another example of the category.

Mirepoix: A style of cutting vegetables. See AROMATICS.

Mushrooms: By nature, mushrooms are very spongy; if soaked in water, they will soak up almost all of the water and consequently lose a lot of their taste. It is, therefore, not a good idea to wash mushrooms too much. Wash them only if they are extremely dirty. Otherwise, wipe off the excess dirt with a paper towel. Also trim off the stem ends. Wild mushrooms, on the other hand, will invariably need to be washed because of dirt and slugs. Slugs will fall off if a bit of vinegar is added to the washing water.

To cook mushrooms for a garnish and use their juices in a sauce, heat some butter, add the mushrooms, and season with salt and pepper. Toss the mushrooms in the hot butter and cover them. The juices will run out of them within 3 to 7 minutes. Separate juices from mushrooms.

To cook mushrooms as a sautéed vegetable, proceed as above, but let the juices evaporate completely and continue sautéing until the mushrooms brown in the butter. Add whatever herb you like.

In light cuisine, omit the butter and cook mushrooms in a nonstick pan, adding a few tablespoons of stock if necessary.

Mussels: Mussels always contain a certain amount of sand; the way to remove it is to soak the mussels in salted water. They will believe that they are in the sea again, especially if you use sea salt, and they will open up their shells to release the sand. Do not soak mussels in plain water since they will lose all their tang.

To clean mussels, scrub them with a knife or a clean plastic pot scrubber. Next, squeeze the shells between your thumb and finger from right to left. This is extremely important since dead mussels will fall apart and healthy ones will let out a "phfft" as the air is squeezed out of their shells. When you steam the mussels, any that remain closed after steaming should be discarded.

Mussel juices are always used in sauces because of the marvelous flavor. But the juices are sandy and they should be strained either through a paper coffee filter or several layers of cheesecloth.

Mustard: Mustard comes dry as a powder or prepared in jars. In French cuisine, the mustard used is mostly prepared Dijon mustard which contains wine and vinegar. Dijon mustard comes plain, strong and yellow, or flavored with purées of herbs such as tarragon, in which case the mustard takes on a greenish tinge and an added delicious flavor.

Needle test: This is to test the doneness of poached fruit such as pears and peaches. The fruit is done when a needle inserted in the body of the fruit comes in and out freely.

Omelet pan: In light cuisine, the best omelet pan has a nonstick coating and needs no conditioning. A good omelet can be made in such a nonstick pan without a trace of any fat, very quickly and very well, to give you beautiful results.

Onions: There are onions and onions ... For cooking use ordinary yellow onions, chopped or sliced. They are excellent in stews, broth, soups and onion soup. For a side dish use either white boiling onions or their tiny little brothers, the silverskin onions. For a garnish in a stew, only silverskin onions look "French." Before cooking them you should cut a tiny cross in the root end to prevent them separating into layers. Red Spanish onions and large sweet Bermuda onions are excellent when thinly sliced in salads. Should they be pungent, soak the slices in salted water.

Ounce: The basic liquid and solid measure of the avoirdupois system is the ounce. There are 16 liquid ounces in a pint, and 32 in a quart in the United States, while there are 20 liquid ounces in a pint and 40 in a quart in Britain.

There are 16 solid ounces in a pound and each ounce is the equivalent to 28 generous grams, most of the time rounded off to 30 grams.

Parisian spoon: See MELON BALLER.

Persillade: This is a mixture of finely chopped garlic and parsley widely used in French cuisine, especially in the provinces south of the Loire. The cooks of Provence prefer *persillade* browned whereas those of Languedoc and Aquitaine prefer it plain.

Poaching: To poach means to cook without boiling. Fish is mostly poached in *court-bouillon* or in a small amount of fish stock and wine in the oven. The term also applies to white meat of chicken cooked extremely fast in a very high oven to obtain a "super tender" texture.

Pots and pans: For all steaming, poaching, boiling, stewing and braising, you can use your regular pots and pans or a pressure cooker. For stir-frying, panfrying and omelet making, use a skillet with a nonstick coating.

Pressure cooker: This is one of the best friends of working cooks. Read the directions carefully and observe them with care. Remember that French cuisine prepared in a pressure cooker does not measure up to French cuisine prepared in those good old slow-cooking pots.

Processors: These are modern implements that simplify certain tasks for the cook and allow hours of work to be done literally in minutes. See BLENDER and FOOD PROCESSOR.

Provençale herbs: In Provence, herbs grow naturally on the *garrigues*. The three main ones are rosemary, savory and thyme. These are often sold in jars or bags labeled "Provençale herbs." Often the blend will also include mint and orégano.

Quatre-épices: Literally, "4 spices," but this spice mixture is often made with 6 spices or more, and sometimes with the addition of a few herbs as well. Available commercially from many spice firms, but you can blend your own if you prefer. Most mixtures contain nutmeg, ginger, cloves and white pepper.

Reduce, reduction: In culinary terms, the verb *reduce* is used to express the action of cooking down a liquid to evaporate moisture and concentrate taste. A *reduction* is the result of reducing a mixture. The best example of a reduction can be found in the base of a Béarnaise sauce, where wine, vinegar and aromatics are reduced together, before the eggs and the butter are added to finish the sauce.

Salpicon: This is a style of cutting vegetables. See AROMATICS.

Sauce: In light cuisine, a sauce consists mostly of the gravy of meat, thickened by reduction (see this word). A sauce can also consist of a more or less reduced gravy thickened by the addition of an egg yolk and evaporated skim milk (*liaison*).

Sauceboat: The best sauceboat is the French type built with a gravy separator. It has two spouts with M (maigre = lean) which will let only lean gravy pass through, and the other with G (gras = fat) which will allow both lean and fat to pour onto food.

Sauce spoon: This is the large oval spoon usually part of basic kitchen spoon sets.

Seasonings: Seasonings are those ingredients that are added to food to modify their basic tastes and make them more palatable. Sugar, salt, pepper, celery salt, spices, herbs and condiments are all seasonings. Note that *cold* deadens the effect of seasonings and that more salt or more sugar should be added to foods that will be served cold, deep-chilled or frozen.

Sharpener, sharpening: Your knives are just as good as your sharpener. Buy a good stone or a good sharpening steel and sharpen your blades by rubbing them on the stone or sharpening steel at a 20-degree angle. There is a sharpener made of carbon material which is expensive, but will last a lifetime.

Skewer test: see also DONENESS. The skewer test is used for meats that have been pot-roasted or braised. If a skewer inserted at the center of a piece of meat goes in and comes out freely, then the meat is done. As long as the meat lifts with the skewer, it is not done.

Skimming: Bouillons, soups, boiled dinner and sauces are skimmed, which means that the impurities coming to their surface can and must be removed with a spoon. Use a large sauce spoon to bring the scum from the center of the pot to its edge. Use the ''belly'' of the spoon, not its tip, and lift off the scum or fat. Discard the scum.

Spatulas: There are several types of spatulas: turners are spatulas for turning over meats; folding is best done with a rubber spatula of a large size, approximately 3½ x 2½ inches, with a plastic or wooden handle; frostings and icings are best spread on cakes with long stainless-steel spatulas approximately 10 inches long and 1 inch wide.

Spices: Herbs are chiefly plant leaves used freshly chopped, or dried and revived; spices are seeds, dried and ground, roots, twigs or even barks. Allspice berries, for example, are dried, and they can be used whole for some preparations, but they are more often ground, as are cinnamon bark, nutmeg seeds, and white and black peppercorns.

Spirits: A spirit is any brandy at least 90 proof which is distilled from wine or fruit. Applejack and Calvados are both distilled from apple cider, Cognac and Armagnac are distilled from wines. Whisky and Bourbon are distilled from grains. All of these are used in cooking to give foods a special aroma, but if added to sauces they must be flambéed to burn off their alcohol.

Stir-frying: This is a Chinese technique for cooking vegetables adopted in France by the modern cooks. It consists of tossing finely cut vegetables (¼-inch-wide julienne strips) in hot oil until they are tender and crisp. The French "doneness" is one tiny stage beyond the "grassy" Chinese taste.

Stock: the technical word for BOUILLON.

Strainer: See CONICAL STRAINER.

Teflon: Teflon is the name of a coating applied to skillets and saucepans to allow cooks to cook without any fat. Please read carefully the paragraphs in the introductory chapter on cooking implements in light cookery.

Scratched Teflon surfaces are ruined and become useless as the food will start sticking to the exposed metal during cooking.

Tomatoes: Fresh tomatoes, good enough to eat or to make sauce with, are only available at tomato season from July (in hot climates) or August (in cold climates) until the end of October. It is useless to try to make a sauce with the "vine" tomatoes "manufactured" for shipping rather than for eating, so in the winter use canned tomatoes. All those coming from the Mediterranean basin (Israel, Greece, Italy, Spain) are excellent. Most of them are the "pear-shaped" tomatoes which the Italians label *pelati*. All countries with a national tomato canning industry can use their own product. Remember that the hotter the climate, the better the fruit.

Peeling tomatoes is easy: Bring a pot of water to a boil. Remove the stem and immerse the tomato in the boiling water for 2 minutes. Lift the tomato with a slotted spoon, rinse it under cold running water, and peel it.

Trussing: This is the tying of a bird so that it cooks evenly. Here is an easy method that does not require a trussing needle: Use a 20-inch piece of kitchen string. Tie a knot around the "parson's nose" (the tail of the chicken) with half of the string in each of your hands. Then tie the string over the two drumstick ends. Pass the string on each side between the leg and the breast, pushing down. Turn the chicken or bird upside down and finally tie across the wings folded akimbo.

Vanilla: Use only pure vanilla, whether it is vanilla extract or vanilla bean.

Vanilla extract is always added to desserts containing eggs to temper the egg taste .whatever the final flavoring of the dessert might be. When using a vanilla bean, cut it or use a small portion of it, and scrape the seeds into your dessert preparation.

To make vanilla sugar: bury the used or unused beans in a jar of granulated sugar.

Vinegars: Vinegars are made with many things: red and white wines; cider; pineapple wine; raspberries; etc. Use the vinegar you prefer and also think of flavoring basic vinegars by adding fresh sprigs of herbs to them, such as tarragon, chives and basil. White alcohol vinegar is not used in French cuisine for cooking purposes, but it is used to pickle such vegetables as tiny gherkins and onions. Sherry vinegar is excellent but very potent. Use it sparingly; see introductory chapter.

Water: Water for boiling pasta or rice should be salted at the very last minute, just before adding the noodles or rice to prevent off-tastes from developing in combination with the starches.

Water bath (bain-marie): This is the *ban maria* of the Italians, who invented it before the Renaissance. It was brought to France by the cooks of the Medici princesses. It then became re-baptized *bain-marie.*

Remember to always proceed this way: bring a kettle of water to a rolling boil. It is important that the water boils so that when you pour it into the baking dish it stabilizes at about 190°F. to help poach the food. Put the baking dish on the oven rack and set the container of food to be cooked in the dish. Pour the boiling water into the baking dish until the water level comes up to ¾ inch from the rim of the container in which the food is cooking. When the cooking is completed, cool the food in the water bath. A hot-water bath is also used to keep sauces hot.

Whisks: Small sauce whisks are a *must* in any kitchen, home or professional. The whisk is the best friend you will ever have in the kitchen. It allows you to gain time by adding hot liquids to hot *roux.* It breaks any lumps that form instantly. Stainless-steel whisks are the best.

Wines: There are two types of wine used in cooking: Natural red and white wines with 10 to 13% alcohol content; remember always to cook these wines down by at least 50% of their original volume so that they completely lose their alcohol by reducing. Fortified wines with 18 to 20% alcohol; these are Madeira, Sherry, Port, Marsala, etc. You may reduce these wines by adding them to a sauce while it cooks, or if you prefer you can add 1 or 2 tablespoons (US) or 1 tablespoon (UK) to each cup of finished sauce. All fortified wines come both dry and sweet. The dry ones are best for savory dishes, and the sweet ones should never be used in light cuisine.

INDEX